D1082983

TOWARD
DISENGAGEMENT
IN ASIA

A Strategy for
American Foreign Policy

Bernard K. Gordon

Prentice-Hall, Inc. *Englewood Cliffs, N. J.*

A SPECTRUM BOOK

BERNARD K. GORDON is Southeast Asia Project Chairman, Research Analysis Corporation; Adjunct Associate Professor, George Washington University; and Lecturer in Asian Studies at the School of Advanced International Studies of Johns Hopkins University. He is the author of *New Zealand Becomes a Pacific Power* and *The Dimensions of Conflict in Southeast Asia.*

SOUTHEAST ASIA AND THE ASEAN NATIONS

INDONESIA · MALAYSIA · SINGAPORE · THAILAND · PHILIPPINES

Current printing (last number):

10 9 8 7 6 5 4 3 2 1

Prentice-Hall International, Inc. (*London*)

FOREWORD

Usually the times make a book. Occasionally it is the reverse. In Dr. Gordon's case it is some of both. With a fresh and original approach, this study examines the critical international issues in East Asia today. Creatively, he also goes beyond the times to offer constructive proposals for the future peace of this massive, volatile continent where half of mankind lives in jeopardy and poverty. He deals cooly and fully with one of the most perplexing paradoxes of contemporary history: a warring Asia that desperately needs to organize for peace. He suggests a new role for the United States to play in keeping with new trends in Asia.

His book is about East Asia, not Asia as a whole, I should first point out. The massive South Asian continent and the vast area of the Indian Ocean do not figure in this study. I should also caution that his concept of "disengagement in Asia" is so relative that it will not confirm the fears of those Asians who are convinced we will soon pull completely out of Asia, nor fulfill the hopes of those Americans who are equally convinced that we should get out now. To understand this book it is essential to remember that Dr. Gordon does not imply or suggest any such all-out withdrawal. Instead, disengagement means to him "a declining direct American involvement in the defense and security" of East Asia.

Here is a book that finally gets to the marrow of the matter in East Asia. It is free of the distortions, misrepresentations, and irrelevancies which have so marred the debate on Vietnam and so filled most of the current literature on crises in Asia. His tone and thrust are positive. They are well stated in the very last sentence of his book: "Americans need no longer be apologetic in suggesting that Asian effort and Asian manpower become the primary means of providing for Asian security." His study seeks to find out how the Asians can take over the primary responsibility for security while the United States decreases its involvement. Thus, he addresses himself to the question of highest priority in all Asia—how can the nations of Asia together organize Asia for its development in peace? He approaches this issue quite rightly in terms of the national interest and relevant role of the United States in Asia in the future.

He makes an earnest and effective effort to dissect and describe our national interests in Asia. Why have we been there in the first place? It is shocking to learn from his analysis that the answer has seldom if ever been wholly or adequately explained to the American public, even long before the Vietnam debate in our time. Since 1900, public understanding has not matched official commitments in East Asia, a dangerous predicament in a democracy.

This book should greatly help to close that gap. Dr. Gordon suggests a three-scale or triple-tiered range of national interests to gauge the extent to which we should become militarily involved in any area of the world. His set of three levels, as he calls them, is a useful tool, even if a rather too general projection of past involvement. However, his reasoning is rigorous and not mechanical. He does not hesitate to denude myths and redress realities about our Asia policies. His conclusions will be especially useful for

246425

rational discussion of what to do about commitments in East Asia "after Vietnam," because he presents several *specific* national interests of the United States in Asia as a whole: the primary one of prevention of Asia's dominance by any single hostile power, the corollary of support for "multipolarity" in an Asian balance of power, and the necessary encouragement of an Asian system of regionalism.

The basic implication of this book is the merit of American support for the concept of counterbalance, for ASEAN (the Association of Southeast Asian Nations), and for creative realignment in East Asia. Regional cooperation for security in East Asia will benefit our national interests and objectives of preventing one-nation dominance of Asia, supporting multipolarity, encouraging Asian-Chinese coexistence, and reducing what I call our overpresence in Asia. Regional cooperation deserves our support. For one thing it would rid our vocabulary of the "domino theory," as there would be no more "dominoes" in Southeast Asia, if indeed there ever were. Southeast Asian nations would either be in the counterbalance which would not succumb to external threats, or outside it, which would not matter. It is a distinct virtue of this study that its concept of the counterbalance accurately reflects the characteristically Asian interdependence of East Asia, also pictured, if crudely, by the over-maligned domino image. Support for regional cooperation and relative disengagement on our part would demonstrate a correct understanding of the intricate interaction among Southeast Asian nations, Japan, and China—an interaction, moreover, that will be undertaken in an increasingly Asian style of diplomacy quite different from ours. For that reason too, we should heed Dr. Gordon's warning of the dangerous time gap between conceiving and achieving regional cooperation in security. He seems to envisage a couple of decades which is not too early. Asia, even modern Asia, has a different time sense than the West. Our countdown is in hours or less. They go by seasons or more. American disengagement in Asia, as envisaged in this book, should not be premature. Indeed, it cannot be, because it will take a long time in any case.

This study, somewhat ahead of the times, will help us in the times ahead to relate ourselves more realistically to Asia's major issues than we have in the past seventy years. Euro-centric Americans need a better informed dialogue and debate concerning our relevant role in Asia in the changing decades ahead. For that, *Toward Disengagement in Asia* is an excellent point of departure.

KENNETH T. YOUNG

CONTENTS

ACKNOWLEDGMENTS

In an earlier book my purpose was to discuss Southeast Asia as a distinct political subregion—a region which in its own right warrants study by international relations specialists. That book was intended to be non-prescriptive, in all respects, and value-free from the viewpoint of American foreign policy in particular. But having identified certain Southeast Asian patterns, it was perhaps inevitable that as a teacher and student of foreign policy I later began to question the relevance of those patterns to American interests. Yet few guidelines were apparent, for scholarship has long resisted asking certain basic questions: What have been American objectives in Asia generally, in Southeast Asia in particular, and how do they relate to America's interests globally?

This book deals with those questions, and hopes to "place" Southeast Asia within the general context of American policy. For the opportunity to make the effort my deep thanks go to Professor Robert E. Osgood, Director of the Washington Center of Foreign Policy Research of Johns Hopkins University, where I was Research Associate during 1967–68. My debt however is much older: ten years before, at the University of Chicago, both Professor Osgood and Hans Morgenthau introduced me to the concept of national interest—a concept which I have sought to operationalize in this book. My obligation to both will be clear to all readers. I wish also to thank Dr. John P. Hardt and others at Research Analysis Corporation for authorizing my leave of absence to write this book, and for encouraging my work on some of the ideas developed here. Of course I am alone responsible for their expression.

Many friends in Southeast Asia have extended kindnesses that hopefully have enhanced my understanding: in Bangkok, Sompong Sucharitkul, Dr. Pracha Guna-Kasem, and Foreign Minister Thanat Khoman; among Indonesians, Ali Alatas, T. K. Adhyatman, Anwar Seni, Dr. Mohd. Sadli, and Foreign Minister Adam Malik; in Manila, former Ambassador S. P. Lopez, Rafael Salas, and Franki Jose; and in Kuala Lumpur, for his great patience and knowledge, Tan Sri Ghazali Bin Schafie. In Singapore, where I was briefly his colleague at the University, I wish to again thank Dr. Wong Lin Ken, Raffles Professor of History and formerly Ambassador to the United States, and also Foreign Minister Rajaratnam.

The comments of Professors Bernard Reich, Robert Tilman, Jack Montgomery, and Young C. Kim were especially helpful, as was the aid of Elaine Clark, Pat Field, Anne Cyr and Susan Hice. Three whose encouragement was crucial at an early stage I must single out: General Robert J. Wood, U.S. Army, Ret., Ambassador Kenneth T. Young, and my wife Anita.

To Anita, with Pam and Josh, this book is dedicated.

One

ON PRIORITIES

Of all the foreign policy issues facing Americans, none is more pressing and divisive than United States involvement in East Asia. The war in Vietnam, of course, has brought debate to a head, and many leading men are questioning daily almost all aspects of American policy in Asia. Among them, former Ambassador Kennan has charged that nothing involved in the struggle in Vietnam warrants the effort being made there by the United States. Senator Fulbright has argued that the Vietnam war is only one illustration of a tendency of the American government to assume the role of global policeman; he has ascribed our Vietnam involvement to an arrogance flowing from our great power. Former Marine Commandant Shoup has dismissed as "poppycock" the President's statement that the Vietnam war relates directly to the national security of the United States.

Such charges, although specific to the Vietnam war, are expressive of even more basic divisions and doubts about American purposes and interests in Asia generally. These doubts arise from a number of questions which have long gone unanswered, including these: What is the United States' national interest in East and Southeast Asia; what kind of relationship does the United States aim for with China; and finally, taking into account both the nature of American interests and what we know of China, what guidelines exist to develop a reasonably peaceful and stable Asia?

These questions can yield rough answers. To find them, however, we must range far beyond the topics of the day, in terms of both time and geography. To learn, for example, what are American interests requires a re-examination of the whole sweep of United States involvements in Asia—not only to see how we got where we are, but also to find what patterns, if any, exist in our foreign policy behavior.

1

It requires also a consideration of Asia in the context of American involvements in other world regions, for it seems clear that not all parts of the globe can be equally relevant to the well-being of the United States. Demands that there be "no more Vietnams" strongly suggest that Americans resist policies which imply universal involvement by their government; they are likely instead to insist that their leaders carefully discriminate among global regions.

But to suggest a need for discrimination implies a sense of priorities —a basis for deciding which events warrant an American involvement. The United States badly needs such a sense of priorities, partly because American resources are not unlimited. Even for a nation with our physical, financial, and human resources, there is objectively nothing to commend United States involvement everywhere on the globe, and much to commend noninvolvement wherever possible. But the limits on our material capacity are not the only reasons for establishing priorities of national interest. A sense of priorities would also bring added meaning to the actions we take, making our policies, and the objectives of those policies, more understandable. As our purposes are understood, it is likely that our policies will be more effective abroad and better supported at home.

Taking the foreign context first, there seems little to be gained, for example, from inviting gross miscalculations about what the United States regards as vital. Japan made such an error when it attacked Pearl Harbor and assumed that the United States lacked the will for a prolonged conflict in the Pacific. The Soviet Union made another when it deployed missiles in Cuba and assumed that the Monroe Doctrine and its implications were no longer meaningful.

In the domestic context, foreign policy priorities are equally important: it is a principle of democratic faith as well as political expediency that no administration can long afford to forego popular understanding and support for its foreign policies. Without that understanding, government runs the risk of having its policies rejected not from informed and deliberate disagreement, but from uninformed popular frustration. In foreign policy that can mean popular rejection not only of steps that are merely desirable, but rejection—*because priorities have not been made clear*—of some vital steps as well. Administrations flirt with that risk when people come to suspect that their leaders are willing to intervene almost everywhere and anywhere.

Today in the United States that belief, even if not grounded in fact, seems widespread. The most common complaint against the government's foreign policy leadership, even among those who could hardly be called traditional "isolationists," is that the United States is somehow "overextended" and "overcommitted." [1] This can be a dangerous belief if it leads to pressures for indiscriminate withdrawals, or if it impedes American involvement in those situations where involvement is essential. One result could be an American "undercommitment" to interests that are in fact of primary significance. If political and military leaders wish to avoid such pressures and to refute the belief that the United States has become an "imperialist" power seeking near-universal involvement, they will need to discriminate more clearly and carefully among their involvements.

Yet some recent actions of the United States suggest that such discrimination has not always been present. Leaders have sometimes acted as if there were no priorities—and when they behave in that manner they not only provide evidence to their least constructive critics (and to foreign adversaries), but they alienate the support of their friends as well.

A case in point may have been the decision, in mid-1967, to dispatch three American military aircraft to the Congo. These aircraft were sent on a mission that was, at least in part, humanitarian, but there was a deeply negative Congressional reaction when it was learned that the United States had dispatched military aircraft carrying combat-equipped servicemen on this mission. Not only Congressmen, but many others as well asked the question: what *interest* and what commitment of the United States was served by this employment of American military capacity? No clear answer was forthcoming, and to many the incident seemed a vindication of Senator Fulbright's warning that American officials regard the United States as the world's policeman.

Perhaps the most significant aspect of the incident was that the strongest Congressional criticism came from men, like Senator Russell, who generally are the firmest supporters of Administration foreign policy—in Vietnam and in most other places. Yet even these leaders were forced to wonder, when American troop transports were flown to central Africa, whether there were any limits at all to the foreign interests of the United States. Senator Russell stressed that such small decisions needed the most careful deliberation; it was just such "small"

---

[1] For a discussion of this critique, in particular the writings of Fulbright, Schlesinger, Steel, and Eugene McCarthy, see Charles Gati, "Another Grand Debate? The Limitationist Critique of American Foreign Policy," a Review Article in *World Politics*, XXI, October 1, 1968, 133–51.

inputs of American military aid that could lead to later calls for added
assistance.[2]

Administration spokesmen insisted that no wider efforts were intended, and the use of American military aircraft and personnel in
the Congo soon came to an end. Nevertheless, "mistakes" like the
Congo flight probably need to be avoided, precisely because they lend
credence to criticisms like that of Senator Fulbright: that the United
States, so impressed with its might, has become characterized by "the
arrogance of power." Policymakers will want to avoid that impression
because, as just suggested, they cannot afford to risk the loss of future
support for actions they deem truly vital. The American people are
likely to expect, in other words, that when their leaders do make use
of great power, it is in the service of great ends; for that proposition
to be accepted some sense of foreign policy priorities is essential.

This task is especially important for a people who have so often
displayed a general distrust of foreign involvements, and in a nation
whose recent diplomatic history can as a result be characterized as
frequently tentative and selective. It is useful to recall, for example,
the "great debates" of the early 1950's regarding the proposed Bricker
Amendment, which was widely supported, and the proposal for large-
scale troop deployments in Europe, which was widely opposed in the
Congress. In that period, only fifteen years ago, the "arrogance of
power" label with which Senator Fulbright brands American policy
today would have been a hardly credible charge. Instead it was then
more accurate to complain that American policy was too hesitant and
unsure in the deployment of its might, and the complaint was essentially correct.

Against that background it is remarkable that the pendulum of
criticism has swung so quickly to a different extreme. For today it is
argued that the deep failing in American foreign policy is its alleged
propensity toward intervention: that "we tend to intervene against
all radical revolutionary movements because we are afraid lest they
be taken over by communists."[3] The Vietnam war is of course cited
as the prime illustration of this impulse, and the whole thrust of

[2] Senator Russell called the action an "unjustified intervention in a local dis-
turbance. I say it is immoral to send even one American boy into a country
where we have *no commitments and where we have no vital interest.*" Another
Senator complained that the action would pave the way for "another Vietnam"
(*The New York Times*, July 11, 1967).

[3] Hans J. Morgenthau, "To Intervene or Not to Intervene," *Foreign Affairs*
(April, 1967), p. 433.

American policy is seen in this view as bent on the creation of a new empire—a *"Pax Americana."* [4]

This criticism contains a number of errors, for the United States has not in fact sought to intervene on a global basis. But the most disturbing feature of the criticism is its tendency to lump all interventions together, when in reality situations that might call for American intervention vary widely. Some, in essence, are much more important than others: the central problem of foreign policy is to determine degrees of importance. In the United States especially, when so many men believe that there are no good guidelines for identifying the most important American interests, the need for establishing criteria is strikingly evident. Seeming "errors" of the sort that led to the Congo airlift need to be avoided, for even the United States—with all its power—must determine which things it genuinely requires as compared to those which it would merely like to obtain. Indeed, it is precisely *because* the United States is so powerful that it must be careful to deploy its power with greater selectivity than most other nations. For action by the United States, especially any level of military action, necessarily leads states like the Soviet Union and China to consider possible reactions, and the United States has no interest in provoking needless reactions by others.

For that external reason, as well as for the domestic reasons already mentioned, the United States needs to develop and make more explicit the interests and objectives that will warrant the use of its great power. It needs, moreover, to define its interests so that their importance in relation to one another will become more clear. A ranking of priorities will result, and only with such a sense of priorities can the United States tailor its commitments to fit the relative importance of its interests.

The task of identifying the major national interests of the United States and the scale of its interest priorities is, of course, not a simple one, but neither is it impossible. The American foreign policy behavior record is a place to begin, and that record—especially in Asia—will be explored in this book to determine what patterns may exist. But a concern to identify the national interest priorities of the United States forms only one of the two main purposes of this book. Its other aim is to help establish a basis for resolving America's Asian dilemma: How can the United States, without forfeiting its security, achieve a stable relationship with China?

[4] Ronald Steel, *Pax Americana* (New York: The Viking Press, 1967).

This has been the order of business since the immediate aftermath of World War II, but it was tragically impeded, first by the Korean conflict and in the sixties by the war in Vietnam. As a result, a legacy of mistrust and hostility has been built up on both sides since 1950. This book is written in the conviction that this legacy can be eroded, and that the security interests of China and the United States do not require a great armed conflict for their satisfaction.

Because Southeast Asia constitutes the major zone of conflict between Chinese and American interests, much of the discussion will focus on that region. Its purpose will be to determine what latitude for peaceful resolution of Chinese and American interests exists in that subregion of East Asia. Perhaps this betrays an assumption which should at once be identified. This is the premise that there are benefits to be gained through the ultimate military disengagement of the United States from Southeast Asia. I suspect that these benefits exist not only in terms of international political stability, but also in terms of America's ability to make better progress toward achieving domestic tranquility. The problem, of course, is to identify the conditions under which Asian disengagement will be feasible, and this leads to the identification of another premise. As a student of international politics, I am impressed with the explosive sensitivity and danger that characterizes bipolar confrontations in world politics. Much to be preferred, it would seem, are conditions of multipolarity, though that configuration is not without its problems. Nevertheless, in the Asian political environment, and with the prospect of an increasingly developed nuclear weapons and delivery systems capacity available to Peking, the dangers of a bipolar Chinese-American military confrontation are awesome.

A multipolar structure *has* characterized the East Asian political system in the past, and the shape of that structure will be presented in later chapters. But the concern of this book is more than to describe what has gone before: it seeks instead to determine whether there is a potential compatibility in the future between the security interests of the United States and a multipolar structure in East Asia. The nature of the American national interest, as developed in Chapter Two and applied specifically to East Asia in the following chapters, suggests at least a strong conceptual compatibility.

In the second half of this book—and only after first identifying the nature of the United States interest in East and Southeast Asia—the subject of Asian regionalism will be closely examined. For, no matter how intrinsically interesting, the concept can be evaluated usefully by those interested in American foreign policy only after answering this question: What part of the American national interest does a given "regional" development or proposal affect?

Another caution is in order because regional cooperation hopes have been raised in Southeast Asia before, and little was achieved. Yet there are political forces now at work in the area which suggest a very durable quality to the phenomenon. Even the most pragmatic and hard-headed leaders have come increasingly to aspire to the goal of a more cohesive Southeast Asia, for they see in this approach a means to achieve potentially conflicting goals. Regionalism, in other words, is seen as an expression of "Asian-ness," and in that sense it responds to the need to reject or at least move away from the Western nations. At the same time, regional cooperation, particularly as reflected in concrete economic cooperation programs, is understood to be accept-able to the West, particularly to the United States. As a result, Asian leaders hope that their assertions of independence, if expressed through Asian cooperation, will not lead to too sudden a break with the West-ern powers on whom they still depend for much support.

To the extent that American interests in Asia can be satisfied by the building of multipolarity in the Pacific region, this may be a very welcome development. The ideologues and nation-builders of the first two postwar decades have begun to recede from power positions in Southeast Asia. The more practical men are replacing them, and as a result there is reason to expect that today's regional efforts will be marked by more pragmatism, and less of the ethereal quality that characterized some of the Asian brotherhood efforts in the 1950's.

If pragmatism and concrete cooperative programs do become the hallmarks of Asian cooperation during the 1970's, there can emerge a realistic basis for the American role in Asia to move away from poli-cies consistent with bipolarity, toward policies appropriate to a multi-polar Asia. Genuine disengagement rests on that outcome, and in the final chapters of this book an approach is suggested which can help the early achievement of that outcome. But the degree of effort which the United States ought to devote toward achieving a multipolar Asia can only be assessed if the nature of American national interests is made more explicit. And that in turn will require, as we suggested at the outset, a sense of priorities.

A framework for ascribing global priorities is outlined in the next chapter; later in this book we will also suggest that by examining subregional patterns of interaction it is possible to identify priorities of interest within global regions. This is another way of saying that global regions can be thought of as subsystems of the international system. In that way some of the key variables (and possibly "key states") should become more apparent. Hopefully this method of analysis will make it possible to identify guidelines for future American policy, for in Asia, as in other areas, it is vital that United States foreign policy be based less on hunch and more on an ordered concept of the priorities of national interest.

Two

INTERESTS, OBJECTIVES, AND POLICIES

Although it is "foreign policy" that we generally read about and discuss, policy is only one of three broad levels of consideration that lead to actions in the foreign environment. The other two can be referred to as *interests* and *objectives,* and they are separated from one another and from *policies* by an important sequential distinction. National interests, that is, are presumed to lead to objectives. Objectives, in turn, shape policies, and policies ultimately dictate the specific actions which the nation undertakes.

These distinctions, which characterize the range of commitments of the United States, can be shown graphically as below. We will call it a commitment continuum:

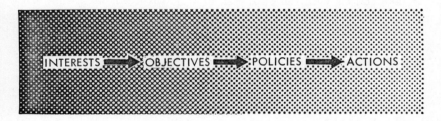

At one extreme, interests are regarded as the least changing and changeable. At the other extreme, specific actions are expected to be constantly subject to change. Moreover, once interests are identified, each of the next characteristics, reading from left to right, can be regarded as the standard by which to judge the next. Thus policies can be understood and evaluated primarily by reference to the objectives they are designed to achieve, and to assess national objectives we require a standard against which they, too, can be judged. That standard is the definition of ultimate purpose to which a nation and its leaders subscribe or are committed. Those ultimate purposes most commonly have been referred to as the "national interests" of the state, and that is the term that will be used here.

These distinctions may be deceptively simple; they imply, for example, that there have been accepted definitions of the national interests and objectives from which leaders have developed their policies and actions. Yet careful study of American diplomatic history and foreign policy shows that this has not been the case except, as in World Wars I and II, in time of major war.[1] For most of the remainder of the American foreign policy experience, and especially in Asia, both the objectives and national interests of the United States have often been hotly debated. The debate on Vietnam today is only the most recent manifestation of this pattern.

But American diplomatic history shows more than debate; it also shows how that vague term "the American national interest" has in actual practice been interpreted and applied during this century. The main behavioral lesson points to a very sharp distinction between what has been expounded as the national interest and what has been in fact a much more limited set of operating principles. On the one hand, the stated tenets of national interest have been global in scope and often moral in content, and indeed the United States has in that sense become "involved" in almost every corner of the globe. On the other hand, the whole globe no longer appears as the field of American action if we judge genuine involvement by willingness to go to war, or take actions with the clear risk of war. Involvement in that sense shows a clear and more restrictive pattern of American action—and it is concentrated in just three of the world's regions: in Europe, East Asia, and Latin America. Moreover, even within those regions only certain kinds of developments have been regarded as important enough to risk war. Such developments (in Europe, East Asia, and the Western Hemisphere) seem in each instance to have touched on what I will call here the question of *regional dominance*. Because they are so closely linked with actual or potential resort to war by the U.S., these events (impacting on the concept of dominance in the European, East Asian, or Western Hemisphere region) are quite distinguishable from all others. They will be referred to here as events

---

[1] In those instances defeat of an enemy has taken on the characteristics of both an interest *and* an objective; seen in that perspective the goal of victory in war has had near-universal support among Americans.

involving the vital, or *Level One* national security interests of the United States.

At the opposite extreme, which will be referred to as events involving *Level Three* United States interests, are those developments around the globe which have led to no actions by the United States. Many events, after all, are either ignored or lead to nothing more than an expression of concern and interest. The massacre of between 200,000 and 300,000 Indonesians in 1965–66 was a major political development in Southeast Asia; it led, however, to no reaction by the United States. Similarly, the Yemen conflict, beginning in 1962, has led to as many as 15,000 Egyptian, Saudi Arabian, and Yemeni deaths, and at least 100,000 wounded.[2] Gas attacks alone have taken as many as 1000 lives, but aside from occasional condemnations by American spokesmen, there has been no official action by the U.S. A similar refusal to be involved, despite great loss of life, characterized the American official posture toward the Nigerian–Biafran conflict in 1968.

There is a category between these two extremes. Into this category, which I will call characteristic of *Level Two* national interests, fall all those developments which the U.S. neither ignores nor regards as likely to lead to war. Instead, to many developments there is a specific American response, but a response that is limited in the sense that it carries little or no implication of an American commitment to undertake military action. Much of contemporary American foreign policy behavior falls within this category, including American relationships with many of the nations to which assistance is given.

These propositions, which begin to suggest both *where* and under *what circumstances* the United States has felt its major security requirements to be involved, can be explained if we re-examine the meaning of the term "national interest." For this purpose it will be necessary to think of the national interest as a concept operative at three different levels—each level corresponding with one of the three main types of American behavior just mentioned. Moreover, if this three-tiered concept of interest is joined with the concept of "regional dominance," guidelines for future policy will begin to suggest themselves.

To make this clear, and in order also to see how well these propositions explain past behavior, let us first consider where the United States has clearly risked and fought its major wars in this century.

[2] Institute for Strategic Studies, *The Military Balance 1967–68* (London: Institute for Strategic Studies, 1967), pp. 50–51.

Wars, especially major wars, are singled out because the conscious willingness to resort to war on the part of a responsible leadership indicates its belief that a major or "vital" national interest is at stake.

A. WAR AND NATIONAL INTEREST: LEVEL ONE

Major wars have been fought by the United States only in Europe and in East Asia, and for the past twenty years the U.S. has signified its willingness again to risk war—nuclear if necessary—in both those regions, and in connection with Latin America as well. In terms of "levels" of U.S. national interest, as we suggested a moment ago, we can call this willingness to risk and resort to general war the symbol of a vital or *Level One* interest. It may be useful to recall briefly *why* this level of interest has been perceived to exist.

In the European case, a victory of the Central Powers in World War I would have faced the United States with a Europe whose political structure would have been dominated by Germany. To help prevent this, and to defeat Germany, the United States allied itself with Britain and France. The same consideration, if anything on a more intensively felt basis, led the U.S. to ally itself with Britain and the U.S.S.R. in 1941 to defeat Germany once more. Finally, since 1948–49, the United States has again been willing to face the prospect of general war in Europe, this time against the Soviet Union.

In each of these three cases there was no direct attack or immediate physical threat to the U.S. or its possessions; instead, it was in order to prevent an outcome, centered on Europe, that the United States acted. There seems no question, certainly in the case of Hitler and Stalin, that the outcome that was prevented was hegemony in Europe. With its vast pool of industrial might, a Europe managed by any single power has been seen as a change in the global international structure much less tolerable than a structure characterized by multipolarity, or balance of power. The security of the United States itself, in its own hemisphere, has been perceived to be endangered by the prospect of the enormous concentration of war-making power that one-nation hegemony in Europe would represent.

In East Asia, and especially in East Asia's wars, the United States has not been active quite as long as in Europe, but it has, nevertheless, been almost continuously involved in conflicts there since at least 1941. The general war that broke out in that year was set in motion

even a few years earlier, as the United States—with increasing firmness—began to oppose Japan's conquest of China in 1937–38. And
although that essentially total war ended in 1945, only five years later
the United States had to resume large-scale hostilities in Korea. In
turn, that "limited war" of very major proportions came to an end
in 1953, and only a year later the United States undertook the guarantees in Indo-China and Southeast Asia that led to its becoming involved in a massive way in Vietnam.

The reason for these repeated involvements in East Asian affairs is
to be found in principles nearly identical with those on which the
U.S. has operated in Europe. Washington has been unwilling, in other
words, to accept an East Asian structure under the main influence, or
dominance, of any single power.[3] For this reason, the post–World War
II period in East Asia has been characterized by a continuation of the
bipolar conflict that began in 1915. For China, under Mao, has appeared to aim for East Asian hegemony, and the United States—having
successfully opposed Japan's efforts to achieve that goal—has been unwilling to accept China in her place.

The essential explanation for this resistance has lain in the belief
that, like Europe (but in the years before World War II with less
immediate intensity), East Asia represents a pool of technological and
human resources which under single management could threaten the
security of the United States. Moreover, and as a region in which this
concept of *regional dominance* applies, the *Level One* interests of the
United States have found application in terms of the three subregions
which taken together comprise East Asia: China itself, Japan-Korea,
and Southeast Asia. By 1941 Japan's conquest of Southeast Asia was
readily achievable, and some have argued that to prevent that outcome alone the U.S. might not have gone to war. But to the extent
that control of China was also within her grasp, Japan clearly would
then have achieved general hegemony in East Asia. China was the
third "leg" of East Asian dominance, and to prevent the completion
of that tripod the United States was compelled to undertake war.

In the postwar era the same three-part conception of East Asia has
seemed relevant. To the extent that China appeared bent on establishing major influence in Southeast Asia (if not by conquest then by

[3] As later chapters will explain in more detail, an American conviction on this
score could be traced as far back as the Open Door notes, and certainly no later
than its specific opposition to Japan's efforts to achieve East Asian hegemony.
In 1915, for example, the U.S. began to express its adamant opposition to the
"Twenty-One Demands," which was only the first of a long string of Japanese
efforts to bring China under its exclusive influence.

achieving on her rim the establishment of states submissive to her will), China has appeared in the American strategic perspective as a successor to Japan's earlier role. For were China to accomplish general dominance in Southeast Asia, Peking would then have achieved two of the three legs of East Asian dominance. The United States has been willing to risk and undertake war to prevent that outcome,[4] a willingness which has been referred to here as the characteristic of a *Level One* national interest.

In both Europe and East Asia, moreover, these post-1945 evidences of American willingness to undertake general war have been accompanied by major dollar support programs designed to assist potentially very strong nations to achieve political and economic stability. In Europe the success of the Marshall Plan, along with the guarantees conveyed in the NATO treaty, have resulted in a Western Europe that does not tempt aggression and subversion today, as it did from 1947–53. In East Asia, United States massive assistance in rebuilding Japan, a policy initially resisted by such friendly states as Britain, Australia, and New Zealand, has similarly helped result in a Japan not readily susceptible to overthrow, or to threats from without.

In this broad portrayal, in which we have discussed two separate world regions, it seems clear that there is much that is common to the U.S. involvements in both Europe and East Asia. The common element appears to have had little to do with ideology, or even with immediate physical threats, for neither Germany nor Japan represented communism, and neither was embarked on direct attacks against the territory of the continental United States when war was undertaken. Instead, the common element has to do with the United States perception of power relations in Europe and East Asia, and the meaning of those power relations ultimately for United States

[4] A China dominant in two-thirds of East Asia would have two awesome implications for Americans. On the one hand, Japan might seek to prevent further Chinese expansion, and a military conflict of large proportions could result. Given the close ties to Japan (formalized in treaty commitments), the likelihood would be very high for direct American involvement in a war with China. Equally disturbing is the other outcome, for a China already dominant in Southeast Asia could lead Japan to seek *rapprochement* with Peking. In that case the enormous industrial and technical power of Japan might be bent to the ambitions of China —an outcome frightening in its implications. Although a decision to resist Chinese power is a somewhat more likely choice for Japan than a policy of alignment (and subordination), either choice represents a situation which the U.S. would hope to avoid.

security. In each case, that is, *the United States appears to have undertaken or risked general war to prevent a nation already embarked on aggrandizement from achieving final dominance in Europe and East Asia.* The fifty-year global behavior pattern of the United States indicates that it will accept general war rather than tolerate that outcome.

The only close parallel, in terms of both constancy of behavior and the importance which the United States appears to attach to the region, is in Latin America. There, the United States has quite often used force to achieve its aims. In 1962, in a confrontation with the Soviet Union on the issue of missiles in Cuba, the U.S. very clearly risked general nuclear war rather than permit to take place what it regarded as a fundamental political change. But there is an important difference, as well as a similarity, in the U.S. perception of Latin America as compared with Europe and East Asia. For the United States is clearly the dominant power, to the exclusion of all others, in the Western Hemisphere, and since 1823 the United States has come to expect that no other great power should challenge this dominance. Indeed, until the Cuba Missile crisis it was not uncommon for observers in recent years to write off the Monroe Doctrine as a dead letter. That famous "eyeball to eyeball" confrontation proved that it is not. The United States knowingly risked nuclear war with the Soviet Union rather than permit the emplacement by a great power of strategic weapons within the Western Hemisphere.

It seems clear, therefore, that the United States believes that certain kinds of change in Latin America can affect the vital interests of the United States. Its willingness to risk nuclear war there suggests that in Latin America, just as in Europe and East Asia, a *Level One* U.S. interest is present. In contrast to its interest in Europe and East Asia, however, the Latin American concern of the United States is of a positive nature. The U.S. has acted to *preserve* its own dominance in that region, while in Europe and East Asia it has acted in order to *prevent* any other one state from achieving regional dominance. The similarity is, nevertheless, sufficient to allow the vital or *Level One* interests of the United States to be expressed in this way:

LEVEL ONE NATIONAL SECURITY INTERESTS OF THE U.S.

IN EUROPE:	*To Prevent One-Nation Dominance*
IN LATIN AMERICA:	*To Preserve the Dominance of the U.S.*
IN EAST ASIA:	*To Prevent One-Nation Dominance*

B. LEVEL TWO AND LEVEL THREE NATIONAL INTERESTS

It would be tempting at this point to present a similarly-drawn formulation, attempting to identify the *Level Two* and *Level Three* national interests of the U.S. But as the discussion will show, that is not readily possible. In large part this is because the three-tiered concept of national interest suggested here is predicated on the assumption that the United States has only *minimum* conditions which it seeks to see satisfied in international relations. This is precisely the opposite of a nation with a developed set of goals and objectives for the globe as a whole. The Soviet Union and presumably China are such states;[5] within more limited spheres so were Nazi Germany and Japan. In contrast, the United States is not presumed here to be an imperialist state with a blueprint for the world. For that reason, and after identifying (as we have just done) the vital or *Level One* interests of the U.S., we can best describe the other ranges of U.S. national interest by suggesting how they are different from *Level One* interests.

To be most specific, it should be emphasized that whereas the hallmark of a *Level One* interest is the willingness to risk general war in connection with dominance in the three named regions, *Level Two* and *Level Three* interests imply no such automatic willingness.

Indeed *Level Three* interests, as they were identified just before, are furthest removed from resort to force. For this reason, and for the purposes of this discussion, the nature of *Level Three* interests can be quickly identified and just as quickly dismissed here: they represent the most general concern of the United States in peace, in a modicum of political stability, and in a diminution of violence everywhere on the globe. But this *Level Three* interest, in peaceful change for its own sake, implies no willingness on the part of the United States to undertake war. It is in that sense that I suggested earlier that the United States has "ignored" events such as the mass murdering of several hundred thousand Indonesians in 1965–66, even though that event took place in Southeast Asia—part of the East Asia region where the United States has a *Level One* interest. A judgment was made, cor-

---

[5] Hans J. Morgenthau long ago coined the term "nationalistic universalism"; it applies to nations with a positive set of foreign policy goals for the globe as a whole.

rectly, that the Indonesian slaughter, however reprehensible and deplorable, was not closely related to the question of dominance in Southeast Asia or in East Asia as a whole.

Between this *Level Three* posture (where an event is essentially ignored) and the other extreme, where an event is seen to touch on the *Level One* interests of the U.S. (because of its connection to dominance in the three named regions), there is, as we suggested earlier, another category. In this category, to be referred to as characteristic of *Level Two* interests, fall those developments which have led to American responses—but responses which have implied no willingness to risk or resort to general war. Because this middle category is likely to present the most difficulty to analysts and policymakers, we will, following a brief and general comparison of *Level Two* and *Level Three* interests, devote the remainder of this chapter to an elaboration of *Level Two* problems.

1. The Middle East and Level Two Interests

There are important economic resources in the Middle East, for example, to which the United States would prefer to have access. More important, the United States would prefer not to have those resources—oil especially—denied to Western Europe, but there is nothing in American behavior that suggests a willingness to risk general nuclear war to prevent that outcome. American behavior has seemed to say, that is, that the United States would risk even nuclear war to protect the territorial integrity of Western European nations, but that the United States would probably not risk nuclear war to ensure the continued access of those nations to the oil of the Middle East.

Conceivably, of course, resources such as Middle Eastern oil might be construed *indirectly* to represent a vital U.S. interest. This would be the case, for example, if Western European states would necessarily fail to retain their independent status without the oil of the Middle East. This is very unlikely, and with technological change it is becoming an increasingly remote possibility. In such a situation, whereby the hegemonic European ambitions of the Soviet Union or other great power were likely to be achieved because of events in the Middle East, then it could be said that a vital interest of the United States had been sensitized. But because of the indirect linkage, it is important not to confuse an essentially one-resource region like the Middle East with the vast economic and industrial power and potential of Western Europe.[6] The two regions do not impact with equal immediacy on the United States. For that reason it would be more accurate to conclude that the oil of the Middle East, or any similar resource, represents not a vital, but a *Level Two* interest to the U.S.

2. *Africa and* Level Three *Interests*

Similar considerations, but perhaps even further removed from immediate impact upon U.S. security, seem applicable in Africa. Behavior toward events there has indicated that the U.S. deplores revolution and violence as the major instruments of African change. Thus the U.S. has worked to prevent or modify some excesses in African political behavior, as in the Congo. It has also welcomed and assisted moderately those few states which seem embarked on developmental programs presumed—hopefully—to have a good likelihood of success, as in Ethiopia. In addition, the U.S. opposes the extension of Russian and Chinese influence in Africa. For that reason it has sought to reduce the effects of their propaganda and subversive activities there.

On balance, therefore, the U.S. appears to have a preference for *access* in Africa: access in trade terms as well as access to the political leaderships of independent African nations. But the behavior of the U.S. suggests that there are no resources in Africa which exercise a critical leverage either on the immediate security of the U.S. or on the continued independence of Western European states—which might indirectly place some interests in Africa in the category of a *Level Two* U.S. interest. Similarly, the activities of China and the U.S.S.R. in Africa, while not to be ignored, are still so tenuous (and political Africa so inchoate) that they bear no significant connection to power relations either in Europe or in East Asia.

For these reasons, most African political developments appear to impact on the national interest of the United States at the level of least criticality and specificity. The American interest in Africa can thus be expressed in terms only of the most general relevance: it is an interest in the maintenance of peaceful change as the dominant characteristic of world politics. This interest in peaceful change, which the U.S. hopes for everywhere, can be differentiated readily from the two more salient levels of U.S. interest already identified. For example, in Africa there is no question of a vital resource (*Level Two*), nor is there any likelihood of events in Africa upsetting the patterns of domi-

[6] Even allowing for the Suez Canal as another "resource" of the Middle East.

nance—in Latin America, Europe or East Asia—which the U.S. apparently regards as vital (*Level One*). Africa, therefore, represents only the generalized American interest, applicable universally, in peaceful change; we can refer to such an interest as a *Level Three* concern.[7] Nothing in past behavior or present trends or obligations suggests that the U.S. would knowingly risk war for this level of national interest.

Level Three and *Level Two* U.S. interests also apply in Europe, Latin America, and in East Asia; this is another way of saying that not everything taking place in those regions affects the *Level One* interests of the United States. For example, the United States would prefer to see peaceful change as the method in those areas, and would for that reason oppose intraregional conflicts in such regions. In this context the U.S. was opposed to the Indonesian confrontation with Malaysia, and would similarly oppose and no doubt try to settle a conflict between Ecuador and Peru—as it did between Bolivia and Paraguay in the Chaco War.[8] Such conflicts (even though occurring in an area of *Level One* interests), would impact upon the U.S. only at *Level Three* of its national interest, and the U.S., although it might act, would not knowingly risk general war to bring an end to such conflicts.

C. The Operational Problem Posed by Level Two Interests

It has to be recognized, however, as the illustration of Middle Eastern oil has already intimated, that some conditions—arising *outside* the areas where regional dominance has been the concern—conceivably could lead the United States to undertake major military action. One such illustration pertains to the American relationship with Israel. It is widely believed that the United States government, despite the fact that no formal mutual security agreement exists, is committed

---

[7] At this point in time the U.S. approach to Africa is much like the "Open Door" initially applied to China in 1900. The difference, however, is that Africa is already divided, whereas China was never quite fully carved up by the European states. If Africa were less divided, and if simultaneously one great external state did seem capable and anxious to achieve dominance over much or all of Africa, the U.S. approach might have to alter.

[8] 1928–1938. See Bryce Wood, *The United States and Latin American Wars 1932–1942* (New York: Columbia University Press, 1966), pp. 62–83.

to the preservation of the integrity and independence of Israel. Such a commitment, if we assume that Soviet military assistance also implies a security guarantee to such nations as the U.A.R. and Syria, could conceivably involve the United States in a war with the Soviet Union. It was just this concern that conditioned much of the American political environment during the Arab-Israeli war of June, 1967.

Such an illustration is not unlike that of the oil in the same Middle Eastern region. The oil, and implied American commitments to Israel, both represent potential *indirect* linkages to an American choice that might have to include the willingness to risk general war. It is precisely because of this indirect linkage, and also because no such broad purpose as the prevention of regional dominance is involved, that the proposition of an intermediate or *Level Two* category of interest is required. Its implication is that certain conditions, which ordinarily would not be expected to lead to a decision to risk major war, could force such a choice on the United States. That describes a very uncomfortable situation; it suggests that whatever those "certain conditions" are, they lack the inherent or objective qualities for which it might otherwise seem "worth" risking war.

1. *The Two Components of* Level Two *Interests*

What are those "certain conditions"? They would seem to fall into two categories, which I will refer to as specific *resources* and *commitments*. Take as an example of *resources* uranium, and assume, as was thought to be true in the first years of the nuclear era, that uranium was in short supply worldwide. If, as a result, the United States would have been prevented from developing its nuclear arsenal without access to uranium in central Africa (an area not previously included in the concept of regional dominance), then access to central Africa would have become a vital interest of the United States. The area as a whole would not have required American hegemony, but access for this specific purpose would have been sufficiently important to raise the possibility of risking war in order to maintain access.

The meaning of the word *resource* is, moreover, not restricted to minerals or other tangibles. Location can be a resource of critical importance under certain conditions of communications and transport technology. It is in this sense that the history of international politics is replete with references to the strategic importance of certain "narrow seas." The Suez Canal and the Straits of Gibraltar and Malacca are famous historic examples; and Britain, in an age of ocean transport and as a nation critically dependent upon foreign trade, would have considered interdiction of those narrow seas as much a security threat as the destruction of some of her capital ships.

Yet the value of any location is not constant, as any home-buyer in densely populated parts of the United States knows. In international politics especially, the value of any location is instead a function of the state of transport and communications technology. Thus the North African bases of the United States Strategic Air Command, which were probably an essential requirement for bombers with Soviet locations as their targets, obviously have decreased in value with the advent of longer-range weapons. Missiles in deep Colorado silos and nuclear-fueled submarines capable of launching their missiles from under the sea have already begun to call into question the military concept of "forward base deployment." [9] The newest C-5A transport aircraft illustrate the same proposition. Their gigantic airlift capacities will lead to a decline in the need for prepositioned military supplies, and *hence the importance of the territory on which they are situated.*

A *Level Two* national interest, in other words, could be expected to vary greatly in its significance over relatively short periods, say a decade. To the extent that it depends for its importance on a specific resource, such as location, and more importantly to the extent that it could lead the United States to undertake war on its behalf, such an interest would appear to warrant constant review and reappraisal. There would be no point in risking general war for a resource whose value could no longer be demonstrated.

Possibly, but not necessarily deriving from a resource, is the other aspect of a *Level Two* interest: a *specific commitment* or obligation. Such a commitment could be contained in a formal mutual defense agreement between the United States and another nation, or it might be a less formal understanding, although widely believed to imply a commitment. Resources *per se* ordinarily have not been the explanation for such commitments,[10] and it is because of the absence of such "objective" factors that this aspect of a *Level Two* interest needs to be mentioned. For commitments have been undertaken by the United

[9] One reflection is in the high-level attention given to the whole question of future American bases in a study undertaken in 1968 under the auspices of the Joint Chiefs of Staff. Reports suggest it was prepared for submission to a new President as a basis for all strategic planning (See *The New York Times,* October 25, 1968).

[10] This is in large part explained by the very slight dependence of the United States on imports of natural materials ("resources" in the usual sense) from outside the Western Hemisphere.

States to nations which do not meet two criteria: nations outside the regions we have identified as corresponding with a *Level One* interest (and for that reason not connected with the concept of *regional dominance*); and nations lacking in some resource on which it might be said the United States was critically dependent. The most prominent example, as we suggested just before, is Israel: for the American relationship to Israel is widely believed to imply a commitment to the continued existence of that state.

Another illustration, and one on which the United States has acted, arises in connection with Australia and New Zealand. Both in the ANZUS treaty and by virtue of its behavior since 1942, the United States has several times shown its willingness to expend major military efforts to ensure the security of those two English-speaking nations.

The most striking evidence comes from decisions taken early in 1942, when Japan's conquest of the Dutch East Indies was imminent, and when the rapid pace of her advance was very impressive. Australian leaders had already concluded that promises of help from Britain were nearly worthless,[11] and "in Washington there was even serious talk of abandoning Australia and New Zealand to the enemy." [12] But Admiral Ernest King, advising President Roosevelt, stressed the common ties of heritage between the two British nations: "We cannot in honor let Australia and New Zealand down. They are our brothers, and we must not allow them to be overrun by Japan." As historian Samuel Morison adds, "And the President agreed," with the result that the United States—*despite the absence of any formally expressed prior commitments*—did undertake to guarantee the security of Australia and New Zealand. King's advice led the President to send major portions of two Marine Divisions to Australia and New Zealand, where their training continued, and from where they were later sent to battle at Guadalcanal. Moreover, and as if to symbolize the United States commitment, General MacArthur moved his headquarters to Australia, and a U.S. Army Division was sent to Fiji—where New Zealand feared Japanese attacks might otherwise occur.

---

[11] Prime Minister John Curtin of Australia delivered a now famous speech in which he made clear that for the future Australian security would become totally dependent upon the United States. That has not yet changed. See Bernard K. Gordon, *New Zealand Becomes a Pacific Power* (Chicago: University of Chicago Press, 1960), p. 147.

[12] Samuel E. Morison, *History of United States Naval Operations in World War II,* IV (Boston: Little, Brown and Co., 1949), 153.

In the years since, Australian governments have continued to regard their security as a direct function of a United States commitment. The ANZUS treaty is today the formal expression of this commitment, and Austrialian officials make no secret of how much they rely upon it. For example, were Australia engaged in a military conflict with Indonesia over disagreements in New Guinea, and were they unable to meet the problem on their own resources, Australian leaders would expect the United States to support their effort. When asked by virtue of what commitment would the United States be expected to engage in military action against Indonesia, Australians promptly respond that ANZUS provides this commitment.[13]

The prospect of a United States military effort in New Guinea, in defense of almost any Australian interest, would seem destined to raise American objections of huge proportions. Yet it is precisely in the nature of an indirect but specific commitment—for which no "objective" United States interest can be demonstrated—that such an outcome might be projected. If readers are tempted at this point to object that the Australian illustration is too farfetched, let it first be remembered that the United States "commitment" to South Vietnam, from 1954 to perhaps as late as 1961, would have been accurately characterized as a *Level Two* interest: A *Level Two* interest reflecting *specific commitments.* To make that more clear, and in order to illustrate how the levels-of-interest concept may be applied, the nature of the Vietnam involvement will be briefly considered within that analytical framework.

[13] Australians justify their interpretation of ANZUS by referring to its coverage of their "island territories." Averell Harriman has said that "the terms of the ANZUS Treaty, to which we are bound, *would cover New Guinea as well as mainland Australia*—in fact—anywhere where your soldiers were involved. That is what I said and I am glad to repeat it . . ." (from Press Conference by Mr. Averell Harriman, transcript provided this author by Australian Embassy, Washington, D.C.; emphasis added).

Australians confidently refer to this statement as a reinforcement of their ANZUS guarantee, and fully expect that the Treaty will cover any contingency, including one that might take place in New Guinea. A leading Australian scholar, Coral Bell, notes that Australia is "unambiguously within the American protectorate area since the signature of the ANZUS Treaty in 1951 . . . [which] could be invoked in the event of a threat to Australian security arising from the part of Indonesia, or even the original source of apprehension, Japan. Furthermore, it covers any armed attack in the Pacific area, not only on the metropolitan territories of the parties, but on 'island territories under their jurisdiction.' This is an important point, *since one major focus of Australian apprehensions about the future is the situation in New Guinea,* which is strategically equally difficult to abandon or to defend." Coral Bell, "South-East Asia Minus Britain," *Survival* (March, 1968), pp. 74–75 (emphasis added).

2. Descriptive and Prescriptive Uses of the Model:
Vietnam and a Hypothetical Case

a. Vietnam. If we consider the nature of the United States relationship to South Vietnam after 1954, and as recently as, say, 1961, it is clear that whatever commitment did exist in that early period was certainly not of the *Level One* variety, for the outcome in Vietnam *during that period* did not yet bear a direct relationship to the question of dominance in Southeast Asia as a whole. The issue of regional dominance was not then involved for at least two reasons: first, because Southeast Asia in the 1950's was much less an interrelated or articulated political region and system than today, and as a result, events in one part of Southeast Asia were much more insulated from other parts of the region than is true today. The second reason is probably even more important: the fact that through the 1950's the United States was openly and publicly far less intimately tied to any outcome in South Vietnam than later became true. The United States had not yet made any suggestion that its role in Asian security (*and interpretations as to the credibility of that role*) was inextricably linked with its ability specifically to prevent South Vietnam from being absorbed by the Hanoi government.

Instead, whatever commitment to South Vietnam did exist in that early period was an incremental combination of *specific commitments.* Among these, for example, were the bilateral military assistance agreements, which carried implications of further support; the protective "umbrella" contained in the SEATO protocol; and finally perhaps, a self-made sense of commitment among some Americans. To officials who knew how much effort and resources had already been invested in the regime of Ngo Dinh Diem, it probably appeared that the United States could not ("in honor"?) do otherwise than invest just a little bit more to "complete" the task of making South Vietnam secure.

Only later (after about 1962), when the United States began to make increasingly clear to the world that its prestige, its good faith as an ally, and the sanctity of its "commitment" were also involved, did the Vietnam conflict take on the characteristics of a *Level One* interest. By 1964–65 this escalation of Vietnam's significance was complete, and where only an indirect interest had existed before—deriving from specific commitments—now a vital interest stood in its place.[14]

---

[14] If this point is not always clear to Americans, it is at least understood in Southeast Asia. For example, Singapore's Prime Minister, commenting on America's role

That this process of interest-escalation took place in *steps* lies at the heart of much of the popular frustration with the Vietnam conflict. For there was no single and formal announcement that it was taking place, and no widespread understanding that it had occurred. When Senator Fulbright and other critics of the Vietnam conflict took Secretary of State Rusk so much to task in the Senate *Hearings* of March, 1968, it was as a product of this frustration. It seemed to the critics inexplicable that the United States should be engaged in so costly a conflict for a purpose of such small proportions: the security of South Vietnam. It could not be demonstrated that this small nation of 17 million, marked largely by poverty, possessed any resources of significance to the United States, or even to another nation. It could not be demonstrated that there was any treaty between South Vietnam and the United States, which in any usual sense had legally "required" the United States ultimately to send more than a half-million troops there. In the absence of that sort of criteria to justify so large an investment, critics understandably are likely to ask, as many Senators asked Secretary of State Rusk, for what purpose is so large an effort being made?

Officials will be loathe to reply in such circumstances that the United States by its own actions had escalated the level of national interest involved. Yet that is precisely what occurred in the Vietnam instance: had the United States not increased its Vietnam role in the early 1960's, South Vietnam probably would have fallen to Hanoi— but it would have been very difficult to argue that such an outcome *then* would have irrevocably damaged perceptions of American commitments, or the American role in Asia. By 1967–68, on the other hand, a defeat or a Vietnam withdrawal by the United States could be expected to have destructive consequences throughout Southeast Asia, and probably beyond. This is precisely the danger inherent in a *Level Two* interest, particularly when the interest derives not from a tangible resource, but from incremental—and separately small—specific commitments.

If there is a lesson in such an episode, it must be that the number

---

in the Vietnam war, remarked early in 1968 that "if, having put the stakes up so high, it [South Vietnam] is abandoned, then I think the neighboring countries, the countries adjacent to Vietnam, will find American will to stay and hold the line not credible, and everybody will shift in posture. And once the shift in posture takes place, what normally might have taken ten, fifteen or more years will be telescoped into five or even less years" (From remarks of Lee Kuan Yew, quoted in David W. Chang, "Nation-Building in Singapore," *Asian Survey*, VIII, September, 1968, 771).

of *Level Two* national interests needs to be kept to the barest possible minimum. The commitments which might flow from such interests have too great a potential for enlargement and intensification, to the point where the military actions necessary to preserve what originally had been a *Level Two* interest cannot be distinguished from those which would be acceptable in the defense of a *Level One*, or vital interest. The result is not only to engage the nation in what could be regarded as an indefensible war, but also to intensify the natural doubts that accompany any war effort—and, as the Vietnam conflict helps illustrate, a democratic political system needs to maintain domestic support for its external actions. That consideration alone makes it essential to limit commitments to interests that are in fact vital, and the three-step levels-of-interest model suggested here can help clarify that distinction.

A major use of the model is that as developments come to the attention of policymakers, the approach suggested here can help to "place" global events. For that reason the model has the potential to assist in developing guidelines for future United States policy, and to underscore that point we might consider a theoretical illustration.

b. Levels of Interest as a Decision Framework: A Hypothetical Case. Let us first assume that an armed conflict has erupted between two African states, and let use even suppose that one of the states involved is the recipient of Soviet or Chinese military assistance. Assume further that the conflict is very intense, with thousands of casualties resulting, and that American military assistance is sought.

Using the levels-of-interest model described earlier, we would know at the outset that the United States has never considered its vital, or *Level One* interests to be affected by developments in Africa. It has instead always acted as if events in only Europe, East Asia, or the Western Hemisphere could affect the global strategic balance with which it is concerned. Based on that consideration, the model would reject any initial effect at *Level One* deriving from a conflict in Africa. Having dismissed any direct *Level One* interest, the question would remain: Does this African conflict concern the United States at *Level Two* or at *Level Three* of its national interest scale?

To answer that, two questions would in turn have to be answered: first, has the United States undertaken any specific (even informal) commitments likely to be called on in connection with this conflict? Second, does any outcome from the conflict threaten to block access to any resource on which the United States is directly or indirectly critically dependent for its security? If both questions were answered negatively, then, no matter how much the conflict seemed to represent an important world crisis, it would represent to the United States an event at only *Level Three* of its national interest scale. That would in turn mean that no justification would exist for any action by the United States that might lead to involvement in armed conflict.

In essence, such a determination would have the effect of foreclosing many potential options otherwise liable to be considered. But such options would, of course, represent different forms of American intervention, and unless one is predisposed toward intervention for its own sake, an early decision not to intervene is not a cause for distress.

Suppose, however, it were concluded that a *Level Two* United States interest *were* affected by this African conflict, either by reason of some resource, or because of an implied or formal commitment to one of the states involved. The case for intervention then would have to be weighed against the possibility that such intervention could lead to exertions of very major proportions. To intervene, in other words, the United States would have to be willing to accept costs not distinguishable from those which it would contemplate bearing were a *Level One* interest involved.

If access to a *resource* was the essence of the *Level Two* interest, the costs of substituting for that resource would need to be weighed. Would the costs of substitution appear greater than the potential costs of general war?[15] If not, then the appropriate course of action would be to adopt methods to substitute for the resource and make no further commitment in support of the *Level Two* interest. If it were a *commitment* which had led to the *Level Two* designation, and were it determined that the cost of forfeiting on the commitment was less than the costs that might have to be borne in its defense, then once again it would be appropriate for the United States to find the most graceful way out of the apparent obligation. In both cases the effect would be to downgrade a previously perceived *Level Two* interest to a *Level Three* category.

Bearing in mind that we have excluded from the illustration crises potentially associated with *Level One* interests (those in which the question of East Asian, European, or Western Hemisphere dominance is raised), the decision to drop an apparent *Level Two* interest to *Level*

---

[15] Charles Wolf, Jr., in an excellent essay, has similarly dealt with the concept of "substitution cost" as a method by which to ascribe values in foreign policy analysis. See Chapter One, "The Value of the Third World," in his *United States Policy and the Third World* (Boston: Little, Brown and Company, 1967). My debt to Wolf's thinking is clear, although I drafted this particular chapter before his book became available to me.

Three is a probable outcome in most cases. Yet it is possible to envisage the reverse; some *Level Two* interests could be judged sufficiently important to warrant early treatment as *Level One* interests. Again, the American commitment to Australia and New Zealand, as well as to Israel, might appear to fit this category, and if something like the model presented here was utilized when reaching such a decision, at least the potential price of the decision could not be overlooked. That is the purpose of suggesting the "levels-of-interest" approach in the first instance: to help identify the criteria on which the United States has in the past, and might in the future, *discriminate* among global developments.

D.   The Tradition of Selectivity

Perhaps because the United States is so often thought of as a "global power," and because it does have lower level interests (*Levels Two* and *Three*) everywhere, it may sometimes be forgotten that in its behavior the United States *has* discriminated among the different world regions. Perceptive observers have recognized this, and they have seen too that the basis for discrimination has lain in the U.S. concern regarding regional dominance in certain regions. Charles Wolf, for example, has defined the Asian national interests of the United States in precisely those terms: "to prevent the domination of the area by a single power, or by a group of powers acting in concert." [16]

But it has remained for such writers as Hans Morgenthau and, a decade before him, Nicholas Spykman to relate the concept of regional dominance to the global position and interests of the United States. Their writings show clearly how the U.S. has differentiated among

[16] Charles Wolf, Jr., "United States Interests In Asia," RAND Corporation Monograph, P-3311 (January, 1966), p. 1. When Wolf wrote that, his contribution may have been unique in the postwar scholarly literature. When work began on this book in 1966, and a similar judgment was reached on the nature of the over-riding American interest in Asia, there seemed little company other than Wolf. Now, however, as scholarship begins once again to explore the purposes—as contrasted with the mere practices—of American behavior in East Asia, it appears likely that fairly wide agreement on the nature of the U.S. vital, or *Level One* interest will emerge. For example, since these chapters were drafted a similar conclusion on the prevention of one-nation dominance in East Asia has been well-stated by Fred Greene, in his *U.S. Policy and the Security of Asia* (New York: McGraw-Hill Book Company, 1968), and asserted by Morton Halperin in "After Vietnam: Security and Intervention in Asia," *Journal of International Affairs*, XXII, 1968, 236–46.

world regions. Fifteen years ago, for example, Morgenthau emphasized that the U.S. interest in Europe, East Asia, and the Western Hemisphere is absolutely and fundamentally distinct from its interest in other world regions. In the Western Hemisphere, he stressed:

> We have always endeavored to preserve the unique position of the United States as a predominant power without rival. We have not been slow in recognizing that our predominance was not likely to be effectively threatened by any one American nation or combination of nations acting without support from outside the hemisphere. This peculiar situation has made it imperative for the United States to isolate the Western Hemisphere from the political and military policies of non-American nations. . . . The Monroe Doctrine and the policies implementing it express that permanent national interest of the United States in the Western Hemisphere.[17]

This fundamental goal, to preserve U.S. dominance in the Western Hemisphere, Morgenthau continued, could be endangered only by support from outside—"historically from Europe." For that reason, he added, the United States has sought to avoid conditions "conducive to a European nation's interfering in the affairs of the Western Hemisphere or contemplating a direct attack upon the United States."

> These conditions would be most likely to arise *if a European nation, its predominance unchallenged within Europe,* could look across the sea for conquest without fear of being menaced at the center of its power; that is, in Europe itself.
> It is for this reason that the United States has consistently—the War of 1812 is the sole major exception—pursued policies aiming at the maintenance of the balance of power in Europe.[18]

Finally, in dealing with Asia, Morgenthau concluded that in that region too the American "interest is again the maintenance of the balance of power." This purpose has been much less clear than in Europe because, as Morgenthau added, the U.S. has been "vitally concerned" in Asia only since the turn of the century, and also because the nature of U.S. interests there has lacked definition. As a result, policies toward the area have not been precise; they have "never as unequivocally expressed our permanent national interest as have the hemispheric and European policies." Yet, Morgenthau concluded,

> . . . underlying the confusions, reversals of policy, and moralistic generalities of our Asiatic policy since McKinley, one can detect a

[17] Hans J. Morgenthau, *In Defense of the National Interest* (New York: Alfred A. Knopf, 1952), p. 88.
[18] *Ibid.,* p. 5.

consistency that reflects, however vaguely, *the permanent interest of the United States in Asia. And this interest is again the maintenance of the balance of power.*[19]

We will need to examine that proposition in this book, partly to determine whether the consistency to which Morgenthau points is in fact apparent, and also to determine whether "balance of power," which many identify as an *interest,* is better understood as only an *objective.* For there are, as we suggested at the outset, important distinctions between the two. As we examine the American record, in Asia especially, the distinction will become more clear.

[19] *Loc. cit.* (emphasis added).

Three

A BALANCE OF POWER IN ASIA

Many readers will not find it easy to accept Morgenthau's conclusion that "balance of power" has always been the main interest of the United States in Asia. Some will question whether there has been *any* important consistency in America's Asian policies, to say nothing of an approach so seemingly calculating as a balance-of-power policy. This and the next chapter will help answer both questions: Are there important and discernible consistencies in the record of American involvement in East Asia? Is it valid to conclude that the United States has pursued a balance-of-power policy in that region?

One excellent way to judge is to re-examine the historic behavior of the United States in the Far East, and to recall how that behavior has been described and understood. To do this, it is necessary to look back to the turn of the century: to the period of the acquisition of the Philippines, the Open Door notes, and other steps that began to signify an active U.S. interest in the politics of East Asia.

Historians do not necessarily agree on which precise U.S. step in that period signals the "beginnings" of a U.S. Asian policy, but they do agree that it was comprised of three ingredients: (1) it derived from considerations of *global politics;* (2) it was concerned with *China;* and (3) because the purpose of policy was to prevent any one state from achieving East Asian dominance, it was characterized by *shifts in American support.*[1]

[1] For some insights, however, on the extent of *disagreement* among historians of American policy in Asia, see Dorothy Borg (compiler), *Historians and American Far Eastern Policy* (New York: The East Asian Institute, Columbia University, 1966).

A. THE FLEXIBLE APPROACH

These shifts in support, amounting to a seemingly pragmatic and flexible approach, are well illustrated in U.S. relations with Japan and China at the turn of the century. In 1894, for example, those two states were at war, and it was a Japanese victory for which American leaders hoped. "American opinion," as John Fairbank writes, "favored Japan in her war against China." [2] Only a few years later, however, in 1900 and 1903, it was China and *her* rights that drew strong support from the U.S., beginning with the first Open Door notes. Then, in just another few years, U.S. actions made it clear that the earlier support for Japan still existed, for in the Russo-Japanese War of 1904–5, Japan was once again the clear favorite of American opinion and leadership.

The interesting point about this seemingly inconsistent behavior is that even early commentators saw it in approximately balance-of-power terms. Often they concluded that the U.S. simply was suspicious of any Asian power that seemed to be in the process of becoming "too" powerful, and this is the judgment to which many of today's historians have come as well. In researching Theodore Roosevelt's attitudes and behavior, for example, they have concluded that he was quite conscious of the purpose and direction of his policy in Asia. Although he had an undoubted admiration for the Japanese, it was never his purpose to favor Japan's unbridled dominance in the East. Instead, and once again in Fairbank's words, the United States "began to turn against Japan after 1904 only when Japan gave promise of being the top dog in the Far East." [3]

Indeed, historians have described Roosevelt's policies as aiming "to leave a weakened Russia and a strengthened Japan facing each other at the end of the war, thereby equalizing the Manchurian balance of power." [4] And as Tyler Dennet has put it, "It is impossible to study the period 1898–1904 and not feel that Japan was fighting the battle of the United States in Manchuria . . . it was apparently

[2] John K. Fairbank, *The United States and China* (Cambridge: Harvard University Press, 1948), p. 317.
[3] *Loc. cit.*
[4] *Loc. cit.*

to American interests that Japan should disturb the Russian over-balance in Manchuria." [5]

The policy of the Open Door itself should be seen in the same light, although it has sometimes been regarded as a merely commercial initiative or as a piece of moral posturing. Instead, the Open Door "was an Anglo-American defensive measure in power politics, without much thought for the interests of the Chinese state." [6] Samuel Bemis, one of this nation's most eminent diplomatic historians, has likened British support for the U.S. Open Door declaration in 1900 to earlier British endorsement of the Monroe Doctrine in 1823. In both cases, Bemis writes, Britain opposed the partition of "vast areas" (Latin America and China) among foreign powers. It was for that reason that Britain invited the U.S. to cooperate in guaranteeing the territorial integrity of China: "once more Great Britain wanted to call in the United States to redress the European balance of power . . . this time in the Far East." [7]

Initially, the United States was reluctant to adopt this view of China, but the acquisition of the Philippines helped enormously to alter that. Direct possession of territory in Asia added weight to the arguments of those who had already been urging a more active Asian policy. Thus, in notes first drafted in 1899, and culminating finally in Secretary of State Hay's famous "circular note" of July 3, 1900, it was announced that "the policy of the . . . United States is to . . . preserve Chinese territorial and administrative entity." [8]

[5] Edward H. Zabriskie (quoting Tyler Dennet) in *American-Russian Rivalry in the Far East*, reprinted in William A. Williams, *The Shaping of American Diplomacy* (Skokie: Rand McNally & Co., 1960), p. 474. On this same point, also see Robert E. Osgood, *Ideals and Self-Interest in America's Foreign Relations* (Chicago: The University of Chicago Press, 1953), pp. 67–68.

[6] Fairbank, *op. cit.*, p. 321.

[7] Samuel F. Bemis, *A Short History of American Foreign Policy and Diplomacy* (New York: Holt, Rinehart & Winston, Inc., 1959), p. 348. George F. Kennan asserts, but provides little persuasive evidence for, a contrasting view: that by 1898–99 Britain "was beginning to move quietly away from the Open Door doctrine" (George F. Kennan, *American Diplomacy, 1900–1950* [Chicago: University of Chicago Press, 1951], p. 27). The view is not concurred with by others; P. H. Clyde, for example, writes that the American policy developed "in the late summer of 1899 . . . was a direct product of British initiative" (P. H. Clyde, *The Far East*, 3rd ed. [Englewood Cliffs, N.J.: Prentice-Hall, Inc., 1966], p. 295). This is also the conclusion reached by Bemis and Fairbank.

[8] These words are the core of the Open Door doctrine. In later statements by American leaders, the words "administrative entity" were recast to read "territorial and administrative *integrity*." For the text of the Hay note, see Dorothy B. Goebel, ed., *American Foreign Policy: A Documentary Survey, 1776–1960* (New York: Holt, Rinehart and Winston, 1961), p. 188.

This doctrine, Bemis adds, should be regarded as "the capstone of American policy in the Far East." [9] To understand why he gives this primacy to the Open Door declaration, it must be understood that the territorial integrity of China was only instrumentally the central concern of the doctrine and of U.S. policy. The more crucial question was whether some other power, or combination of powers, would be permitted to control China, for it was assumed that the nation or combination of nations that could achieve that objective would already be in possession of a considerable power base elsewhere.

B.   China, the Open Door, and the Global Balance

Perceived in that light, events affecting China have always been the central concern of American Asian policy. At the time of the Open Door this central concern for China was focussed upon China as an acted-upon state—"on the brink of dissolution"—as Bemis writes.[10] China continued to be weak, if not on the brink of dissolution, until the victory of Mao Tse-tung, and until that time the purpose of American policy was to help prevent its dissolution or control by an alien power.

The reason for this policy was the belief that control of China would fundamentally alter the distribution of power in Asia. Thus, while initially the purposes of the Open Door doctrine were explained in terms of commerce, its main thrust was to help prevent the partition of China by European states. The United States opposed this partition, and aligned itself with Britain in that objective, because it believed that reduction in Britain's relative power globally (which Britain expected would result from a European partition of China) was destructive of U.S. interests. It is in this sense that Fairbank argues that the Open Door should be seen as "an Anglo-American defense measure in power politics, without much thought for the interests of the Chinese state." [11] The proper explanation of

[9] Bemis, *op. cit.*, p. 352.

[10] *Ibid.*, p. 348.

[11] Fairbank, *op. cit.*, p. 321. Goebel concurs in this view, and writes that Hay's note represents a "striking innovation in American policy, a departure from the traditional isolationism. . . . Formerly, three of the great powers signified their agreement with the United States' stand; but their concurrence was motivated by national rivalries and *the struggle for balance of power in Asia*" (Goebel, *op. cit.*, p. 186; italics added).

the Open Door policy, therefore, lies in the U.S. desire to preserve two fundamental interests: (1) *the maintenance of a balance of power in Europe* and (2) *continued U.S. hegemony in the Western Hemisphere*, for that in turn had depended upon balanced power in Europe.

Shortly after the establishment of the Open Door doctrine, its wider implications became more apparent. American leaders enlarged its meaning from a doctrine of opposition to the break-up of China to a doctrine of opposition to any nation's control of China. Nicholas Spykman, one of this nation's foremost strategic thinkers, recognized what this reinterpretation of the Open Door meant. He wrote in 1942 that the doctrine "soon became an end in itself, a political consideration inspired by concern with the preservation of a balance of power in the Western Pacific." [12] Another writer, a diplomatic historian with a quite different world-view, has stressed the same point: "American diplomacy in Asia between 1900 and 1912 was designed to extend the power of the United States in the Far East . . . to apply the old principles of balance-of-power politics in the form of the Open Door policy." [13]

C. JAPAN AND THE EXPANSION OF THE OPEN DOOR DOCTRINE

Although it is debatable that American statesmen in that period consciously desired to "extend the power of the United States" for its own sake, it is clear that World War I did lead directly to a re-interpretation and expansion of the Open Door doctrine. For after 1915, Japan attempted to fulfill what it believed to be its great-power destiny, and the United States found itself more and more opposed to Japan's aims.

The circumstance that opened this developing confrontation was the withdrawal from China of the European states, as they turned the whole of their energies and attention to the war in Europe. Japan, now the only state with the capacity and will to expand its influence into China, moved to fill the void. The United States in turn now remained the only state with an interest and capacity to arrest that

---

[12] Nicholas J. Spykman, *America's Strategy in World Politics* (New York: Harcourt, Brace & World, Inc., 1942), p. 141.
[13] William A. Williams, *op. cit.*, p. 440.

development. The result was a fundamental change in the *structure* of the East Asian political environment. Where before 1914 it had been the scene of traditional balance-of-power policies, in which the United States was just one of several actors, the structure now became more clearly polarized. As a result the role of the U.S. was soon to become one of direct counter-power.

The first clear sign of this new U.S.-Japanese pattern came in 1915 when Japan, in the form of the "Twenty-One Demands," [14] attempted to impose her own authority on China. The U.S. response was quick. Secretary of State Bryan informed Japan that the U.S. "cannot recognize any agreement . . . impairing the treaty rights of the United States and its citizens in China, the political or territorial integrity of the Republic of China, or the international policy . . . commonly known as the open-door policy." [15] Later, and especially in the 1930's, this pattern of American opposition to Japanese aims was, of course, to be many times repeated. Some of the signposts to that opposition are found in Stimson's nonrecognition doctrine (1932); in Roosevelt's Quarantine speech (1937); and the denunciation of the U.S.-Japan Commercial Treaty (1939). The sequence of these steps suggests that U.S. policies of opposition to Japan were early in origin as well as quite constant and consistent.

Nevertheless, and perhaps because American responses in Asia were so often ineffectual (and usually accompanied to this day by much debate), the underlying single-mindedness of American policy is too often forgotten. It is argued as a result that American responses have been *ad hoc,* and provide no guidelines for logical development and projection. If that is not true, and if instead past guidelines do exist to help shape an effective Asian policy, the roots of that policy must not be hidden. Where, moreover, there are consistent patterns, to which we will now point, these should be uncovered.

1. Consistency: The 1920's and 1930's

One of the foremost post-World War II studies of American foreign policy, undertaken at the Brookings Institution, argues that in the

[14] The "Demands," as a famous State Department publication has put it, "would have made China a virtual protectorate of Japan" (*United States Relations with China* [Washington, D.C.: Department of State Publication 3573, 1949], p. 7).

[15] From *Foreign Relations of the United States* (1915), p. 146, reprinted in Goebel, *op. cit.,* p. 195. Note that Bryan referred specifically to the Open Door, and note too that he paraphrased the Hay note of 1900, with its reference to the U.S. desire to "preserve Chinese territorial and administrative entity. . . ." Bryan altered this to read China's "political or territorial integrity."

1930's American leaders were unsure of their purposes—that they were unaware of the nature of the world context in which they were acting. The global power position of the U.S. was fundamentally changed, this argument correctly stresses, but leaders did not realize the extent or significance of the change:

> The nature and operation of the old equilibrium of power in Europe, the essential requirements for establishing an equilibrium of power in the Far East, the role that Great Britain had played . . . and finally the part that the United States might be obliged to play because of its own growing strength . . . were not clearly brought into the discussion.[16]

The record of the '20's and '30's hardly supports this view. It shows instead that American leaders well understood how Japan's goals collided with U.S. interests and that they took the lead in opposing the Asian aims of Japan during this period. For example, and after Bryan's rejection of Japan's "Twenty-One Demands" in 1915, the first postwar U.S. effort aimed at Japan was in the conferences leading to the Washington Naval Treaty and the Nine-Power Treaty of 1921–22. The U.S. dominated both the proceedings and the events that led to them.[17]

The significance of these meetings is that the U.S. succeeded in having incorporated in the resulting treaties the fundamental declarations of America's Asian policy—the Open Door doctrine of 1900–1903 and insistence on China's integrity. In the meetings, moreover, the positions taken by Secretary of State Hughes shows convincingly that the primary concern of the U.S. leadership was with Japan's aims and interests in the Pacific. Japan, too, recognized this, and "from start to finish Japan was an unwilling participant in the Washington conference." [18] Indeed, Japan tried to prevent the agenda from touching on her interests in China, but that was precisely what the U.S. insisted must be included, and its view prevailed. The result was that the world's major powers accepted and endorsed the objectives of U.S. national interest in Asia: that no one state should be dominant in the Pacific.

To the extent that the U.S. succeeded in having other nations support its Asian doctrines (so that "after 1921 the United States was

[16] Reitzel, Kaplan, and Coblentz, *United States Foreign Policy, 1945–1955* (Washington, D.C.: The Brookings Institution, 1956), p. 18.

[17] The first and informal initiative for these conferences came from Britain, but the initiative was quickly seized and held by the U.S.

[18] A. Whitney Griswold, *The Far Eastern Policy of the United States* (New York: Harcourt, Brace & World, Inc., 1938), p. 298.

no longer the sole proprietor of these policies"),[19] the initiative taken by the U.S. in convening these meetings was successful.[20] But Japan failed to honor these commitments, and the arms-reduction effects of the conference, leaving "Japan in a position of paramount military and naval power in the Far East," [21] came eventually to present the U.S. with a dilemma.

This became most clear after 1931, as Japan undertook the conquest of Manchuria and the establishment of the puppet "state" of Manchukuo. As in 1915, when Secretary of State Bryan first warned Japan that the U.S. could not accept incursions on China's sovereignty, American reactions in 1931–32 were, on their face at least, quite bold. In this instance the response found Secretary of State Stimson taking a highly unusual step: in notes to Japan (and China) he wrote that the U.S. would *not recognize* any treaty or agreement "which may impair the treaty rights of the United States . . . including those which relate to the sovereignty, the independence, or the territorial and administrative integrity of . . . China, or to the international policy relative to China, commonly known as the open-door policy. . . ." [22]

This announcement, which originated the "nonrecognition" policy of the United States, went well beyond what any other nation had declared either privately to Japan, or in League discussion up to that time. The conquest of Manchuria, it was felt, would add considerably to Japan's capacity to become Asia's most powerful state, and would at the minimum severely impair China's capability to play a role of independent influence.[23] That the U.S. leadership was more sensitive

[19] Bemis, *op. cit.*, p. 696.
[20] Griswold wrote in 1938 that by 1920 it was clear that "the balance of power that had existed in the Far East since the nineteenth century had collapsed. Political circumstances . . . had left the United States to confront Japan—alone" (Griswold, *op. cit.*, p. 268). The Washington Conference, a year later, has to be seen in this light, as "the apotheosis of the traditional Far Eastern policy of the United States . . . the treaties constituted the most dynamic and the most comprehensive attempt on the part of the United States to uphold the territorial integrity of China and all that it believed to depend on it; to make the open door in China an enduring principle . . . and *to confine within barriers manufactured in Washington the hungry expansionism of Japan*" (*ibid.*, p. 331; italics added).
[21] Bemis, *op. cit.*, p. 803.
[22] In W. W. Willoughby, *The Sino-Japanese Controversy and the League of Nations* (Baltimore: The Johns Hopkins Press, 1935), p. 206.
[23] In his discussions of Japan's expansion, and declarations of 1931–34, Bemis writes that Japan had entered on a clear policy of hegemony, and that "such an empire, erected on the ruins of ancient China, accompanied by a German empire built on the ruins of a conquered Europe, *presaged an unbalance of power in the*

to this danger than were other nations is attested to by the fact that the Stimson "nonrecognition" doctrine, however ineffective we know it today to have been, was a more severe reaction than any other nation was prompted to make. It underscores two points: The first is that in 1931 American leaders recognized Japan as their adversary. The second is that the Manchurian aggression helped emphasize to Americans that Asia was now bipolar, for it showed that only the U.S., and not the European powers, was strongly resistant to Japan's expansion. As a result of this realization, and despite the fact that news and public attention were heavily focussed on depression and New Deal recovery (and later with the rise of Hitler), Japan's actions after 1932 were given much attention in the U.S. At each step, U.S. responses show that there was no lack of discussion on the developing confrontation.

In 1934–35, for example, Tokyo released a series of statements on China, and on Japan's way to "peace in East Asia." In these statements, especially one in April, 1934, Japan warned that it would oppose efforts by other nations to supply China with aircraft, military equipment, and instructors. It was a general warning against interference with what Tokyo called its "mission and special responsibilities in Eastern Asia." [24] These views, which were soon repeated and amplified, were promptly labeled by Americans as "Japan's Monroe Doctrine." In an article with that title, a former Under-Secretary of State wrote soon afterwards that Japan's policy would: (1) "make China a vassal State to Japan"; (2) close the Open Door; and (3) be a "flat repudiation of the Nine-Power Treaty of 1922." [25]

The State Department responded in a similar vein. It released a public note that restated America's interests in the integrity of China, and in response to Japan's assertions of "special rights" in China, Washington stressed that "no nation can, without the assent of the other nations concerned . . . make conclusive its will . . . where there are involved the rights, the obligations and the legitimate interests of other sovereign states." [26] Press reactions also show that there was no mistaking either Japan's intent or, in 1934, the American

---

Old World which ought to be the nightmare of every anxious American. . . . It brought back the danger that had been removed for a generation by American intervention in the First World War . . ." (Bemis, *A Diplomatic History of the United States,* p. 821; emphasis added).

[24] Text in *The New York Times,* April 21, 1934.

[25] William R. Castle, "Japan's Monroe Doctrine," *New York Herald Tribune,* May 6, 1934.

[26] State Department announcement of April 30, 1934, quoted in Willoughby, *op. cit.,* p. 638.

attitude to her acts. This attitude was typified in one *Washington Star* editorial comment that "Japan means to set herself up as the supreme, if not the sole, arbiter of Far Eastern, especially Chinese, destinies." [27]

Finally, a series of scholarly books and writings on the subject began to appear, and these helped put in perspective the continuity of Japan's aims, as well as the continuity of American opposition to them. One, published in Washington in 1935, said simply that:

> In the Twenty-One Demands made upon China in 1915, Japan made evident her desire to obtain a control over China that would bring that country under her suzerain control. This result she was not then able to obtain, and as a result of the agreements into which she was persuaded to enter at the time of the Washington Conference, it was hoped . . . that this ambition had been abandoned. *However, it would now appear that this ambition still exists and influences the national policies of Japan.*[28]

The final steps in the chronology came not long after, when Japan resumed open war in China in 1937. President Roosevelt, in his famous "Quarantine Speech," tried to rally public support behind the Government's understanding of Japan's threat. The next day, in order to leave no doubt that it was Japan he had in mind, the State Department said that:

> . . . the United States has been forced to the conclusion that the action of Japan in China is inconsistent with the principles which should govern the relationships between nations and is contrary to the provisions of the Nine-Power Treaty of February 6, 1922. . . .[29]

There is no need to continue to retell these events here, for the detailed record of events after 1937 and immediately prior to Pearl Harbor is too familiar. In gross terms, the remainder of that record shows that the United States in 1938 resumed its naval building program and formally rejected Japan's "new order" in Asia;[30] in 1939 announced that it would abrogate its trade treaty with Japan; and in 1940 worked to stop all shipments of scrap and strategic goods, by tightening up on the "moral embargo" that Roosevelt had asked for even two years earlier.

In the light of this record, there is little to support the view that America's Asian policy lacked direction and sense of purpose. Amer-

---

[27] This and other press reactions are in Willoughby, *op. cit.*, pp. 632–33.

[28] *Ibid.*, p. 627 (emphasis added).

[29] In U.S. Department of State, *U.S. Relations with China*, p. 19 (full text at Annex 20, p. 451).

[30] See Statement by Ambassador Grew to Japanese Foreign Minister Arita, December 30, 1938, in *U.S. Foreign Relations*, Annexes, pp. 459–63.

icans who discussed and wrote about Asia in the 1930's saw that the
U.S. goal of a general Asian balance must lead to a confrontation
with Japan. Willoughby made this clear in a book published as early
as 1935. He concluded with reluctance that the U.S. effort in 1915
to stop Japan's expansion, hopefully "institutionalized" by the Nine-
Power Treaty in 1922, had failed.

D. POLICIES, OBJECTIVES, AND THE U.S. INTEREST

But the main concern in this discussion has not been only to show
that United States *policies* consistently opposed Japan in the 1920's
and 1930's. The point is instead that those specific policies flowed
from an objective; that objective derived from an interest so fundamental that the policies in support of it led inexorably to war: The
U.S. opposed Japan *because that policy served the more basic objective of trying to achieve a balance of power in Asia.* That objective
in turn was sought *because it would best serve the U.S. national
interest of preventing one-nation hegemony there.*
It is not merely the wisdom of hindsight that leads to this conclusion;
it was understood and so stated at the time. In his previously mentioned book, published in 1942, Nicholas Spykman, for example, was
already able to place the war with Japan in its balance-of-power context. Looking beyond the war, he reminded Americans that "the
danger of another Japanese conquest of Asia must be removed, but
this does not inevitably mean the complete elimination of the military
strength of Japan and the surrender of the Western Pacific to China
or Russia." [31] He went further, and predicted that "the main difficulty
of the postwar period will be not Japan but China, [whose] power
potential is infinitely greater than that of (Japan)." [32] In words that
must have seemed strange in 1942, Spykman's conclusion is striking:
"If the balance of power in the Far East is to be preserved in the
future . . . *the United States will have to adopt a . . . protective
policy toward Japan.*" [33]
The obvious implication of Spykman's perceptive and prophetic
analysis is that, despite the friendship that Americans had developed
toward China since at least the 1920's, the United States would have

[31] Spykman, *op. cit.*, p. 460.
[32] *Ibid.*, p. 469.
[33] *Ibid.*, p. 470 (emphasis added).

to oppose China's political ambitions once her leaders succeeded in achieving unity and power. That, of course, is precisely what did develop soon after the end of World War II, not primarily because a Communist revolutionary took control in China but because Mao Tse-tung restored unity and embarked on great-power politics. In that sense, China's behavior—especially Peking's efforts to remove all other great-power influence from East Asia—has reawakened an old American concern. For China has appeared bent on achieving general dominance in East Asia, filling a role that Japan attempted to play a generation earlier. In that earlier case, and given the three-part concept of East Asia which I suggested earlier, Japan's conquest of China —because it would have meant Japanese dominance in East Asia generally—would also have implied a fundamental change in world politics.

Today, the same three sub-regions of Asia—China, Japan-Korea, and Southeast Asia—still appear to constitute the whole of the East Asia region, but today it is China that represents the source of anxiety.[34] For China's policy, even though it has generally avoided overt and direct military aggression as its technique, nevertheless has seemed designed to remove any other great-power influence from the states on China's rim. Nowhere has this been more apparent than in Southeast Asia, and as scholars have noted, China's goals apply to Japan as well.[35]

Yet even considering Southeast Asia alone, the prospect of Chinese

[34] U.S. anxiety about China's aims, while centering on China, was reinforced in the first post-1949 period by fears of Russian-Chinese combination. It is increasingly clear however that the "Sino-Soviet bloc" which so worried Americans in the 1950's was only a temporary Chinese convenience. The wonder is that the two were able to present a united front for so long. See John Fairbank's comments on Mao in the *Washington Post* (Book Review) July 17, 1967.

[35] In a book published after this study was largely completed, Professor Fred Greene notes, for example, that China sees an American presence in Asia as "its chief obstacle" in the path of "China's desire for predominance in the eastern half of Asia . . ." (Fred Greene, *U.S. Policy and the Security of Asia* [New York: McGraw-Hill Book Company, 1968], p. 195). Greene notes that China seeks to bring Japan "under Chinese political control, thereby shifting the balance of power dramatically and perhaps decisively." Concerning Southeast Asia, Greene's analysis is parallel to this author's: that China seeks to remove all opposing great-power (and especially American) influence from the region. He remarks, for example, that "the undoubted Chinese desire for predominance does not necessarily entail direct control," and could accept a "situation in which most states remained independent . . . *but with all outside influences but China's excluded*" (emphasis mine). In any event, Greene stresses, China would not "treat a political status quo in Southeast Asia as anything more than a temporary expedient on the way to communization." All references are to pp. 195–97, *ibid.*

dominance there has resurrected the anxiety that one nation might possess what I referred to before as two of the three "legs" of East Asian dominance. American leaders, having at such great cost denied that role to Japan in the years 1941–45, are not now prepared to accept China in her stead.

Four

MYTHS AND REALITY
IN AMERICAN ASIAN POLICY

If, as described here so far, American purposes and objectives in
Asia have been so constant and so clearly aimed to protect the vital
interest of the U.S. of preventing one-nation dominance in Asia, why
have they always been so intensely questioned and debated by many
Americans? Today this debate is reflected in deep and widespread
questioning of the purposes of the Vietnam war; but historically, debate and disagreement have characterized the entire 70-year period
of America's Asian involvement. Is there a reasonable explanation for
this pattern of doubt and disagreement?

Part of the answer, it would appear, lies in the strikingly wide
gap between the public and official *explanations* for U.S. Asian policy
and the underlying purposes which those policies have been designed
to achieve.

A. CONSTANT PURPOSES AND INCONSTANT EXPLANATIONS

Historically, American official pronouncements on Asia have been
less than candid. At the beginnings of U.S. policy toward China, for
example, the discussion was framed in terms of "commercial interest."
The Open Door policy itself was publicly justified in those narrow
terms, whereas the balance-of-power aims shared by Britain and the
U.S. in 1900 are recognized by historians as the more accurate explanation for that historic American initiative. Similarly in 1915, 1922,
and in 1937–38, the United States justified its opposition to Japan's
policies in false terms. Instead of explaining to Americans the need to
counter Japan's expansion *per se,* officials justified their policies in

terms of the "sanctity of treaties" and "orderly international processes."

The most striking illustration came in 1938, when American opposition to Japan was becoming undeniably clear, and when Americans were demanding to know the reason for it. In this instance the demand came from the Senate, in the form of a request from Vice-President Garner to Secretary of State Hull. The Senate wanted to know, Garner wrote, precisely what was the extent of American "interests" in East Asia: what was the extent and dollar value of our Asian trade and of investments in the East, and how many Americans were living in China?

Hull's answer is of classic importance, for it represents one of the first instances in which the official and public definition of U.S. national interests in Asia broke loose from its traditional trade and commercial mooring. Thus Hull, after first detailing the China trade and the number of Americans residing in China (in order to comply with the Senate's request to quantify U.S. "interests") wrote this to Garner:

> The interest and concern of the United States in the Far Eastern situation, in the European situation, and in situations on this continent are *not measured* by the number of American citizens residing in a particular country at a particular moment nor by the amount of investment of American citizens there nor by the volume of trade. There is a broader and much more fundamental interest—which is that *orderly processes in international relationships be maintained.* Referring expressly to the situation in the Far East, an area which contains approximately half the population of the world, the United States is deeply interested in supporting by peaceful means influences contributory to preservation and *encouragement of orderly processes. This interest far transcends in importance the value of American trade with China or American investments in China; it transcends even the question of safeguarding the immediate welfare of American citizens in China.*[1]

Hull's answer shows that statesmen groped—almost pathetically—for a meaningful definition of U.S. national interest in Asia, a definition that would go beyond the usual catechism of investments, trade, and the rights of U.S. nationals in China.

But Hull's letter also shows that statesmen were still unwilling to state frankly both to Americans *and* Japanese—even in 1938—that the U.S. would not accept an Asia dominated by Japan. *That* was the irreducible American national interest for which the United States

[1] Department of State, Press Releases, January 15, 1938, pp. 100–105, in T. A. Bisson, *American Policy in the Far East, 1931–1941* (New York: Institute of Pacific Relations, 1941), p. 151 (emphasis added).

ultimately went to war, but officials declined to say so openly. Instead, and by way of definition, the State Department sought comfort in the nonoperational concept of "orderly international processes" as the statement of United States national interest—as if the U.S. would risk and face war anywhere and everywhere for that vague goal. Because the goal was not real, the dialogue and the debate continued to be conducted in mythological terms, just as very often today the war in Vietnam has been justified in terms of American support of "self government for Asian peoples," or the need to bring democracy to Vietnam.

As a result of this pattern, and it amounts to an unfortunate and unintended deception, Americans have too often been unprepared for actions which their government has later found it necessary to take. This was certainly the case in the 1930's, when despite Japan's increasing aggression, the U.S. continued to explain its policy in ways that did not help Americans to understand the enormity of the problem. It was no doubt for that reason that despite the clarity with which Roosevelt may have recognized the Japanese threat to U.S. interests in Asia, his famous "Quarantine" speech in 1937 met with so little public acceptance and approval.

B. The Roots of Involvement

This lack of general understanding can be traced to the way in which the U.S. first became heavily involved in Asia, particularly in the acquisition of the Philippines. That step was the most momentous foreign policy decision that the U.S. had taken since independence. It was hotly argued against at the time and in terms that are perfectly compatible with the tone of debates over Vietnam today. Just as today there have been teach-ins, "open letters," and demonstrations calling for a halt to the war in Vietnam, so there was in 1898 an "Anti-Imperialist League." It campaigned "on grounds of policy and morality against territorial expansion in the East and . . . over alien peoples in distant islands," and President McKinley himself admitted that he "had to look the Philippines up on the globe; he could not have told their locality," he said, "within two thousand miles." [2]

But the War with Spain, while it originated in Cuba, had placed the U.S. in *de facto* control of the Philippines. Fortuitous or not, highly

[2] Bemis, *op. cit.,* p. 291.

influential men saw how this fitted in with their design to maintain a balance of power in Asia, and in particular to ensure that the aims of Germany and Japan in China were countered. The most prominent spokesmen were the men associated with Theodore Roosevelt: Captain Mahan, Senator Lodge, and others who advocated a "large" policy for the U.S. They urged that the Philippines was the necessary strategic location from which the U.S. could exercise its influence in Far Eastern politics, and argued for acquisition of the islands. While other advisers tried to persuade the President that the *whole* of the Philippines was not necessary for that task, there were compelling military arguments for taking the entire archipelago. Indeed, Japan already had privately "volunteered" to help the U.S. bear its burden in the Philippines, and Germany entertained an even greater goal until the last moment.

Thus the President took the Philippines, and if in retrospect he seems to have had little choice, the relatively unplanned, almost accidental, and certainly sudden character of the whole venture can hardly be denied. Moreover, it was clear even then (as it is today) that no commercial interest of the U.S. required a major involvement in East Asia,[3] and it was ludicrously clear that one of the "reasons" McKinley gave for taking the Philippines—to bring Christianity to the heathen Filipino—was patently false. The Philippines had already converted to Catholicism, and even today Filipinos resent the ignorance that McKinley's statement disclosed.

These almost accidental roots of our first major involvement in Asia helped make it difficult for American leaders to explain and justify ensuing American involvements there as well. Clearly, an "interest" was created by acquiring the Philippines, for "policy is the fruit of history and experience, seldom of some abstract design," as then Assistant Secretary of State William Bundy has remarked.[4] Yet the unplanned origins of our East Asian involvements have added to the doubts and uncertainty that have accompanied our actions there ever since. For as long as statesmen were unwilling to say frankly that the United States was interested in and required a balance of

[3] Julius Pratt has shown that "big business" was opposed to the 1898 war and to expansion of U.S. territorial control (see *The Expansionists of 1898: The Acquisition of the Spanish Islands* [Baltimore: Johns Hopkins University Press, 1936). The specific opposition to control of the Philippines, moreover, was centered in New England, at the time still the home of major business interests.

[4] "American Policy in South Viet-Nam and Southeast Asia," Address by William P. Bundy, January 23, 1965, in *Department of State Bulletin* (February 8, 1965), pp. 168–75.

power among the nations in Asia, how could they honestly explain
their Asian policies?

Aside from prospects of potential Asian "trade," they were unable
to point to the convenient myths that have been ostensible "guiding
principles" for our European and Western Hemisphere policies. Unlike
the situation for policymakers concerned with Latin America, when it
came to Far Eastern problems there was nothing like a Monroe
Doctrine, with which every schoolboy was familiar. Americans had
satisfied themselves that that doctrine was justification enough for
U.S. dominance in Latin America. Similarly, and unlike those responsible for European affairs, U.S. leaders who dealt with Asia could
not cite George Washington's warning against "entangling alliances"
with which Americans had justified staying out of Europe until 1917.
There were, in effect, no hoary guidelines for a U.S. Asian policy
because in the early days of this republic East Asia was not yet a
part of world politics. Thus, in the absence of guidelines and for a
generation after 1900, policymakers responded to specific events in
Asia as they had had to respond to Admiral Dewey's sudden capture
of Manila Bay and Luzon: intuitively and uncertainly.

Intuitively, too, they responded to some larger changes in Asian
and European politics which coincided with their control of the
Philippines. For by 1900 it was no longer true, as it had been during
the nation's first century, that East Asia was not a part of world
politics. That loose and easy background was forever destroyed when
the European powers began their efforts to carve up China into
spheres of influence. Putting this another way, it is clear now that when
the rivalries of the great European states were expanded to East Asia,
it meant *the incorporation of China and Japan into the global international system.*

C.   THE U.S. IN BRITAIN'S ROLE

The extension of European politics to East Asia coincided, moreover,
with the point in history at which Great Britain was ceasing to be
dominant in the system of world politics, and that timing proved to
be crucial for the future development of U.S. foreign policy. It was
British dominance of the global system, after all, that had insulated
the U.S. from Europe, and allowed Washington's warning against
European alliances to be a feasible policy. It was also British power

that had guaranteed the Monroe Doctrine, because Britain, too, wanted to keep Latin America free of European control. By 1890–1905, as Whitehall knew, other nations were achieving great-power status, most notably Germany and most surprisingly Japan. These changes in the global structure implied a *relative* decline in Britain's power and proved to be crucially important for the U.S. In sum, the *pax Britannica*—which had given the U.S. almost a century of indirect national security protection—was coming to an end.

In Asia this meant that London would not be able to prevent a division of China into spheres of influence (or worse yet, the dominance of China by one nation alone).[5] The behavior of American statesmen, particularly their tacit and informal understanding with London leading to the Open Door, indicates that they sensed the effect of these changes on the United States: If, by controlling much of China, one of the great European powers were able to eclipse Britain's power, that would overwhelm the global balance, and U.S. insulation from Europe, as well as U.S. dominance in Latin America, depended on that balance being preserved. Thus it was in the interest of United States security to prevent any further decline in Britain's relative power globally, and the United States did precisely that in the years after 1898. It did this in two ways: *indirectly*, by helping to prevent the expansion in the Pacific of powers like Germany (and by helping to prevent the break up of China); and *directly*, by going to Britain's aid in 1917. For U.S. leaders not to have acted in the years around 1900—for example, *not* to take the Philippines, or to acquiesce in the division of China—would in effect have been to help diminish British power by allowing others to continue their rise. Thus when U.S. leaders acted in ways that were parallel to British interests, they acted most essentially to protect the security of the United States.

Except for a few leaders like Theodore Roosevelt and Captain Mahan, it is unlikely that the full shape of these steps was clearly understood at the time. Nevertheless, the actual behavior of the U.S., whatever its specific intent, meant that the U.S. was succeeding to and reinforcing the global balance-of-power policies that Britain had exercised to preserve its own security. This pattern took shape only gradually, and as we have seen, only in response to the force of

[5] "The general expectation was that these spheres would soon become protectorates supported from the naval bases, that their extension and transformation into actual dominion would be only a question of time . . . . Let it be said, too, that each of the European powers, *notably Great Britain*, was more or less impelled to establish its sphere *for fear that a rival would dominate China exclusively*" (Bemis, *op. cit.*, p. 293; emphasis added).

specific events, such as the Twenty-One Demands in 1915. Yet American statesmen, even if they did gradually recognize the import of their behavior, were hardly able to proclaim publicly that it was their objective to maintain the world "balance of power" by going to the aid of Great Britain. But that, of course, is what the United States did do, on several occasions, until in 1945 the United States emerged with its own power unchallenged.

Partly because of the pragmatic and *ad hoc* beginnings of U.S. involvement in East Asia (and also because of the extent to which U.S. behavior was essentially a reaction to events) no meaningful and explicit statement of U.S. interests and objectives existed up to the time of the war with Japan. In a book completed just before Pearl Harbor and devoted to the entire Japanese-U.S. relationship, William Johnstone concluded as late as July, 1941 that there had been a "failure of the American people and the American Government to agree on a definition of what our national interest in the Far Eastern situation really is." [6]

D.   The National Interest of the United States

The best attempt at a "definition" of the national interest was in the Hull letter of January, 1938. There, finally, it was at least stated that "there is a broader and more fundamental interest" that "transcends the value of trade with China or American investments . . . it transcends even the question of safeguarding the immediate welfare of American citizens in China." But what was this "broader and more fundamental interest"? In the Hull letter and other official documents it was identified only as the U.S. concern "that orderly processes in international relations be maintained." [7]

This definition was not false. It was merely vague. Rather than focussing on the *condition* of Asia that it was in the U.S. interest to see achieved, it focussed instead on the *method*—"orderly processes."

[6] William D. Johnstone, *The United States and Japan's New Order* (New York: Oxford University Press, 1941), p. 345. See his discussion of this point on pp. 345–56 and 350–52.

[7] *Ibid.*, p. 32. Professor Johnstone has pointed out to me recently that Hull presaged his letter to Garner in an earlier statement (of July, 1937). Hull announced, in response to Japanese actions in China, that "any situation in which armed hostilities are in process . . . is a situation wherein rights and interests of all nations . . . may be seriously affected." In later comments, Hull repeatedly referred to this 1937 statement as a major expression of U.S. "interests."

Yet, just as in the past when statesmen had tried to explain U.S. Asian policies in terms of commercial interests, friendship for the Chinese people, or treaty obligations, their emphasis now on "orderly processes" remained unconvincing. The true interest of the U.S.—an East Asia in which no one nation exercised dominance—had to be deduced, and only with great difficulty, from the official explanations. A few did this, and Johnstone himself came close. After listing among the "basic objectives" of U.S. Far East policy such things as the Open Door, "the independence of China," and the need "to protect the lives and property of its citizens in the Far East," Johnstone included with his list the recommendation that the U.S. should "continue to oppose the domination of large areas of the Far East by one nation to the exclusion of the rights and interests of other nations . . . ." [8]

But it remained for Nicholas Spykman, writing at the same time, to elevate that objective to its proper position and to state it in terms relevant to U.S. security. He saw that Japan's conquest of China, and its resulting dominance in Asia "would mean the final destruction of the balance of power in the transpacific zone which would have ultimate repercussions on our power position in the Western Hemisphere." [9] And he stated frankly that *our power position in the world . . . had always depended on the existence of a balance in Europe and Asia . . . ."* [10]

That objective, not simply the desire to see "orderly processes" in world affairs, lay behind the policies of U.S. opposition to Japan. But the official propensity not to face that reality, reflected in a generation of misleading explanations of policy, resulted in a double failure in the 1930's: it caused our adversary to misjudge us, and it allowed the American people to misjudge how Japan's actions affected them.

In that failure, and especially the failure to inform the people, lies the explanation for the historic and repeated difficulties faced by American leaders when they have sought eventually to protect the nation against dangers emanating from Asia. The American people have not had honestly driven home to them that in Asia, just as in Europe, their nation's vital interest has been to prevent one-nation dominance. They have not been told that the necessary objective flowing from that interest has been, at the minimum, a multination balance of power (when

[8] *Ibid.*, p. 352.
[9] Spykman, *op. cit.*, p. 155. In his conclusions, Spykman wrote that "a balance of power in the transatlantic zones is an absolute prerequisite for the . . . preservation of the power position of the United States" (p. 457).
[10] *Ibid.*, p. 195 (emphasis added).

that has been feasible), and that sometimes the objective has been direct counterpower.

In the absence of that explanation, almost every important step in U.S. Asian policy, from as early as 1937 to the present, has been subjected to greater doubts, with consequent official indecision, than the facts and the interest warranted. In the confrontation with Japan, as Spykman realized, administrations never felt free to make clear to Japan how adamant was U.S. opposition to one-nation dominance in Asia. "We have employed," he said, "all the methods available in international relations except one. We have tried persuasion, barter . . . but we have never been willing to go to war and that explains . . . the reason why our diplomacy has had so little success":[11]

> Every time a situation emerged which demanded that the United States decide on a course of action in the face of Japanese expansion, the debate was re-opened. Should we attempt to check the growing power of Japan or should we take the point of view that the Far East is far away and that its balance of power does not concern us?[12]

Despite that debate, however, the main thrust of American policy remained the same, and as this discussion has argued already, the trend and tendency of that policy was increasingly hostile to Japan. From 1915, it was a constant policy, and if even on the eve of the Pearl Harbor attack U.S. officials still refrained from explaining why the nation was opposed to Japan's actions, some unofficial observers did not.

One of these, ironically, was Walter Lippmann. Writing during the war, he stressed that because Japan understood U.S. aims, they *had* to attack Pearl Harbor:

> For the Japanese would not have attacked Pearl Harbor if we had accepted the terms they offered us. They did not attack Pearl Harbor for the sake of sinking our Pacific fleet. They tried to sink our Pacific fleet because we were opposing them on matters that they were determined to carry through.
> There is no mystery about what these were. Japan was committed to the conquest of China . . . . The Japanese were willing to negotiate, to compromise, and at least to postpone, their demands *outside* of China. There was the irreconcilable issue. *When the United States refused finally to assent to the conquest of China,* and to desist from opposing Japan in China, *Japan went to war.*[13]

[11] *Ibid.,* p. 155.
[12] *Ibid.,* p. 140.
[13] Walter Lippmann, "The Mystery of Our China Policy," in Ralph A. Goldwin, ed., *Readings in American Foreign Policy* (New York: Oxford University Press, 1959), pp. 257–69. Emphasis added.

Then, emphasizing precisely the continuity in policy which we have stressed, Lippmann concluded that:

> . . . the American nation reached this momentous decision gradually, reluctantly, but with increasing unanimity and finality, over a period of about forty years. The remarkable thing about the record of these forty years is the constancy with which the United States government has stood for the integrity of Chinese territory.[14]

Remarkably, it was only after the war, and only when the Communists had completed their conquest of China, that the U.S. Government finally acknowledged that this had been the true purpose of American policy. As we saw, earlier statements had refused to face the fact squarely: in the fullest prewar statement of national interest Secretary Hull had only with difficulty acknowledged that our "interest" in Asia transcended the usual litany of material and economic interests. Suddenly, however, in a famous "White Paper" of 1949 the Department of State changed its public explanation of prewar Asian policy. It emphasized—as if it had been clearly stating it for a generation— that the United States has "asserted that the domination of China by any one Power or any group of Powers is contrary to the interests both of China and the United States." [15] The fact, however, is that the U.S. had *not* explicitly asserted this objective, although its *behavior* for fifty years had been clearly and consistently aimed in that direction. Despite the varied and often irrelevant statements with which the U.S. Government explained its Asian policies from 1898–1945, a consistency of purpose, based on a good understanding of American interest, has in fact always characterized America's Asian policies.

These policies, as the State Department acknowledged in 1949 but avoided saying for the entire fifty-year period before that, were motivated by one aim: to prevent any one-nation dominance in Asia.[16] The U.S. security requirement that justified that interest, and led to the objective of preventing China's conquest by Japan, was the conviction that any nation which could dominate China would have within

---

[14] *Ibid.*, p. 259.

[15] This appears in the first paragraph of *United States Relations With China* (Washington, D.C.: Department of State Publication 3573, 1949), p. 1.

[16] In his *Letter of Transmittal* accompanying the "White Paper" of 1949, Secretary Acheson said—as if everyone knew it all along—that "The record shows that the United States has consistently maintained and still maintains those fundamental principles of our foreign policy toward China which include the doctrine of the Open Door, respect for the administrative and territorial integrity of China, *and opposition to any foreign domination of China*" (*ibid.*, pp. iv; emphasis added).

reach the dominance of all East Asia[17]—and that would threaten the global balance on which U.S. security was seen historically to have been founded.

In pursuit of that interest, as I have stressed, the United States took steps that were, in their general direction, increasingly opposed to Japan, and ultimately led to war. These were, however, only incremental steps, not designed to bring war, but, nonetheless, making it more likely. From the history of that period two conclusions should be drawn: the first pertains to the previously outlined concept of levels of interest, and the second to the concept of balance of power.

E. UTILITY OF THE "LEVELS" APPROACH

We have seen that although efforts were made to explain American policies in Asia, there was no agreement as to the nature of the United States *interest*. As a consequence there was no clear conception of how much conflict potential there was between Japan's aims and the requirements of the United States, with the result that until the outbreak of war itself, the policies adopted by the United States were ineffective. In other words the United States behaved as if Japan's actions affected, at most, a *Level Two* national interest, and if Secretary Hull's statements are taken as an indication, as if only a *Level Three* interest were involved.

But the issue, of course, was not simply "orderly international processes"; it was instead the question of whether the United States would acquiesce in Japanese policies that must have led to Tokyo's general dominance in East Asia. Yet as long as only a *Level Three* interest was seen to be involved, then it was appropriate for the United States to do little more than issue formal denunciations of Japan's behavior. To the extent that a *Level Two* interest was perceived (in terms of American "commitments" to the Open Door principles), then it was perhaps appropriate to undertake some specific actions opposed to Japan. The oil and scrap metal embargoes can be understood in that context.

---

[17] I believe it no longer in doubt that Japan in fact aimed to become dominant in East Asia; as James Crowley states in his exhaustive analysis of Japanese policy from 1930–38, "Japan's foreign and security policies of the 1930–38 period were designed to realize one cardinal objective, a hegemonial position in East Asia" (James Crowley, *Japan's Quest for Autonomy, National Security and Foreign Policy, 1930–38* [Princeton: Princeton University Press, 1966], p. xvii).

But more than that is involved in a *Level Two* interest, for its distinguishing characteristic is that when effectively challenged it is liable to upward or downward movement. A *Level Two* interest, in other words, is unstable, and when it is challenged the choice posed by the challenge or threat should become clear: is the value symbolized by this *Level Two* interest of sufficient importance to warrant its upgrading to a *Level One* interest? If not, the rules of this model suggest that whatever specific commitment, resource, or other value has been subsumed under the *Level Two* heading must be treated as a *Level Three* interest.

Had such a model operated in the late 1930's, it might have been more clearly understood that the *Level Two* commitments to Chinese territorial integrity were merely the formal expression of what was in fact a *Level One* interest: the American concern to prevent dominance in East Asia by any one state. In that circumstance, and making use of this hierarchical concept of interest, the choices before the United States could have been revealed in their properly stark terms: again, it is the central quality of a *Level Two* interest that it can force into the open the elements of a decision.

Thus, had the commitments to China been understood as a *Level Two* interest, it could have become inescapably clear to American leaders, no later than 1940, that their policies regarding Japan were inclining toward a collision course. For the real choice in 1940–41 was what to do with the *Level Two* interest represented by a generation of untested expressions of good will and vague commitments to China. Had a Japanese conquest of China been perceived to have little or no significance to the security of the United States, then it would have been incorrect to allocate any more resources to prevent that outcome. In effect the previous *Level Two* interest (represented by commitments to China) would have been dropped to *Level Three* category. If, on the other hand, a Japanese conquest of China would have been perceived as an unacceptable outcome, then it was incumbent on the United States to revise quickly its *Level Two* interest to *Level One* category, *and make clear to Japan its willingness to resort to war to prevent that outcome.* Simultaneously, of course, it would have been incumbent on the United States to prepare immediately for war, with the added hope that the sheer weight of its power might deter the Japanese from further attempts at conquest.

In the actual event, of course, no such hierarchical model was employed, and the United States avoided making the decisions which its *Level Two* behavior implied. It continued, that is, to send aid to

China, and it reinforced those economic measures designed to impede Japan's war potential. That is not a viable approach, as some of President Roosevelt's advisors understood—in particular, Secretary of War Stimson, Treasury Secretary Morgenthau, and a few others. Ambassador Grew in Tokyo put the case very well in a telegram dated September 12, 1940:

> Japan is today one of the predatory powers; having submerged all ethical and moral sense, she has become unashamedly and frankly opportunist, at every turn seeking to profit through the weakness of others. American interests in the Pacific are definitely threatened by her policy of southward expansion, which is a thrust at the British Empire in the East. Admittedly America's security has depended in a measure upon the British Fleet, which has been in turn and could only have been supported by the British Empire. If the support of the British Empire in this her hour of travail is conceived to be in our interest and most emphatically do I conceive it, we must strive by every means to preserve the *status quo* in the Pacific, at least until the war in Europe has been won or lost. This cannot be done, in my opinion, nor can we further protect our interests properly and adequately merely by the expression of disapproval and carefully keeping a record thereof. Clearly, Japan has been deterred from the taking of greater liberties with American interests only because she respects our potential power; equally it is clear that she has trampled upon our rights to an extent in exact ratio to the strength of her conviction *that the people of the United States would not permit that power to be used.* It is not impossible that once that conviction is shaken, the uses of diplomacy may again become accepted.[18]

Military leaders argued, however, that the nation was not physically prepared for stronger measures, and Secretary of State Hull continued as always to argue for caution. The result was that the President took no firm action, and by late 1940 it could no longer be argued that the compelling reason for inaction (as in 1937) was public apathy or resistance. Instead, polls showed that a majority favored strong measures to restrain Japan, including measures that would comprehend the risk of war.[19] Nevertheless, it was only very late in 1941, and then quite suddenly, that the President took steps that made war truly inevitable, and the nation was still not well prepared physically for war.

War might have come in any case, but had a model of the sort proposed here been applied, say in 1940, the timing and/or circum-

---

[18] Quoted in William L. Langer and S. Everett Gleason, *The Undeclared War, 1940–41* (New York: Harper & Row, Publishers, Inc., 1953), p. 19 (emphasis added).

[19] See account of editorial opinion and public opinion poll of September 30, 1940, in *ibid.*, pp. 33–34.

stances of the outbreak of war could have developed on terms more favorable to the United States. For in mid-1940 Japan made unalterably clear its intentions to create a "new order" in East Asia and announced as well that if the United States continued to "refuse to understand the real intentions of Japan . . . there will be no other course open . . . than to go to war." [20] The same warning was repeated in several ways, and at one point in late 1940 the Japanese Ambassador told Secretary Hull directly that American embargoes on scrap iron shipments constituted "an unfriendly act."

Certainly no later than that, and perhaps precisely at the point at which Japan signed the Tripartite Pact with Germany and Italy,[21] a three-level model of the national interest would have required the United States to choose: either to acquiesce in Japan's ambitions or escalate its *Level Two* interest to *Level One* category. In the absence of such a formulation the United States seemed content to rely on condemnations of aggression (the symbols of a *Level Three* interest), while continuing to make the type of commitments (implying a *Level Two* interest) that could lead to war. That was not eminently responsible behavior in 1940–41; in the nuclear environment of today, when even greater dangers can derive from causing an adversary to mistake American intentions, such behavior could be suicidal.

A second lesson that can be drawn from this period pertains to the belief that the term "balance of power" can be used both to describe the nature of the American *interest* in East Asia and to characterize U.S. *policies.* The answer to the question we raised at the beginning of the previous chapter, "How valid is the notion that the U.S. has played a balance-of-power policy in East Asia?" now seems clear: the U.S. has not always followed a balance-of-power policy, but it has generally sought an overall Asian balance. The distinction is important, especially when it helps to underline the remarkable constancy that has marked U.S. involvement in East Asia. It is a constancy of purpose, that is, of *interest.*

In contrast, *objectives* and *policies,* the latter more clearly, have been much more subject to change. In the early years of the growing confrontation with Japan, as in the 1920's, the United States certainly did attempt to follow balance-of-power policies. American leaders believed that the Asian environment was still characterized by multi-

[20] Statement of Prince Konoye (Japanese Prime Minister) October 4, 1940. For an excellent account of these events and the remarkable role played by Hull, see *ibid.,* Chapter II.
[21] September 27, 1940.

polarity, and in that structure a balance-of-power policy is perfectly appropriate. Later, as the United States and Japan came into increasingly direct confrontation, it was no longer possible for the United States to behave as merely one among several actors in a system. Its relationship to Japan became more direct, for there was no other actor with which the United States could "side" in the hope of balancing Japan. For that reason we can conclude that although an overall Asian balance remained the American *objective,* the policies for achieving that objective had of necessity altered. We can further conclude that the United States sought as its objective an overall Asian balance because, by definition, such a balance would be the manifestation and reflection of the United States national interest: that no one nation achieve general dominance in East Asia. Thus the quality of constancy in the American record in East Asia has been not so much a matter of policies or even objectives, but of adherence and attachment to the overriding national interest there.

Five

THE U.S. AND MULTIPOLARITY IN ASIA

Although a constant purpose has characterized American involvements in East Asia, the methods chosen to achieve that purpose have varied. Sometimes the method, as we suggested in the previous chapter, has been through unilateral declarations and efforts, as in the Open Door itself. At other times the method has emphasized multilateralism, although even in a multination framework the U.S. often found itself in the lead. The reason was that over the years Washington was forced to conclude that no other capital was as anxious and able to prevent one-nation dominance in East Asia. Thus in 1922, when the Nine-Power Treaty incorporated the essence of the Open Door doctrines, this was undoubtedly a multilateral achievement, but in a more important sense it was merely a multilateral endorsement of essentially American interests.

In the 1930's, when it became clear that multilateralism was ineffective, the U.S. often tried to achieve its aims unilaterally, but those efforts were generally restricted to ineffective declarations. Finally in 1941, the U.S. had to resort—essentially unilaterally—to full-scale war to prevent Japan from upsetting its national interest in East Asia. Ever since that time the U.S. has had to repeat regularly its unilateral, or near-unilateral, behavior pattern, but it has never entirely discarded multilateralism. Instead, it has frequently sought to enlist the help of others in policies that supported American interests. The massive military involvement in Vietnam since 1965 was only the latest instance of this behavior pattern, which we might say began just before the war with Japan: *to take action alone if necessary, but with others if possible.*

Thus the U.S. has seldom, if ever, resisted at least the trappings of multilateralism when that was the aim of other states as well. This was the pattern in 1943 when the U.S. established a "Pacific War Council";[1] in 1950 when it obtained U.N. endorsement for its resistance to aggression in Korea; in 1951 and in 1954 when ANZUS and SEATO were established; and in 1966 when it convened a meeting in Manila of the nations actively supporting its Vietnam war effort. As in 1950, the U.S. today seeks to provide at least the color of multination endorsement for military actions which it would undertake alone if necessary.

A. RETURN TO MULTILATERALISM

Most recently, however, the United States has once again begun to encourage the other side of multilateralism: the one that looks beyond useful, but temporary, military alliances toward groupings of Asian states based on wider and more enduring convergencies of interest. This tendency has become apparent since 1965; it is reflected most clearly in the hopeful interest that U.S. leaders now express in Asian regional cooperation generally, and particularly in the regional "initiatives" recently undertaken by Thailand, Indonesia, and Japan.[2]

The United States encourages these steps toward Asian regionalism for two kinds of reasons. The first lies in the expectation that regional

[1] The "Pacific War Council," with the U.S. President as Chairman, included Britain, Holland, China, Canada, Austrialia and New Zealand. It was primarily the result of the urgings of Australia and New Zealand that they be better apprised of wartime military decisions taken by the U.S. against Japan, and of decisions which would effect the ultimate Pacific peace. The Council, like every other multilateral body set up in Asia and the Pacific since, did not amount to much. One delegate commented, even during the war, that "Usually all we did was to listen to Mr. Roosevelt discuss what had been going on in the Pacific, and we generally already knew that through earlier talks with the military staffs." (See *The Dominion* [Wellington, New Zealand], December 19, 1944, cited by Bernard K. Gordon, *New Zealand Becomes a Pacific Power* [Chicago: University of Chicago Press, 1960], p. 172.) For other references to early attempts at Pacific regional cooperation, see Daniel S. Cheever, *Organizing for Peace* (Boston: Houghton Mifflin Co., 1955), pp. 810–11.

[2] President Johnson initiated this shift in American policy when he announced, in his Johns Hopkins speech in April, 1965, a $1 billion program to encourage regional development in Southeast Asia. Since then, both the President and Mr. Walt Rostow, his Assistant for National Security Affairs, have on several occasions pointed to the strong U.S. encouragement of regional cooperation in Southeast Asia. The foremost example of Presidential encouragement came in Mr. Johnson's speech in Hawaii in October, 1966. In addition, the administration has included in the Foreign Assistance Act of 1967 a specific provision authorizing expenditures in support of this goal.

cooperation, especially among smaller developing countries, can aid in speeding the processes of economic development. This conviction explains, for example, American support for regional economic cooperation in Latin America. There, the U.S. is pressing for the establishment of a Latin American common market, and it also encourages other steps aimed at economic integration. In Asia, however, few would suggest that a common market approach is worth considering now, and for that reason the U.S. encourages other forms of economic regionalism. The best-known example is in the establishment of the Asian Development Bank, which owes much to American support. The U.S. is also encouraging a variety of other, lesser-known cooperative steps in Southeast Asia.[3]

But these efforts reflect only the essentially economic aspects of regional cooperation. The other aspect, the one that has become increasingly apparent since 1965, is based more clearly on political considerations. This side of the American interest stems from the belief that as regional cohesion develops in Asia, especially to the extent that it includes Japanese participation, it will help establish an added power center in Asia. Such a development, if successful, would loosen the tight bipolarity that has characterized the East Asian international system since at least 1937.

Judging by recent American actions and the statements of the most senior U.S. officials, American policy is already embarked in this direction. Since 1965, statements by the President and his closest advisors reflect the belief that Asian regionalism will be directly in support of U.S. national interests in Asia. Both immediate and long-term objectives are involved.

The short-term objective is a pragmatic one and will be touched on only briefly here. This is essentially the belief that with the added development and stability that regional cooperation may bring, Asian states will grow ultimately less susceptible to subversion, and also better able to bear the costs of defending against it. But the more fundamental U.S. objective relates to the structure of international

---

[3] Among these, for example, is a series of Southeast Asian Ministerial Conferences on Higher Education and on Transporation. The U.S. has given these very strong encouragement through a Regional Development Office in the Bangkok Embassy, and the Agency for International Development (AID) seeks to support such efforts with American financial assistance. In 1968, for example, AID asked the Congress to authorize (for fiscal year 1969) more than $18 million in support of certain regional projects in Southeast Asia—an approximate doubling of the amount requested in each of the previous two years (see Agency for International Development, *Program Summary*, "East Asia Regional," p. G-7).

politics in East Asia. This is the American hope that Asian regionalism will lead to a multibloc system in the 1970's—something akin to
the balance-of-power system that operated before World War I.

It cannot be proved, of course, that the earlier balance-of-power
structure—the one that ended in 1915—did in fact provide for security and stability in East Asia. But it is clear that when that multibloc
structure deteriorated, thirty years of increasingly tight bipolarity in
Asia did lead ultimately to war.[4] It is in hope of avoiding another
such general conflagration, which may be the product of *any* international structure that is too tightly bipolar, that the U.S. encourages
today the building of other power centers in East Asia. Such a multicentered Asia would be consistent with U.S. interests because the U.S.
does not require an American-dominated Asia; it requires only that
no one state or combination of states achieve all-Asian dominance.

B.   SHIFTS IN U.S. OBJECTIVES: A MULTIPOLAR
ASIAN STRUCTURE

If the new direction of U.S. policy is to encourage Asian regionalism and the re-establishment of a multipolar Asian structure, this suggests that, historically, U.S. Asian policy will look something like the
swing of a pendulum. The pendulum might be described by saying that
on one side of its arc multilateralism was the dominant characteristic
of U.S. behavior in East Asia. On the other side, U.S. behavior has
been characterized by unilateral responses.

As the accompanying illustration suggests, we would say that U.S.
policy began, at the turn of the century, with multilateralism. In the
1920's and 1930's it swung gradually away from that policy; its tendency was toward increasing self-reliance. Finally, in 1941, U.S. policy reached the extreme point of unilateralism (and unilateral armed
force) in the war to defeat Japan. Today this pendulum appears for
the first time to be moving away from self-reliance; it seems to be
shifting once again toward multilateralism.

This is the meaning (evident since at least 1965) of American policies which strongly encourage Asian regionalism and welcome the

---

[4] For a fuller discussion of the stability characteristics of a "tight" bipolar
system, as compared with one that is "looser," see Morton A. Kaplan, *System
and Process in International Politics* (New York: John Wiley & Sons, Inc., 1957).

renewal of Japan's active role in Asia.[5] For such policies, if they are successful, will mean an Asia that is neither balkanized nor characterized by the two-power confrontation of China and the United States alone. They will mean an East Asia in which several actors are of major significance—implying U.S. behavior in a multipolar Asia for the first time since 1915.

Until 1915, East Asia was clearly a multicentered international system. The U.S. participated in that system much like other states; it followed balance-of-power policies. The system itself guaranteed that the U.S. interest was preserved, for the U.S. interest was identical with the purpose of the system: to prevent any one nation from dominating the whole. After 1915, however, East Asia's structure became bipolar, and after 1931–32 its bipolarity was intensified. The United States, still aiming to prevent one-nation dominance, found itself more and more impelled to rely on its own counterpower; this tendency reached its highest point in the 1941–45 war.

This bipolarity continued in the postwar era, for, since 1949, East Asia has been characterized by an indirect China-U.S. confrontation, just as between 1915–45 it was characterized by the more direct Japan-U.S. conflict.

Today, however, this bipolar structure is eroding—under the impact of three important developments. One pertains to the re-emergence of Japan in East Asian politics. The second, which will be fully discussed in the next two chapters, concerns the renewed and now widespread interest in regional cooperation in Southeast Asia itself. The third, which we will explore in a moment, is the active American support now being given both those trends—particularly the Southeast Asian interest in regionalism. However, before we deal with the United States role, brief mention should be made of Japan.

That there is now taking place a gradual revival of Japanese interest in Southeast Asian affairs can hardly be denied, although specialists differ in their estimates of its pace and intensity. State-

---

[5] An interesting discussion of the growing role of the Asian subsystem in global international politics is in Oran R. Young, "Political Discontinuities in the International System," *World Politics* (April, 1968), pp. 369–92. On the U.S. objective of encouraging what I have called here "the building of other power centers in East Asia," Young comments, for example, that the "United States [and the Soviet Union as well] is currently beginning to show an interest in supporting the continued development of Japan . . . to provide a balancing force that is likely to become increasingly important as a function of the emergence of China as an important actor in the Asian subsystem" (p. 386).

DIRECTION OF U.S. POLICY
IN A CHANGING ASIAN STRUCTURE *

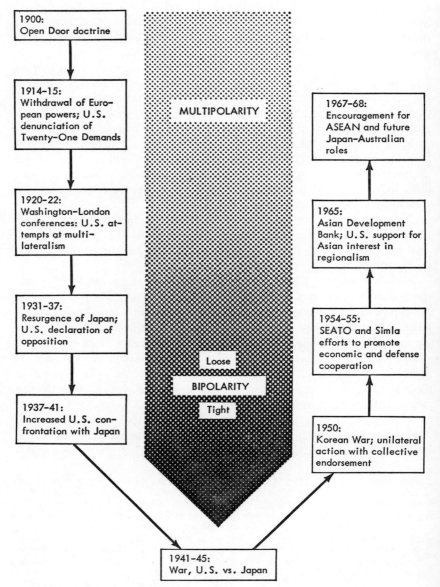

1900:
Open Door doctrine

1914–15:
Withdrawal of European powers; U.S. denunciation of Twenty–One Demands

1920–22:
Washington–London conferences: U.S. attempts at multilateralism

1931–37:
Resurgence of Japan; U.S. declaration of opposition

1937–41:
Increased U.S. confrontation with Japan

MULTIPOLARITY

Loose

BIPOLARITY

Tight

1967–68:
Encouragement for ASEAN and future Japan–Australian roles

1965:
Asian Development Bank; U.S. support for Asian interest in regionalism

1954–55:
SEATO and Simla efforts to promote economic and defense cooperation

1950:
Korean War; unilateral action with collective endorsement

1941–45:
War, U.S. vs. Japan

* Illustration by Anita M. Gordon.

ments of the Japanese Premier and Foreign Minister certainly indicate expectations of an increased role in East Asia, and in Tokyo there is open and frank support today for the goal of improved regional cooperation among the developing Southeast Asian nations. One reflection of this interest is in Japan's sponsorship of three successive Ministerial Conferences on Economic Development in Southeast Asia, of which only the first and organizing meeting was held in Japan. Another and more familiar reflection is in Japan's role in the economies of Southeast Asia—she is the principal trading partner of all but one of the Southeast Asian nations. Finally, there is in the intellectual and leadership community in Japan a clear renewal of interest in all aspects of the affairs of Southeast Asia. In part this is seen in the remarkable growth of scholarly attention directed to the Southeast Asia region by such University centers as the one in Kyoto, and by research institutions in the capital. Some of these apparently gain their sponsorship from the Japanese Foreign Office and other government departments.

Yet partly because Japanese leaders were determined to give their main attention to domestic economic development during the 1960's, this interest in Southeast Asia has not yet been expressed in large financial terms. The major exception is Japan's willingness to share the largest burden in establishing the Asian Development Bank (an initial subscription of $200 million was promised, equivalent to the United States obligation). At the same time, there is a widespread belief among both leading Japanese and foreign observers of Japan's foreign policy that Japan must come to play a larger role in the security of East Asia,[6] and in that context Southeast Asia will of course be a first-order consideration. Against this pattern of thinking, however, some analysts caution that Japan is not yet ready to take the plunge once again into Asia—that many internal forces inhibit a renewed policy of activism.[7] On balance, these different estimates appear to be largely a matter of emphasis and timing. Those specialists on Japanese affairs most sensitive to international politics expect Japan's broadened role to become apparent relatively sooner; those whose studies concentrate on the complexities of Japanese domestic politics are prepared for a longer wait. Few, however, believe that Japan can permanently

[6] See the comments, after numerous discussions in Japan, of Robert E. Osgood, "Japan and the United States in Asia," *SAIS Review*, 11, No. 3 (Spring, 1967), 3–21.

[7] George R. Packard, III, "Living with the Real Japan," *Foreign Affairs*, 46, No. 1 (October, 1967), 193–204.

remain an economic giant and a political pygmy in the affairs of East Asia.[8]

But even if Japan's reinvolvement is not so quick as some of her own leaders might hope, it is becoming clear that the other Asian states— by their own renewed concern with regionalism—have helped to facilitate Japanese participation in Asian affairs. The Southeast Asians have not *caused* this, to be sure, but their former resistance to almost any Japanese role is receding, and in part this is a result of their own growing sense of self-confidence. For example, when the United States has attempted in the past to encourage greater Japanese participation in Southeast Asian developments, that goal has been hindered by Southeast Asian fears of Japanese dominance. These apprehensions—especially concerning Japan's great economic might—and latent resentments growing from the wartime experiences cannot be erased altogether, but a greater degree of collaboration among Southeast Asian states is expected to better enable these small states to stand up to Japan. Lacking some degree of cohesion, the developing states of Southeast Asia must otherwise remain too easily susceptible to Japan's sheer weight in Asian affairs. Southeast Asian leaders are indeed the first to stress this, and their recognition acts as an additional incentive toward regional cooperation. For they too believe (as do many Americans) that the objective factors of location and Japan's economic interest will lead her inexorably to more involvement in Southeast Asia;[9]

[8] On this point I am indebted to Professor Donald Hellmann, Associate Director of the Center for Japanese Studies at the University of Washington. In addition to a forthcoming book on party politics in Japan's foreign policy process (to be published by the University of California Press in 1969), Dr. Hellmann is the author of a study on "Japan and the postwar East Asian International System," to be published in 1969 by the Research Analysis Corporation (RAC).

[9] During any given week the Japanese press is sprinkled liberally with articles that in some way deal with Japan's role in Southeast Asia, and especially with her economic involvement. Business interest is so intense that late in 1967, with respect to Indonesia, *Asahi* commented that "Indonesia fever is running high in industrial circles" (*Asahi Shimbun, December* 21, 1967). The article listed such fields as oil, lumber, nickel, non-ferrous metals, and other areas in which Japanese industrialists expected to operate in Indonesia. On the political side the Japanese Foreign Ministry has been endeavoring since 1965–66 to lead opinion (and other Ministries) into accepting a greater role for Japan in East Asia. In May, 1968, former Foreign Minister Miki called home for a four-day conference all Japanese Ambassadors to the "Asia-Pacific" area, in order to outline his four-point "Asian-Pacific bloc Establishment Plan." One of its points is the critical role which he hopes Japan will play as the "bridge" between the developed Pacific nations (Australia, the United States, and Canada) and the states of Southeast Asia. Miki hoped to press for a greater Japanese role as the Vietnam war subsides, and the main obstacles he faced were not within the Foreign Ministry (see *Mainichi Shimbun,* May 5, 1968).

regionalism among the weaker and smaller Southeast Asian nations appears to them as one more way by which to be better able to deal with the Japanese.

For its own reasons the United States, too, has been urging a greater Japanese role in Southeast Asian affairs. Simultaneously the U.S. has also begun, as a second aim, to give special encouragement and assistance to the development of regional cooperation in Southeast Asia. Whatever precise mix of Asian regionalism results from and is affected by that support, one point is clear as the United States works to achieve both objectives: the effect of American behavior will also be to help restructure the nature of East Asian international politics.

C. THE U.S. NATIONAL INTEREST AND ASIAN REGIONALISM

This restructuring of the East Asian system appears to be no accident, or mere by-product of American actions: it seems instead to have been the conscious goal of the most senior United States officials, including the President himself. But to say that the United States hopes to help reshape the East Asian system—in this case by virtue of Japan's resurgence and the prospect of a more cohesive Southeast Asian sub-region—is only another way of saying that American *objectives* in East Asia are changing. The U.S. *interest*, in contrast, remains the same—to prevent any one-nation dominance in the region—but there is no desire to press that interest to the point of a conflict with China. A bipolar Asia could lead to such a conflict, and in that sense there was a deep truth in Roger Hilsman's warning, in early 1966, that U.S. policy in Asia was on a "collision course with China." The desire to avoid such a collision explains the American concern today to develop conditions that can lead to a new multipolar Asia, and no better evidence for this intent can be found than in the statements of the man who was President during much of the 1960's.

Probably the clearest expression of White House thinking on this subject can be found in a major address delivered by President Johnson in October, 1966. That speech, given in Hawaii, is notable on several counts. But perhaps its most striking feature is that it represents one of the rare public occasions on which a president has frankly acknowledged the overriding national interest of the United States in

East Asia. *"No single nation,"* the President said there, *"can or should be permitted to dominate the Pacific region."* [10]

This was no off-hand comment. Instead, the President's statement represents a crucial part of a major speech in which he sought to welcome a new spirit of pragmatism in East Asia. This new spirit, he correctly said, is concerned more with the hard tasks of development than with the kind of sloganeering and ideologizing best symbolized by the Bandung Conference a decade earlier. Thus, when the President listed the "realities" that typify Asia today, he pointed not only to the interest in not allowing any one-nation dominance, but also to the new spirit of regional cooperation in Asia. "One after another," he said, "the nations of Asia are casting off the spent slogans of earlier narrow nationalism . . . one after another, they are grasping the realities of an interdependent Asia."

To illustrate the "new spirit" of pragmatism and cooperation now evident in Asia, the President cited the establishment of the Asian Development Bank, the Asian and Pacific Council (ASPAC), and a number of other initiatives which the U.S. welcomes.[11] The hope, as the President put it, is that eventually "the cooperative tasks of assistance and defense will be assumed more and more by others." This was a theme he had also expressed just a few weeks earlier, when he frankly acknowledged the relationship between regional cooperation and United States interests:

> Our purpose in promoting a world of regional partnerships is not without self-interest. For as they grow in strength . . . we can look forward to a decline in the burden that America has had to bear this generation.[12]

[10] From the President's address at the East-West Center, Honolulu, October 17, 1966. For full text see *Department of State Bulletin, November 28, 1966,* pp. 812–16. For comments on the speech, see *The New York Times,* October 18, 1966, and the *Christian Science Monitor,* October 19, 1966. Saville R. Davis, the *Monitor* correspondent, described the speech as one "of intent and changing attitudes . . . expected to take its place among the more earnest and meaningful policy documents of the time."

[11] The President was, of course, under no illusions as to the pace of this development in Asia; it was expected to be slow. Until the security burden, in particular, can be handled effectively by indigenous Asian states, the U.S. does not mean to abdicate its responsibility: "We recognize that our strength, our size, and wealth may impose a special obligation upon us in the transition to the new Asia." But he acknowledged, too, that while "the process of cooperation will be slow . . . the important thing is that all these things are happening . . . with Asian leadership and at Asian initiatives" (from the Honolulu speech).

[12] From the President's address at Lancaster, Ohio, September, 1966, quoted by Walt Rostow, Assistant to the President for National Security Affairs, in an address at Middlebury College, June 12, 1967.

Near-identical views are found in the remarks of one of the President's closest advisors, his Assistant for National Security Affairs. On several occasions Mr. Rostow sought to put regional cooperation into postwar historical perspective. One major speech he titled "Regionalism and World Order," and in another, more recent talk, he said that

> We are finding . . . in regionalism, a new relationship to the world community somewhere between the overwhelming responsibility we assumed in the early postwar years—as we moved in to fill vacuums of power . . . and a return to isolationism.[13]

In these and other talks, as well as in the remarks of the then Assistant Secretary of State for East Asian and Pacific Affairs, William Bundy, at least two points have been frequently emphasized. First, that in its Asian policy the United States now "is actively supporting . . . regional cooperation," and, second, that developments in Asian regionalism are seen in connection with Vietnam. It is not held that the U.S. defense effort in Vietnam has "caused" regionalism, but that it has helped to create a suitable environment for Asian cooperation.[14] Thus Mr. Rostow has remarked that "the most dramatic emergence of a new regional spirit and policy is, of course, in Asia," and when he spoke in 1967 about Vietnam, he made the linkage quite explicit:

> In the couple of years since we have made the decision to fight there, the people of Asia have gathered confidence in their future. They believe that we are going to see it through and on that basis they are beginning to build their futures, and in one of the most exciting of the postwar developments I know, namely this move toward Asian regionalism. This is not a view confined only to those who have put fighting troops in. The people in Singapore and in Indonesia and in Malaysia have drawn the same conclusion.[15]

Mr. Rostow is probably correct in emphasizing the extent to which regionalism in Southeast Asia represents an important development in Asian affairs. It is not that the idea is altogether new, for South-

---

[13] Walt W. Rostow, address at Middlebury College (Vermont), June 12, 1967 (mimeo).

[14] Rostow has also said that "As a historian . . . I know of few more remarkable developments than the new atmosphere of hope and determination to cooperate now sweeping Asia . . . . There has been slow movement forward in this direction for some time, but *the present phase of intense cooperative activity is closely linked on two historic actions:* the decision taken by President Johnson early in 1965 *to do whatever was necessary to defeat aggression in Viet-Nam* and second, the articulation of his vision for Asia in the Baltimore speech of April 7, 1965" (see *Department of State Bulletin,* December 19, 1966, p. 911 [emphasis added]).

[15] From transcript of "Meet the Press," interview with Walt W. Rostow, Sunday, July 9, 1967 (mimeo).

east Asian leaders have been talking vaguely about "regionalism" since at least 1946. But it is only in the 1960's that the concept has begun to take on a level of political significance potentially of major interest to the United States.

That degree of "political significance," as this book may help to show, derives from the contribution that regional cooperation might make toward a multipolar Asia. A Southeast Asia that remains divided will not only make no contribution to multipolarity, it will instead add to the prospects for continuation of that tight bipolarity that is recognized as so dangerous today. For to the extent that Southeast Asian states are weak and aim to go their separate and diverse ways in search of both security and development, two outcomes can be envisaged and both would tend to maintain (and perhaps even intensify) East Asia's present bipolarity.

One outcome would represent the successful achievement of Communist China's objectives—whether (as an impressive group of authorities have concluded) those goals include a conscious drive for dominance in East Asia,[16] or whether (as a few analysts still insist), China's seemingly bellicose attitude reflects only defensive reactions to the provocations of others. David Mozingo, for example, shares that latter view, but even Mozingo states quite flatly that China's "basic objective" is "a belt of weak, friendly, pliant states which refrain from taking actions contrary to Peking's important interests."[17] If that objective were achieved the likely result would be to lead the United States into policies even more hostile and suspicious of China than is the case today. Ultimately it is probable that this would be the impact upon Japan as well, and certainly the effect would not be a loosening of the present bipolar confrontation between the United States and China or a movement in the direction of multipolarity.

[16] As we have seen, Professor Fred Greene has concluded that China's desire is "for predominance in the eastern half of Asia" (U.S. Policy and the Security of Asia, ibid., p. 195). Professor Robert Scalapino, in testimony before the Senate Foreign Relations Committee on March 30, 1966, succinctly identified the foreign policy goals of China: "To remove all Western influence from Asia; to encourage by a variety of means an ideologically politically uniform Asia cast in the image of 'the new China'; and to enlist this 'progressive' Asia in the global struggle against both the 'revisionists' and the 'imperialists.' The words are those of the Chinese. These are scarcely the goals of an élite that is primarily oriented toward defense, and posing its objectives in very limited terms." For Scalapino's full statement, and other testimony on Chinese aims, see Congressional Quarterly Service, China and U.S. Far East Policy (Washington, 1967), pp. 278–311.

[17] David P. Mozingo, "Communist China: Its Southern Border Lands," SAIS Review, 12, No. 2 (Winter, 1968), 45.

The other outcome of continued weakness and division in Southeast Asia would represent precisely the other side of the coin: the continued need by Southeast Asian leaders to rely on the United States, and relations with the West generally, for their security. That result is a logical projection of much of the present condition in Southeast Asia; for example, the Thai and Philippines alliances with the U.S., and the increasing tendency of the Indonesian leadership to look to Washington for assistance. Such an outcome can be expected only to heighten China's suspicions and aggravate all those tendencies that lead her today to aggressive behavior in Southeast Asia.

Asian regionalism needs to be considered in this political context. The endorsement given the concept—by such spokesmen as the former President's Special Assistant for National Security Affairs and by President Nixon himself in his celebrated article of 1967 in *Foreign Affairs*— can be understood only if its relevance to the national interest of the United States is made quite clear. That relevance, in the first instance, derives from the American objective of loosening east Asia's dangerous bipolarity—to substitute for it an Asian structure in which there is less chance for a direct China-U.S. confrontation.

That objective, rather than Asian regionalism *per se*, is the development endorsed under President Johnson by Walt Rostow in the White House and Assistant Secretary William Bundy in the State Department. To be sure, any movement toward "regional cooperation" among developing nations in any part of the globe is probably favorable to American interests. African regionalism, for example, as well as the more advanced efforts in Central and South America, will facilitate the foreign economic assistance programs of the United States by making possible a more rational allocation of resources. In addition, to the extent that such regional efforts might aid in reducing intra-regional conflicts, they would also contribute to a more peaceful international environment. But those outcomes, however favorable, do not relate significantly to the national security requirements of the United States in Africa and Latin America—given the types of U.S. national interest in those two global regions that we identified earlier.

In East Asia, by contrast, the hoped for objective of a multipolar Asia is the rationale that justifies American interest in the concept of regional cooperation. We said earlier that however intrinsically interesting regionalism may be in any area, its ultimate relevance can be judged by Americans only after answering this question: What part of the United States national interest does regional cooperation affect? Hopefully we have answered that question and shown here that the

Asian interest affected is identical with the historic *Level One* interest of the United States in Asia: that "No single nation can or should be permitted to dominate the Pacific region."

Conceivably, of course, the United States could aim to preserve that interest, not working toward multipolarity, but by relying on and possibly resorting to force—largely its own overwhelming force. If it chose, the United States could doubtless erase the industrial and nuclear power potential of China with relative ease and perhaps even with relative impunity. But it chooses not to act in that manner. It chooses instead to de-escalate the confrontation between China and itself by altering the structural condition of Asia. That is the present objective, and the policies the United States pursues in support of the objective are to favor and support those forces that will ensure that no one nation can exercise general dominance in East Asia.

Thus to understand the contemporary meaning of Asian regionalism, it is essential first to recognize how closely it relates to the concept of multipolarity in Asia. It is also essential to recognize how closely *that* concept, multipolarity, relates to the interests and objectives of the United States in Asia. These considerations describe the framework within which Asian regionalism can most properly be considered, and in the remainder of this book we will deal with the environment and prospects for closer connections among states in Asia.

Six

THE ENVIRONMENT FOR REGIONALISM
A Case of Incentives

The American concern with multipolarity in Asia, as I have stressed already, is not new—Secretary of State Dulles, for example, may have hoped that he was laying some of its foundations when he created SEATO in 1954. It needs to be asked today, however, whether this long-standing interest in the concept of multipolarity, and the evidences of renewed American concern with Asian regionalism, are relevant to the realities of the contemporary Asian environment. In testimony prepared for a Committee of Congress, the author put the question this way: "Why, in essence, is the goal of a multipolar Asia any more realistic today than it was before?" [1]

In large part the answer to that question derives from changes in Asian attitudes toward the concept of regionalism, and broader changes in the Asian political environment that have taken place during the past decade. Previously vague notions of "regionalism" have begun to assume a more pragmatic and practical flavor—usually related now to specific programs concerning economic development. The best-known examples are found in the Asian Development Bank and in several smaller-scale institutions and groups created in the 1960's.

In addition, however, Asian nations that have traditionally avoided regional efforts have begun recently to evince a major interest in the prospects of regionalism, and have devoted considerable effort to bring meaning to the idea. A good illustration of such attention in Southeast Asia is Indonesia. Under the government headed by General Suharto, Indonesia began early in 1966 to work for the creation of

[1] See U.S. House of Representatives, Committee on Foreign Affairs, Subcommittee on Asia and the Pacific, Statement of Bernard K. Gordon, *Hearings*, March 7, 1968.

Southeast Asia's newest regional group: the Association of Southeast Asian Nations (ASEAN). Its origins and potential meaning will be discussed in the next chapter. There are, moreover, indications that Japan also seeks to establish an Asian grouping,[2] and even in Rangoon, the concept of cooperation is not treated with the same indifference—and sometimes hostility—that was common even two years ago. As we will see in a moment, the idea of regionalism in Southeast Asia is in a state of transformation today. It has shifted from an environment of low intensity to one in which almost all states in Asia seek to give the concept of regionalism their own imprint.

One result of this new interest is that in the '60's there is even a certain competitiveness about the activity. For in addition to such wholly economic bodies as ECAFE (the U.N. Commission for Asia and the Far East) and the Asian Development Bank, there are now several organizations aiming to promote more broad-based cooperation. Among these have been the Association of Southeast Asia (formed in 1961), the Asian and Pacific Council (formed in 1966), and ASEAN (established, we have just mentioned, in 1967). This newest group, perhaps the most promising, includes Indonesia, Singapore, Thailand, Malaysia, and the Philippines.

In the face of this activity, it is most reasonable to ask two questions: Why have Southeast Asian leaders renewed their interest in the concept of regionalism, and how meaningful are any of these regional efforts? To help answer the second question, the next chapter will analyze the most politically important regional groups, but it is important first to explain why the concept is so widely discussed in Southeast Asia today. The reasons are not hard to find. They lie in the nature of Asian perceptions of Communist China, in the nature of the development problems faced by the smaller Asian states, and finally, in the role played in Asia by the United States. Of these three main elements, we will consider the impact of China first.

[2] In a Tokyo speech before the *Keizai Doyuaki* (Committee for Economic Development) in May, 1967, Takeo Miki (then Foreign Minister) said that there are "four aspects" to Japan's "Asia-Pacific policy." The second is "regional cooperation" in Southeast Asia; the third is "promoting cooperation among the advanced nations of the Pacific area," and the fourth, he said, is Japan's role in the familiar North-South developmental issue. Miki hoped to combine all of these in a way which will allow Japan's economic and technological skills to be used in the most efficient way in Southeast Asia, and the greatest efficiency not only implies some degree of cooperation in Southeast Asia, but also represents "the rising trend among the participating nations for the realization of regional cooperation in Asia" (from "Foreign Minister Miki's Concept of an Asia-Pacific Sphere," *Japan Report*, 13, No. 12 [June 30, 1967], 3–4).

A.   The Negative Incentive: China

China's role in East Asia, for our brief descriptive purposes, can be readily identified: China intends to achieve great-power status, and like a great power, her leaders expect to be regarded as dominant in the region of the globe in which they live.[3] To achieve such a condition, China must seek the withdrawal of powerful and significant Western influences in East Asia, especially as they are represented by the United States.[4] To put it most bluntly, this means that China aims to achieve a position of dominant influence in East Asia.[5]

In the short term, in the view of many analysts of Chinese behavior, China's thrust must be in the direction of Southeast Asia.[6] This is in part because the more traditional buffer areas of concern to China—in her North and Northwest—are now blocked to her influence by the powerful presence of the Soviet Union. Similarly, China is prevented for the time being from attempting to exercise much

---

[3] Although debate continues on the method and style likely to be pursued by China's leaders, this is the conclusion to which most analysts have now come. See, for example, Greene, *ibid.*, pp. 45, 195–97, and O. Edmund Clubb, "China and the Western World," *Current History*, September, 1968. Clubb remarks that since at least 1964 "The Maoist strategic aim was now more than the recovery of the Manchu power position in Asia: it envisaged *the creation of a dominating world position for China*" (p. 150, emphasis added). For earlier analyses of "great-power" ambitions, see A. Doak Barnett, *Communist China and Asia* (New York: Random House, Inc., 1960), pp. 65–66; Richard G. Boyd, *Communist China's Foreign Policy* (New York: Frederick A. Praeger, Inc., 1962), p. 87; and Vidya Prakash Dutt, *China and the World* (New York: Frederick A. Praeger, Inc., 1966), p. 29.

[4] On the removal of "Western influence," see Boyd, *op. cit.*, p. 87 and O. Edmund Clubb, "China's Position in Asia," *Journal of International Affairs*, XVII, No. 2 (1963), 115.

[5] China's perspectives on her role in Asia are discussed in Barnett, *op. cit.*, pp. 65–66 and H. Arthur Steiner, "Communist China in the World Community," *International Conciliation*, No. 533 (May, 1961), p. 401.

[6] Some of the reasons for China's immediate interest in Southeast Asia are dealt with in Boyd, *op. cit.*, p. 87 and Harold C. Hinton, *Communist China in World Politics* (Boston: Houghton Mifflin Co., 1966), p. 394.

With regard specifically to Indochina, Oran Young has recently commented that the United States and the Soviet Union have parallel interests in that region because each is opposed to accepting domination of the area by any one power, and "there is every reason to suppose that the development of new patterns of outside dominance in Indochina *would effectively mean Chinese dominance*" (Oran R. Young, "Political Discontinuities in the International System," *World Politics*, XX [April, 1968], 386, n. 23).

influence on her Eastern flank in Japan. A dynamic and enormously prosperous Japan makes it pointless to attempt to achieve major influence there at this time.

Southeast Asia, on the other hand, represents a power vacuum, relative to other areas of traditional interest to China. Moreover, and in contrast to those other areas of interest, Southeast Asia is near-ideal for the application of Mao Tse-tung's modern revolutionary doctrines. As a region still overwhelmingly characterized by an often poverty-ridden rural population (though the proportion of town-dwellers is not so high as in the first postwar years), Southeast Asia holds the promise of greater gains with a lower level of risk and effort—for example by aiding local insurgents—than is involved in other regions adjacent to China.[7] Finally, it is in Southeast Asia where the power and policies of the United States—China's self-proclaimed major adversary—are seen as most provocative, and need, from Peking's perspective, to be neutralized.

Yet it must be said that, in the view of some commentators, China's foreign policies in the years since Mao took power appear only as defensive-responsive reactions. As we noted earlier, David Mozingo takes this view: he has argued that China is willing to live at peace with any Southeast Asian state that does not associate itself closely with the United States.[8] And Henry Steele Commager, a dean of American historians, has asserted flatly that "Chinese expansion is pretty much a figment of our imagination." [9]

But China's own words and actions strain this interpretation. Peking's repeated calls to overthrow the "Rahman puppet clique" in Malaysia, a government that is not tied formally to the United States, is one case in point.[10] Similarly, to the extent that there was Chinese involvement in the abortive 1965 effort to stage a *coup* in Indonesia —a nation with intimately close ties to Peking at the time—that involvement must also call into question the thesis that China is merely

[7] The lesser risks involved in this area as compared with others are discussed in Boyd, *op. cit.*, p. 53 and Hinton, *op. cit.*, p. 121.

[8] David Mozingo, "Containment in Asia Reconsidered," *World Politics,* XIX, No. 3 (April, 1967), 361–77.

[9] In *The New York Times Book Review,* July 16, 1967, p. 23.

[10] The "Malayan National Liberation League," an organization based in Peking, said through a China news release recently that "All genuine Malayan patriots must therefore step up their struggle against modern revisionism . . . at the same time as stepping up their struggle against U.S.-backed British imperialism and the Malayan (Rahman-Lee Kuan Yew) puppets, in order to crush 'Malaysia' and the new-type colony of Singapore and achieve the genuine independence of a unified Malaya" (New China News Agency, May 14, 1967).

defensive in her dealings with other Asian governments.[11] Even in Cambodia, there is evidence that Prince Sihanouk now suspects Chinese support for groups opposed to his government. This, despite the fact that the Prince has often referred to China as Cambodia's "best friend," and has argued that the war in Vietnam is a civil war in which there should be no American intervention. Yet in 1967–68, in the wake of increasing insurgency in several Cambodian provinces, Sihanouk has several times publicly warned against the activities of the "Khmer [Cambodian] Reds." Most recently he acknowledged that insurgents in Laos and Thailand act on the orders of North Vietnam and China, as when he announced that:

> The Pathet Lao's dependence on Hanoi is known to everybody, including Souvanna Phouma. Everybody knows that the Viet Minh are behind the Pathet Lao. The Viet Minh have already swallowed Laos and are now contemplating pushing the Pathet Lao ahead to devour Cambodia. You will realize this more clearly when I come to the third category [of Cambodia's enemies]. *The Thai Patriotic Front was born in Peking; it depends on Peking.* Peking recognizes our frontiers but the Front does not. You can see that there is not much of a guarantee from the communist side.[12]

Unlike the government of Malaysia (or as we will see in a moment,

[11] The subject of Chinese involvement in the attempted Indonesian *coup* of September 30, 1965 is a matter of some debate. A number of scholars point to reports of secret arms shipments from China to Indonesia in the weeks just before the *coup*. See, for example, Arthur J. Dommen, "The Attempted Coup in Indonesia," *The China Quarterly* (January–March, 1966), p. 168, and J. V. Van der Kroef, "GESTAPU in Indonesia," *ORBIS* (Summer, 1966), p. 467, where he cites reports in the *Sabah Times* of September 14, 1965. The belief, substantiated by these reports, is that China supplied arms disguised as building supplies, in a conspiracy approved by Subandrio, allowing for arms to enter Indonesia without customs inspection. Nevertheless, some specialists find it difficult to believe that China engaged in this activity.

The Indonesian government and many Indonesians are persuaded that China was involved, and this is the view also accepted by most leaders in Southeast Asia. China has of course not admitted complicity, but a new twist came recently when the remnants of the PKI (Indonesian Community Party), based in Peking, released their "self-criticism" designed to explain the failure of the *coup* attempt. The gist of the self-criticism (called precisely that by the Peking group) is that the *coup* failed—and was destined to fail—because the PKI misapplied the revolutionary principles of Mao and Lenin. The statement *does not deny that the purpose of the PKI was to bring about a Communist regime in Indonesia.* It says only that the PKI "did not prepare" Indonesia for "the possibility of a nonpeaceful road" to communism: "the most striking proof of [this error] was the grave tragedy which happened after the outbreak and the *failure of the 30 September movement*" (New China News Agency, July 8, 1967; my emphasis). This can be interpreted as a *mea culpa*.

[12] From Sihanouk press conference in Phnom Penh, May 23, 1968 (emphasis added).

that in Burma), Prince Sihanouk has not yet had to face China's open call for his overthrow, but his remarks suggest that he at least will not be too surprised if that developed sometime soon. Sihanouk, moreover, has sought to preserve friendly relations with Peking with at least as much concern as has Burma's General Ne Win, yet after mid-1967 Rangoon found that Ne Win was branded as a traitor. Peking has frequently called for "all the Burmese people to rise up to strive for the complete overthrow of the Ne Win military government and the establishment of a people's democratic and united front government . . ." [13] By late 1968, amid reports of the creation of a mysterious new China-assisted "Northeast Command," [14] (and declining Chinese support for the faction-ridden Communist Party of Burma), it seemed likely that Peking might be laying the basis for just such a united front. In sum, China's generally stern, and often threatening posture toward Burma—considering particularly that General Ne Win has gone out of his way to placate Peking—suggests again that if China is merely reactive, she reacts to threats that few others can perceive.

It would instead be more accurate to conclude that if Peking does seek friendly relations with governments in Southeast Asia, the only governments "acceptable" are those subject to major Chinese influence.[15] This may be simply another way of saying that China, emerg-

[13] Statement of the Central Committee of the Communist Party of Burma (based in Peking), and released by the New China News Agency, July 1, 1967.

One year later, it was reported that both Burma and China sought reduction in the tensions that had characterized their relationship during much of 1967–68, and some observers were quick to suggest that China's attitude in 1967 could largely be explained by the excesses of the "cultural revolution." It has to be noted, however, that in September, 1968, Peking was continuing to charge that Burma (in allegedly persecuting local Chinese) was "deliberately further worsening the relations between China and Burma . . . for no other reason than that of catering to the needs of U.S. imperialism and Soviet revisionism" (New China News Agency, September 19, 1968). Similarly, Japanese correspondents in Burma reported increases in China-supported "anti-government guerilla activities" (Asahi, Tokyo, September 16, 1968). The whole affair seems hardly consistent with the Mozingo thesis that China opposes only those who are closely tied to the United States.

[14] See the Far Eastern Economic Review, September 26, and October 17, 1968.

[15] Even Mozingo regards China's aims as one "of turning the region into a weak, neutral zone responsive to Chinese interests in policies" (Mozingo, in SAIS Review, p. 46). He has difficulty in explaining why China has become so bellicose toward a pliant state like Burma, and concludes that this "may be a function of the continuing conflict generated by the Cultural Revolution," or that Peking may have become upset with "insults" to its prestige that derived from Burma's suppression of pro-Peking demonstrations on the part of Chinese resident in Rangoon. In any event, China's decision to associate itself with vehement attacks on the government of Burma ("Down with the reactionary Ne Win military government!") certainly does not support the general proposition of

ing from more than two centuries of decline, is beginning to behave in ways consistent with the traditional behavior of Great Powers, and for this reason will aim for predominant influence on her rimland. Yet some analysts, when they deny the need for a continuing U.S. involvement in Asia, fail to see this. A prominent Australian scholar has remarked, for example, that those who deny the need for counter-vailing power around China reflect "an exceedingly optimistic view of the way Chinese power is likely to be used . . . [and] an assumption that China is somehow a Power unlike all other Powers, neither needing to be checked by countervailing power nor susceptible of so being." The unreality of this proposition, she has concluded, "is apparent as soon as it is made explicit":

> To argue in 1966 that China could never be expected to acquiesce in a rival power structure in South Asia is precisely equivalent to arguing in 1946–47 that Russia could never be expected to tolerate a rival power structure in Western Europe. Such a situation was possible and Russia did in fact come to accept it, and twenty years after the process began . . . the prospects for peace look a good deal better than when it was initiated. To assume that China must be conceded unchecked hegemony in South Asia is to acquiesce in so substantial an addition to her future power-base (taking into account manpower and resources and nuclear weapons) that it is difficult to see the consequent world finding a way to live quietly or to keep its crises manageable. There is of course no *present* similarity between the situation of South Asia and that of Western Europe. That is why the intervention of the outside Powers over a long transition period (perhaps twenty years) is likely to remain necessary.[16]

In broad terms, this is the view increasingly held by the political leadership, and much of the intellectual leadership, too, in most Southeast Asian states today. It is not a universally held view to be sure, and there are articulate spokesmen for the view that China poses no major security threat to Southeast Asia. But this is not a view held by the leaderships in Malaysia, Indonesia, Thailand, or Singapore. It is not even the view held by Prince Sihanouk of Cambodia, who has said often that "China does not swallow Cambodia because of the Americans." [17] Indeed, in the wake of the American bombing-halt of North Vietnam in November, 1968—an event which led to some fears that

---

those analysts who hope to argue that China reacts only to stimuli connected with the United States and other "manifestations of imperialism."

[16] Coral Bell, "Towards a Stable Asia," in *The World Today* (April, 1966), reprinted in *Survival* (June, 1966), p. 190.

[17] From press conference remarks in Phnom Penh on September 18, 1967, reported by Radio Cambodia, September 18, 1967, and reprinted in the *Christian Science Monitor*, October 16, 1967.

a precipitate U.S. withdrawal from Southeast Asia might be forthcoming—the Prince stated publicly what close students of Cambodia have recognized for some years to be his genuine preference: *a continued American presence in Southeast Asia.* An American withdrawal, he said, would mean Chinese dominance in the region, since "the weight of China will be too heavy." To avoid this, and although "I don't like the United States . . . I want to have some cards in my hand to maneuver to keep Cambodia for the Cambodians." A continued American role in Thailand and the Philippines, he added, would help retain the "balance of threats" between China and America, and thus "indirectly help to keep Cambodia free." [18]

Prince Sihanouk has frequently sought to exploit this "balance," sometimes in barely-concealed warnings to China. Early in 1968, and in response to increased insurgency problems which he believes are aided and endorsed by Peking, he warned that should there be insufficient arms and ammunition to cope with a rebellion, "I would have to retire and hand over [power] to the Army, which would be obliged to the Americans." [19] And even in 1965, in a letter to American readers, he wrote that "after the disappearance of the U.S.A. from our region and the victory of the Communist camp, I myself and the People's Socialist Community that I have created would inevitably disappear from the scene." [20]

Southeast Asian leaders find less difficulty in reaching this conclusion than Americans, whose perception of China has for years been complicated by a number of myths and contradictions. There is in Southeast Asia, for example, no real equivalent to the China Lobby that existed in the United States, and little parallel to the imagery and literature about China's travail that sparked the sympathy of millions of Americans before World War II. Instead, China represents to politically aware Southeast Asians three important elements, and only one of those has given rise to a sympathetic and friendly view of China.

[18] These statements are from the Prince's remarks to Stanley Karnow, in *The Washington Post*, November 4, 1968.

[19] Recently, in the face of continued insurgency in four provinces, Prince Sihanouk warned that if Cambodian "Reds" "go on creating insecurity . . . it will be necessary to . . . hand over power to the military authorities, which would be led by Lon Nol [Defense Minister], who will be like Suharto in Indonesia . . . . It will be up to him to decide whether we should accept U.S. aid again" (Sihanouk speech of February 28, 1968, reported by BBC *Summary of World Broadcasts*).

[20] From the Prince's letter to *The New York Times*, June 4, 1965. For a brief analysis of Cambodian foreign policy, see Bernard K. Gordon, "Cambodia: Where Foreign Policy Counts," *Asian Survey* (September, 1965), pp. 433–48.

B. The Three Meanings of "China"
in Southeast Asia

The first element is simply that in the Southeast Asian view China is the traditional and alien great power of the region, with a long history of exercising much influence. Considering the fact that China represents one of the few truly great and cohesive world cultures, it is not surprising that her presence has long overawed the more primitive peoples of Southeast Asia. When those people did achieve a higher degree of culture, as they did in Vietnam, their culture was very much the product of Chinese influence. But being deeply influenced and even shaped by Chinese culture and behavior norms has not endeared China to the peoples on her rim, as the history of Japanese and Vietnamese relations with China helps demonstrate.

Secondly, in modern Southeast Asia, the "normal" anxieties which a small state might anyway feel toward the giant of its region are intensified by the role of the Nanyang (or "overseas") Chinese populations. It is a truism too well known to elaborate here that throughout Southeast Asia the Nanyang Chinese exercise a position of economic dominance that is widely resented, feared, and distrusted. The movement of Chinese to Southeast Asia is relatively recent; it was much accelerated by the economic and administrative policies of the colonial regimes of the past few centuries. Yet despite their recent arrival, the Chinese have, nonetheless, been the dominant ethnic group in economic (and sometimes political) matters in Malaysia, Cambodia, Thailand, and in some important respects in Indonesia and the Philippines.

There are qualifications, to be sure: in Cambodia, the Nanyang have shared pre-eminence with Vietnamese;[21] in Thailand they have achieved a degree of assimilation which has smoothed the roughest edges of anti-Chinese sentiment; and in the Philippines the Chinese have not occupied quite the role of influence typical elsewhere in the region. But

---

[21] In Phnom Penh, Cambodia's capital, ethnic Cambodians (Khmers) are in a minority: Chinese and Vietnamese dominate the life of that city. In the economic life of Burma, a similar pattern existed for decades, but on a lower scale and with different players. In that case, colonial policy resulted in the dominance in Burmese life of alien Indians, as well as Chinese. Burma has for some years been embarked on a policy of evicting Indian businessmen, bankers, and shopkeepers, but the anti-Chinese activities in Rangoon in mid-1967 would indicate that this policy had not yet caught up with the local Chinese population.

these qualificatons do not detract from the intensity of a basic racism, aimed at local Chinese, which is one of Southeast Asia's most distinguishing characteristics. In the years since independence it has resulted in numerous instances of abuse and intimidation, and where free rein has been given (as in Indonesia), murder, too, has not been uncommon. The presence of this strong ethnic resentment means that there are "two Chinas" in the minds of many Southeast Asians: "China" the great and perhaps fearsome nation, and "China" the source of the despised and dominating alien group at home. The two mental images are probably mutually reinforcing, and neither is a positive factor from Peking's viewpoint.

It is only modern "political" China that has sometimes been sympathetically viewed among some groups in Southeast Asia. By that I mean simply that there has been much admiration, and not only in the overseas Chinese communities, for modern China's accomplishments. This dates back to the *Kuomintang* period, and to the fact that even under Chiang Kai-shek China was able to assert her independence and her identity, especially against the Westerners. When the communists came to power after 1949, and capped Chiang's limited achievements with the establishment of an effective central government, it was inevitable that many millions in Southeast Asia would be moved and encouraged by Mao's successes. In part this is because they could be understood not only as China's successes but as Asia's success against the West. To Southeast Asian elites who had smarted under generally oppressive colonial restrictions the banners that Mao carried had to be vastly appealing: the banners of anti-Westernism, anti-colonialism, and the welfare of the masses.

This one aspect of China's image in Southeast Asian eyes, the only favorable aspect, might have outweighed the two negative elements, and for a very brief period it did. From 1954 to 1958–59 China emphasized an Asian policy of friendship and reasonableness, symbolized by Chou En-lai's masterful performance at Bandung in 1955. But by 1959 something approaching a "hard line" was reinstated, and the 1960's have seen China dissipate much of the favorable capital that it had accumulated in Southeast Asia. Her strained relations with India, Indonesia, and Burma (to say nothing of Peking's regular vilification of the Thai, Malaysian, and Filipino governments) have led many leaders in Southeast Asia to re-examine their perception of China.[22] Many, that is, would have preferred *not* to see China in nega-

[22] It is often suggested that China did not begin a propaganda campaign aimed at such nations as Thailand until those nations allowed the use of their territory

tive terms; they have hoped that Peking would accept a "live and let live" approach. But China's behavior has made that view difficult to sustain, and this has been one of the prime elements leading Asians increasingly to think of ways to provide for their long-term security.[23] It is in that perspective that the already familiar concept of regional cooperation in Southeast Asia has begun to take on new meaning recently.

China's increasing unfriendliness, that is, has provided something the "environment" for regional cooperation has long lacked: a common perception of threat. As long as that was absent, the concept of regionalism had no special urgency. Even the idea that there might be practical benefits from regional cooperation, a belief urged for years by some economists and by the ECAFE staff,[24] went unheeded because

for American military purposes—Mozingo, for example, dates China's vilification of the Thai leadership from 1964–65. It is worth noting, however, that in *June 1959*, the *Peking Review* bitterly castigated Bangkok for becoming "the most active accomplice of the U.S. imperialists . . ." "If they persist," the article concluded, "history will eventually bring them before the bar of justice" (*Peking Review*, II, No. 25 [June 2, 1959], 23). This was long before there were American troops based in Thailand.

In 1962 the *Peking Review* charged that the United States and the "Sarit Thanarat clique" were collaborating to "wipe out the Thai patriotic forces" (*Peking Review*, V, No. 15 [April 13, 1962], 8). But most significantly, in *October, 1963*, Peking broadcast a talk which charged, *inter alia*, that Thailand "is still under U.S. control and enslavement [and] . . . . until this heavy stone is removed the people of Thailand will be unable to lead a better life" (Peking broadcast entitled "The Great Misery Brought to Thailand by U.S. Aid," October 23, 1963). I believe it not unreasonable to characterize this plea as at least an implied call for the overthrow of the Thai government, a call which was made explicit, as Mozingo and others have pointed out, late in 1964. At that time China broadcast to Thailand a message which said "If we succeed in overthrowing the dictatorial, reactionary regime . . . we will be able to enjoy the true independence and peace for which we are longing" (Peking radio broadcast in Thai, December 13, 1964).

[23] This statement is based in part on the author's interviews with senior officials, especially Foreign Ministers, in Singapore, Indonesia, Thailand, the Philippines, and Malaysia, most recently in February, 1967. Public remarks, however, can also be cited, for Southeast Asian leaders, as will be seen later, are no longer as reluctant as in earlier years to name Communist China as the source of their anxiety.

[24] See A. D. Goseco, "Underdeveloped Countries: A Multilateral Trading Scheme," *The Eastern Economist* (September 1, 1961); Donald B. Keesing, "A Proposal for a Small Common Market," *Malayan Economic Review* (1965) and "Regional Trade Cooperation: An Exploratory Study With Special Reference to Asia and the Far East," *Economic Bulletin for Asia and the Far East*, Vol. XII, No. 1 (June, 1961); "Report of the Consultative Group of Experts on Regional Economic Cooperation in Asia" (Bangkok: ECAFE, December 17, 1961 [mimeo]; D. T. Lakdawala, "Trade Cooperation Within the ECAFE Region," *Pakistan Development Review* (Summer, 1962), pp. 543–57; and "Approaches to Regional Harmonization of National Development Plans in Asia and the Far East,"

there was little *political* reason to pay attention. Since approximately
1962–63, however, the idea has been gaining momentum, and has now
got to be recognized as one of the arresting features of the Southeast
Asian political environment. There seems little doubt that one of the
reasons for this change, although by no means the only or most important reason, is the realization that China cannot be regarded as a
permanently passive element in Asia's affairs, and may indeed become
a very troublesome and active participant.

C.   THE POSITIVE INCENTIVES: POLITICAL COHESION
AND ECONOMIC DEVELOPMENT

It is with this consideration in mind that Southeast Asian leaders,
searching for means to enhance their overall security posture, have
given renewed attention to regionalism. But it must be said immediately that they do not think of regional cooperation as an input to
present defense needs. No Southeast Asian leader deludes himself
into believing that short-term defense requirements can be met with
local resources, and all—even those not tied militarily to the U.S.—
recognize that an American military "presence" in the Pacific must
for some years provide an indispensable security framework. But this
is not seen as the most comfortable or acceptable long-term arrangement; even Thai and Filipino leaders regard SEATO as a mildly distasteful, though presently essential element of security. Nonmembers
of SEATO, moreover, would not join this or any other arrangement tied
directly to the U.S., for their distaste for "military pacts" is even
stronger.[25]

Instead, leaders in Southeast Asia see in regional cooperation a
means of achieving some kind of *solidarity*, and although that goal
was always attractive in emotional terms, cohesion in balkanized
Southeast Asia has become important to them for the first time for
political reasons. For some leaders, of course, there is no difficulty in

---

E/EN.11/CAEP.2/L.5 (September 25, 1964), available from ECAFE offices
in Bangkok.
    [25] For both groups this attitude stems from similar origins: from the non-
alignment ideology generated in the 1950's. That ideology held that military
"pacts" sponsored by the U.S. reflected a "cold-war mentality," and although
Asian leaders themselves increasingly accept the American view that China does
represent a threat, the old slogans die hard.

admitting that the ultimate rationale behind all this is security. For them, and Thai Foreign Minister Thanat Khoman is a good illustration, regionalism admittedly represents a fundamentally political purpose.[26] For most others, by contrast, it has been more comfortable to speak about regionalism only in economic terms, and that has been the main publicly expressed justification so far. But even in that framework, and in order to help understand why there is so much indigenous Asian interest in the idea of cooperation today, it is important to ask what leaders expect to gain from economic cooperation. There is no certain answer to this question, and a good deal of disagreement. Some Western economists, for example, suggest that there can be no important benefits from interconnecting a series of poor, agriculture-based economies whose present mutual trade is very low, and whose exportable products do not show the kind of complementarity that might lead to intraregional trade increases.

There are, however, a number of Asian economists who have for years thought differently: they have consistently urged that many benefits *will* come from regional cooperation. They point out that it is incorrect, albeit familiar, to look at intraregional trade alone as the index of potential economic regionalism. They stress instead that many of the developmental needs of Southeast Asian economies—in technical know-how, improved agricultural productivity, capital availability, and infrastructure—can be met on an improved basis through intra-Asian cooperation. One of the best known of these economists, Professor Hiroshi Kitamura of ECAFE, has long urged that the Southeast Asian economies can reap considerable benefits through the regional "harmonization" of their industrial development programs. At least several benefits might flow from this approach. First, some areas of needed industrialization (steel, fertilizers, aluminum, and so on) are so capital intensive that any one of the smaller Southeast Asian economies, acting unilaterally, may not be able to manage the necessary outlay. Second, the world money markets are more likely to be attracted to opportunities which—because they reflect a regional plan —are not redundant. This might be achieved, as the Governor of the Bank of Thailand has also said to this writer, if two or more countries

[26] Thanat has long been willing to suggest this privately; quite recently, however, he has expressed this conviction for publication: "Especially Thailand has been in the forefront in reference to building a regional grouping, regional entity. The motivations are *not only economic, social;* the motivations are certainly—I do not shy from saying that—*are certainly political*" (Interview, in the *Far Eastern Economic Review*, October 17, 1968, p. 156). My emphasis.

agreed not to duplicate facilities.[27] Finally, these and other economists believe that intra-Asian trade will expand *as a result* of such joint planning or "harmonization." [28]

Without an exhaustive economic analysis of the pros and cons of regional cooperation, no one can say with certainty whether marked improvement will come to the economies of the region from the kinds of cooperative measures presently being proposed. It is clear, however, that some leading Asian bankers and economists have been ardent proponents of the concept for some years, whereas non-Asian specialists often minimize the significance of economic cooperation among developing countries generally. Nevertheless, the proposals of the Asian specialists have maintained their momentum, and have helped persuade both foreign and local leaders that it is worth listening to the arguments for cooperation. One result of this indigenous momentum is that by 1965–66 the governments of both Japan and the United States began to reconsider their previous, and often negative, assessments of the future prospects of regionalism.

The Asian Development Bank, for example, was suggested some years ago in ECAFE, as well as by one of Thailand's most brilliant young banker-economists.[29] The reason for these suggestions was the widespread conviction that regional cooperation was an essential aspect of accelerating the economic development goals of Southeast Asian states. Until almost the last minute, however, the United States (speaking primarily through the Treasury Department) was cool to the

---

[27] Dr. Puey Ungphakorn, in conversation during the past several years in Bangkok. Also see: United Nations, "The Asian Development Bank and Trade Liberalization," Regional Economic Cooperation Series No. 2 (U.N. Publication No. 65.II.F.15, 1965), and Hiroshi Kitamura and Ajit Bhagat, "Regional Harmonization of National Development Plans and Trade Co-Operation: Approaches to Economic Integration in the Developing ECAFE Region" (available from University of Wisconsin, Department of Economics), 1967.

[28] This is also the view expressed by Professors Kyoshi Kojima, the late Lim Tay Boh, Noboru Yamamoto, and Saburo Okita, as stated in interviews in Tokyo, Singapore, and Bangkok from 1962–67. For more detailed discussion of this subject, see Chapter V in my book, *The Dimensions of Conflict in Southeast Asia* (Englewood Cliffs, N.J.: Prentice-Hall, Inc., 1966), pp. 141–61.

[29] See, for example, the speech and article by Paul Sithi-Amnuai, "A Regional Bank as a First Step Towards an Asian Common Market," *Bangkok Bank Monthly Review* (March, 1963), p. 76. Sithi-Amnuai is now a Vice-President of the Bank, based in New York. In several extended conversations with this writer over the past few years he has reaffirmed his conviction that regional cooperation will be a permanent feature of the Southeast Asian scene. His ideas for an "Asian Bank" have already been vindicated, and it is likely that he will continue to be very influential.

idea, but suddenly reversed itself in 1965.[30] Japanese officials, too, represented primarily by MITI,[31] were not enthusiastic about either the Bank idea or cooperation generally until quite recently. Both governments, however, appear now to be very much in support of the concept of Asian regionalism, and this support is likely to reinforce the view of those Southeast Asian leaders who have been advocates of regional cooperation for some years. Their own hunch that regionalism will have an economic payoff is enhanced, for example, by the commitment of Japan and the U.S. to subscribe $200 million each to the Asian Development Bank. It is an added incentive to know that leading outsiders are also in support of the concept.

D. THE IMPACT OF THE AMERICAN COMMITMENT

It may be, finally, that outside support has been indirectly the most important of the three incentives for Asian regionalism. For even taking into account the other two—that is, a perception of China as a threat, and a belief that cooperation will aid economic development— the role the U.S. has played in the area has been critical for the development of regionalism. The essence of this role is that the United States has provided *time* for Southeast Asia: time for leaders to come to their own realization that China's great-power interests are a threat to their independence, and time to begin the process of restructuring the regional politics of Southeast Asia. The "long-range hope," as Thai Foreign Minister Thanat Khoman said in 1966, is "to build an effective Pacific community—to forge one that will be a successful deterrent to aggression." [32]

The function that the U.S. has performed, reflected especially in its strong determination not to lose in Vietnam, is to have shown Asian leaders that there will be time to work toward this goal. Of course, national leaders did not quickly accept the thought that Southeast

[30] Based on a conversation with a former senior Treasury official now associated with the Asian Development Bank. A member of the Policy Planning Council in the State Department has also commented that "as late as March, 1965, we were unwilling to participate in the Asian Development Bank . . ." (Policy Planning Council, Department of State, "The Future of Economic Cooperation in Asia," [June, 1966], mimeographed, p. 69).

[31] The Ministry for International Trade and Industry.

[32] Quoted in *Washington Post*, October 30, 1966, citing Thanat's remarks to correspondents in Bangkok on October 29.

Asia might benefit from the American commitment in Vietnam—and given their experience with external colonial powers this should not be surprising. Nevertheless, the understanding has grown that Vietnam reflected a firm and ultimately welcome American commitment to the security of the region; some of the best evidence for this is found in Southeast Asian attitudes that anticipate the end of the Vietnam conflict and its consequences. Where only a few years ago it would have been reasonable to expect that the imminent departure of the United States would have been accompanied by many cheers in the region, the Asian response today is considerably more complex. While none will deny that there are still spokesmen in Southeast Asia who would welcome American withdrawal from the region, the more instructive point is that there are today many leaders—Cambodian, Indonesian, and Malaysian among them—who wish to be assured that the United States will not "leave" Southeast Asia under conditions that could lead to Chinese hegemony.

Indeed, the most striking impression of conversations held with a number of governmental and academic specialists visited in Southeast Asia in 1966–67,[33] in strong contrast to views expressed to the author by many of the same persons in several earlier visits since 1962, was precisely this new recognition: that there are major positive aspects to the American role in Southeast Asia. In interviews, the extent to which the U.S. purpose in Vietnam was understood and endorsed by these leaders was impressive, as was the connection they drew between American resolve and their own rising enthusiasm for regional cooperation. But nowhere is this better summed up than in a recent article by Denis Warner. He, too, found a close connection between U.S. firmness in Vietnam and the accelerating pace of efforts aimed at Asian regionalism. "The U.S. stand in Vietnam," he wrote, "has

[33] The most recent interviews were conducted early in 1967 and included conversations with the following officials:

Philippines: Hon. Narciso Ramos, Foreign Secretary; Pablo Pena, Under-Secretary for Political Affairs; Manuel Collantes; and Rafael Salas, Executive Secretary, Office of the President.

Malaysia: Tan Sri Ghazalie, Permanent Secretary, Ministry of External Affairs and Jack De Silva (now *Chargé* in Saigon).

Indonesia: Foreign Minister Adam Malik and Anwar Seni, Under-Secretary for Political Affairs in the Foreign Ministry.

Singapore: Foreign Minister Rajaratnam.

Thailand: Foreign Minister Thanat Khoman, Sompong Sucharitkul, and several of Thanat's immediate subordinates.

In almost all cases these meetings were the most recent of a series begun several years earlier (when interviews included Dr. Subandrio in Indonesia, and former foreign secretaries in the Philippines), and frank conversations were possible.

both stimulated interest in and opened up the prospect of much closer relationships between the free Asian states." Warner (an Australian) is one of the two or three most reliable and experienced reporters in East Asia, and to emphasize his point he referred to the frank remarks of Lee Kuan Yew:

> "Are you people really serious in Vietnam?" Lee Kuan Yew, Singapore's acerbic and sometimes seemingly anti-American Prime Minister asked a senior Washington official. "If you are, we are with you." The conviction now that the United States is serious—and this persists despite the sound and fury of the far-off debate—*has helped to stimulate an interest in regional self-help and cooperation* that even the most optimistic observer could scarcely have hoped for when the Communist capture of state power in Vietnam and Indonesia seemed imminent and Communism the wave of the future throughout the area.[34]

Although Warner may have chosen too optimistic a title for his article—for "An Asian Common Market" is hardly in the immediate offing—his conclusions are potentially reassuring. For he has found, too, that "instead of fretting about how to live with Communism, the Southeast Asians have now become concerned about finding a way to live with each other, conscious as never before that by hanging together they will avoid the danger of being hanged separately."[35] This is precisely what President Johnson had in mind when he said that one of the "realities of the New Asia" is the disenchantment with the "spent slogans of narrow nationalism," which has given way to Asia's new interest in "interdependence." These new developments and realizations mean that the deepest purpose of a decade of U.S. policies in Southeast Asia is now being vindicated. Costly as they have been, American actions have allowed Asians to learn two facts for themselves: that the American goal was never imperialism or "neo-Colonialism," and that only behind the American military shield, which so many of them denounced, has it been possible to plan for the new direction represented by Asian regional cooperation.

One measure of this accomplishment is the extent to which Southeast Asian leaders themselves now frankly assess the meaning of communism in East Asia. Although not all of the region's leaders feel they can yet be as publicly candid as those in Singapore, some recent remarks of Singapore's Defense Minister are not at all atypical:

> There is a widely held misconception about the nature and appeals of Communism in backward countries. . . . Communist appeal and

[34] Denis Warner, "First Steps Toward An Asian Common Market," *The Reporter*, May 18, 1967, pp. 24–30 (emphasis added).
[35] *Ibid.*, p. 25.

Communist strength are sometimes believed to be the result of poverty, oppressive domestic government, or frustrated nationalism. *This pays the Communist movement an undeserved compliment. . . . The Communist Party in any country has only one purpose—the revolutionary seizure of state power.*[36]

The other measure of the American accomplishment—though most emphatically and most importantly it is an indirect accomplishment— is the new emphasis on Asian regionalism. While the United States favored and supported efforts at regional economic cooperation in the 1950's (as at the conference in Simla, India, and occasionally in the SEATO framework), the local environment was not ripe. Consequently, outside urgings never were able to make regionalism take hold then. Now, in contrast, the time very clearly is ripe, as leaders in Southeast Asia have been unable to sustain the hopeful belief that it might be possible to adopt a "live and let live" relationship with Peking.

This is a development of momentous proportions. It means, first, that China has succeeded in dissipating much of the favorable capital that automatically belonged to her in the 1950's. Secondly, it means that by her own actions China has forced Southeast Asians—without the prodding of the West—to think of ways to provide for their security against China's threat. Leaders who would have been unwilling just a few years ago to name China as a potential threat to their security are no longer so hesitant, and as a result they are anxious to strengthen the whole region of Southeast Asia. Mochtar Lubis, one of Indonesia's most prominent journalists and writers, is typical of many in this respect. In late 1967 he remarked that although China was presently coping with internal difficulties, and for that reason was probably not an immediate threat, he nevertheless "personally favored a military cooperation between the Southeast Asian nations." [37] Although many would not yet endorse the concept of military cooperation, the same general view is widely shared in Southeast Asia —certainly to the extent of identifying China as the region's primary external security problem. The Prime Minister of Malaysia is far from alone in the conviction, as he expressed it early in 1968, that China is among "our dangerous enemies. . . . If People's China would change its aggressive and hostile attitude aimed at dominating other countries it might be possible that Malaysia could maintain friendly relations with Peking." [38]

[36] From remarks of Dr. Goh Keng Swee, quoted in *ibid.*, p. 24 (my emphasis).
[37] Reported in *ANTARA* (Indonesian Press Agency), September 4, 1967.
[38] *ANTARA* despatch from Kuala Lumpur, February 12, 1968.

These views reflect a marked change in the political environment in Asia, and they have led to the widespread acceptance by Asian elites that the goal of Asian regional cooperation is in the national interest of the Asian states themselves.[39] As a result, the leadership in the movement to achieve concrete progress toward that goal is now quite clearly indigenous. For that reason, and also because Asian regionalism is so clearly consistent with the U.S. objective of a multi-polar Asia, it is especially important that these efforts be well understood by Americans. The next chapter is designed to help achieve that aim.

[39] The *Far Eastern Economic Review*, a journal which on the whole has endeavored to present China in sympathetic terms, was forced in August, 1967, to conclude that "the excesses of the Cultural Revolution *have brought a new unity* to the rest of Asia. The five nations in ASEAN . . . have *come together partly as a result of what they conceive to be the menace from China.* It is hard for the other countries in the region to see how they can maintain relations with China on the basis of reason and mutual self-interest" (August 24, 1967, p. 359; emphasis added). Soviet analysts, no doubt for their own purposes, have come to the same conclusion with regard to ASEAN, and they now blame China to a great extent for the acceptance of American policies in Southeast Asia. Vikenty Matveyev wrote in *Izvestia* in mid-1967 that "fear of China also helped the United States draw Indonesia, the Philippines, Thailand, Malaysia, and Singapore more deeply into the American orbit" (*The New York Times*, August 31, 1967).

Seven

ASIAN REGIONALISM
The Focus in Southeast Asia

Indigenous interest in regional cooperation is not evenly spread throughout the whole of Asia. The "Asia" represented in ECAFE, for example, reaches from Iran across to Japan, and from there south to Australia and New Zealand. Yet there are no significant political forces hoping to achieve regional cooperation in that enormous geographic construct. Instead, patterns of political interaction in Asia today suggest an indigenous interest in *subregional* cooperation—and this interest very clearly centers on the subregion of Southeast Asia.

Occasionally observers have suggested a considerably broader format for Asian regionalism; in particular, it has sometimes been proposed that India and Japan might take the lead in somehow bolstering the weak states of Southeast Asia. Those three areas together, this strand of thinking has argued, might begin to form a counterweight to China.[1] But present trends (and reasonable projections from them) do not support even that view, for it is only in Southeast Asia where cooperative patterns have begun to develop and where there is an increasing pace of "regional activity." Japan, as we saw in an earlier chapter, is not altogether removed from this pattern, but India would appear a most unlikely participant.

[1] An illustration of this concept is found in Bruce M. Russett, "The Asia Rimland as a 'Region' for Containing China," in John Montgomery, ed., *Public Policy* (Cambridge: Harvard University Press, 1967), p. 226. Professor Russett discusses there some of the factors that militate against relying on so broad an area as a factor in "containment." As he shows, "Asia" so broadly construed that it includes all those states "from Afghanistan through India, Southeast Asia . . . and up to Taiwan, Korea, and Japan" has not much political meaning.

A. Southeast Asia and the Different Roles of India and Japan

The reasons for this lie both in Southeast Asian perceptions of what India represents and in India's own relative lack of interest in Southeast Asian nations—with the exception of Burma. For their part, Southeast Asian leaders (with Burma again excepted) have seldom regarded India as a part of the region in which they live. This is not to say that there is any precise delineation of what constitutes a "region"; patterns of interaction in Southeast Asia are of such recent vintage that some analysts still ask whether Southeast Asia fully qualifies for the label. Yet quite intensive communications links, sometimes all the more "tight" because they have developed out of conflict situations, have begun to take shape between Manila, Bangkok, Singapore, Kuala Lumpur, and Djakarta.[2] These patterns have given rise to a strong sense of regional consciousness among leaders in those states, and in the perceptions of those leaders India is simply not considered to be an integral part of the Southeast Asia region.

Most interestingly, a different perception applies to Japan. Not only because of its World War II involvement in Southeast Asia, but also because of its increasing economic presence, Japan in the 1960's is commonly considered to be a part of the same East Asian international system to which Southeast Asian leaders feel they belong. In trade terms, as suggested earlier, Japan is already very much a part of the economic life of Southeast Asia. As *Table 1* shows, almost all Southeast Asian nations rank Japan as their number one trading partner, and for three of them (Thailand, the Philippines, and Indonesia) trade with Japan accounts for at least a quarter of total trade. From *Japan's* viewpoint, of course, Southeast Asia does not represent a primary trading partner—that position is held by the U.S. Nevertheless, Japan's trade with Southeast Asia is now a considerable portion of its total: 15 per cent of Japanese exports (by value) were to South-

---

[2] In 1964, Professor Richard Butwell wrote that "not for centuries has there been the extent of interaction among Southeast Asians themselves that exists at the present time" ("Malaysia and Its Impact on the International Relations of Southeast Asia," *Asian Survey*, IV, 7 [July, 1964], 946). I elaborated on this point in "Foreign Affairs in the Wake of *Konfrontasi*," a paper read before the 1967 Annual Meetings of the Association of Asian Studies.

Table 1 TRADE OF EAST ASIAN COUNTRIES WITH JAPAN AS A PER-
CENTAGE OF THEIR TOTAL TRADE (1965)*

(MILLIONS OF U.S. DOLLARS)

	Export		Import		Total		Rank
	Amt.	Per cent	Amt.	Per cent	Amt.	Per cent	(Total Trade)
Burma	22.0	9.8	71.5	29.4	39.5	19.8	1
Cambodia	5.5	5.2	17.5	17.0	23.0	10.9	2
Communist China	202.3	10.0	269.8	15.4	472.1	12.4	1**
Nationalist China	139.8	31.0	223.4	40.3	363.2	36.1	1
Hong Kong	68.0	6.0	271.4	16.7	339.4	12.5	3
Indonesia	133.9	19.7	225.2	37.7	359.1	28.2	1
South Korea	45.8	26.2	166.6	36.9	212.4	34.9	2†
North Korea	13.2	72.1‡	18.1	52.9	31.3	60.0	1
Malaysia	265.5	24.0	216.0	16.2	481.5	19.9	1
Philippines	216.7	28.3	212.9	23.8	429.6	25.9	1
Ryukyus	78.8	89.0	188.1	77.4	261.8	80.5	1
Thailand	115.6	18.4	231.9	77.4	346.7	25.6	1
South Vietnam	3.7	10.3	32.8	9.2	36.5	9.3	2
North Vietnam	10.3	52.9‡	4.0	35.0	14.3	44.7	1

* Table drawn from Donald E. Hellmann, *Japan and the Postwar East Asian International System* (McLean: Research Analysis Corporation, 1969), p. 27.

** Japan continued to be the leading trading partner of Communist China in 1966 as the total value of transactions rose to $621 million (*Japan Times Weekly,* February 11, 1967).

† In 1966 Japan became the leading trade partner of South Korea.

‡ The total trade figure used to compute the percentage for North Vietnam and North Korea does not include trade with Communist nations.

east Asia in 1961, exactly twice what they were in the prewar year of 1936.

Japan is likely to have an increasingly important economic role in selected Southeast Asian states. Japanese investment in the quite prosperous Thai economy has been one of the major features of the 1960's, and even before the downfall of President Sukarno, much of Djakarta's planning for economic development hinged upon a close Indonesian relationship with Japan. Since 1966, with economic recovery now a goal in Djakarta, the likelihood of closer Japanese-Indonesian economic ties has greatly increased, for Indonesia could become a primary source of raw materials important to the Japanese economy. Moreover, along with the United States and several West European nations, Japan is a party to several bankers' groups which have a strong interest in assisting Indonesian economic recovery. In sum, the prospects for increased Japanese trade and investment in Indonesia are quite strong.

These particular activities are one reflection of a larger and more general resurgence of Japanese economic involvement in the affairs of Southeast Asia. This renewed interest has become more clear since 1965, for Japan has begun to shift perceptibly away from the "low posture" that characterized her relationship to Southeast Asia after the end of World War II. We mentioned earlier that in 1966 the Japanese government sponsored the first of an important series of Asian Ministerial Conferences on Economic Development, and set the tone of the proceedings.[3] At the second meeting, convened in Manila, Japan once again played a large role—so much so that some Filipino newsmen complained of Japan's easy dominance in Asia's economic affairs.[4]

These activities merely reflect Japan's already heavy involvement in the economies of Southeast Asia. From the viewpoint of the Southeast Asian states the relationship is one of considerable dependence. Moreover, much political discussion in contemporary Japan suggests that Japanese leaders accept the proposition that inevitably, and as a requirement of their own security, they must give high priority to the goal of Asian, and particularly Southeast Asian, regional cooperation. Although the politics of factionalism is likely to restrain and retard somewhat any strikingly bold initiatives, the "Asia-Pacific" policy outlined in Tokyo since 1967 appears to represent a durable trend. Despite their factional and intra-party differences, it was endorsed from the outset both by Prime Minister Sato and his then Foreign Minister, Takeo Miki. In this policy, Southeast Asia is designated as the region of Japan's primary attention, in terms of both assistance and trade, and the Foreign Ministry in particular can be expected continually to urge an activist Japanese policy in Southeast Asia.[5]

[3] See *Asahi Shimbun,* April 5–8, 1966 and *The New York Times,* February 10, 1966.

[4] For discussions of the second Japan-initiated "Ministerial Conferences," see the *Manila Times,* May 1–4, 1967, particularly the series of articles by Satur C. Ocampo.

[5] See, for example, Miki's speech, "Asia-Pacific Policy and Japan's Economic Cooperation," given at the monthly meeting of the *Keizai Doyukai* (Committee for Economic Development), May 22, 1967. A translation is available in *Japan Report* (New York: Consulate General of Japan, June, 1967).

While Japanese thinking is far from unanimous on this point, it is clear, too, that Japanese defense officials are also urging a greater Japanese role in assist-

In contrast, the East Asian role of India has been negligible, and in some instances negative. While occasionally some Indian spokesmen have expressed an interest in Southeast Asian affairs, the leadership in Delhi has not followed Southeast Asian developments at all closely.[6] Southeast Asian leaders know this and tend to expect little from India. On one of the rare occasions when a Southeast Asian leader has looked to Delhi for some initiative—for example, when Singapore suggested that India give thought to the concept of regional cooperation—the result was deeply disappointing. The occasion was the visit of Singapore Premier Lee Kuan Yew to New Delhi late in 1966, a period when Indonesian and Thai leaders had begun to actively discuss a new effort at Southeast Asian regionalism, and when Singapore leaders were forming their position on the subject. During his visit, the Singapore Premier apparently suggested that leaders in Delhi give thought to an "All-Asian security arrangement":

> Without being specific Lee proposed that India and Singapore, as well as other Asian countries, begin thinking about how they could group together to defend themselves against any Chinese threat . . . after the Westerners pulled out. Lee told friends here (New Delhi) the Indian officials showed no interest and abruptly changed the subject.[7]

Lee is reported to have been quite distressed at this negative Indian reaction, and it would be fair to state that reports of this development simply reinforced earlier convictions, held by most Southeast Asian leaders, about India's role in Asia. Generally, they simply do not believe that India will have the capacity—to say nothing of the will— to play a role of any significance in their region during the foreseeable future. Japan, on the other hand, although likely to continue for a few years longer to hold to the "low posture" it has so far adopted toward Southeast Asian affairs, is considered in the region to be an almost inevitable and perhaps intimate participant in the subregion's developments.

In the light of this expected role for Japan, regional cooperation has a special relevance for Southeast Asian leaders. As Thai Foreign Minister Thanat has said, regionalism holds out the prospect that acting together the Southeast Asian states can deal more effectively not only

---

ance for Southeast Asian nations. An illuminating article on Japan's security perspectives is in the *Christian Science Monitor*, August 4, 1967, where the point is also made that Japanese defense officials stress aid to Southeast Asian nations in terms of improving their capacity for resistance to subversion.

[6] Again, with the exception of Burma, and particularly Burmese treatment of Indian nationals residing in Burma.

[7] *Washington Post*, September 17, 1966.

with Japan but also with the world's other major powers.[8] And from the American perspective, which aims for Asian multipolarity, one value of regionalism is that it may help to ease Japan's reinvolvement in the system of Asian politics. Lucian Pye has put it very well: "even limited cooperation among Southeast Asian states can provide the necessary formula for bringing Japan effectively into the process of supporting the Asian balance of power." [9]

Regardless of whether every one of these great-power considerations is persuasive to Southeast Asian leaders (to some the grand issues *are* relevant), at least this much can be said of their present thinking: faced with a resurgent China and uncomfortable with the prospects of long-term dependence on *either* the United States *or* Japan, regionalism has an attractive quality that was not apparent in the 1950's. To a few the concept even appears as the only feasible approach to their long-term security problem, and as a result—among leaders in states like Thailand and Indonesia—the goal receives a priority that would have seemed remarkable a few years ago.

The measure of this change is in the pace of developments specific to Southeast Asia, and the clearest reflection is in the Association of Southeast Asian Nations, or ASEAN, the five-nation group established there in August, 1967. ASEAN is both the logical product of much that has been taking place in the 1960's and the likeliest format for future trends in Southeast Asian regional cooperation. But it did not develop without precedent—indeed it is strikingly similar in important respects to the Association of Southeast Asia (or ASA), a smaller group established in 1961. That similarity suggests some preferences and some relative constants in the format for cooperation. For that reason it will be best to introduce our discussion of regional organization with an examination of the Association of Southeast Asia, an early group that appears to have had an impact on later efforts.

B. The Association of Southeast Asia (ASA)

ASA operated during 1961–67 and marked what I will call a second phase in the development of Asian regionalism. Because of the special

[8] For Thanat's views on regionalism as a means for Southeast Asia to deal with major powers, see his interview with Drew Middleton in *The New York Times,* April 12, 1967. He has expressed similar views in conversations with this author in October, 1966 (in New York) and in February, 1967 (in Bangkok).

[9] Lucian W. Pye, "China in Context," *Foreign Affairs* (January, 1967), pp. 234–35.

and highly favorable circumstances of its termination in 1967, ASA warrants more attention than might ordinarily be given to a 3-nation group which had a lifespan of six years. For ASA was not terminated because it failed; instead, it was the most successful effort so far in Asian regional cooperation, and the success had much to do with the creation of ASEAN. Indeed, within a few weeks after ASEAN was established in August, 1967, spokesmen for Malaysia, the Philippines, and Thailand announced that most ongoing ASA activities and plans would be incorporated into ASEAN. In essence, the creation of ASEAN (which also includes Indonesia and Singapore) means that ASA, rather than disappearing, has simply been enlarged and given a new name.

The sense in which ASA represented a "second phase" in the development of Asian regionalism was in its indigenous and pragmatic nature. For unlike earlier ("first phase") efforts like ECAFE, the Colombo Plan, or SEATO, ASA was not created on the initiative of extraregional powers, nor did it include extraregional powers. And unlike the Asian Relations Conference of 1948, or the Afro-Asian Conference at Bandung in 1955, ASA established permanent administrative machinery providing for multilateral meetings and working sessions at regular intervals. Moreover, ASA was not an avowedly ideological group. In the words of Tunku Abdul Rahman, the Prime Minister of Malaysia and one of the ASA's first sponsors:

> . . . this organization is in no way intended to be an anti-Western bloc or anti-Eastern bloc, or, for that matter, a political bloc of any kind. It is not connected in any way with the various organizations which are in existence today; it is purely a Southeast Asian Economic and Cultural Cooperation Organization and has no backing whatsoever from any foreign source.[10]

To the extent that any ideological basis did exist, it derived from the general hope that if regional cooperation could improve developmental prospects, that would in turn make more difficult the prospects for successful subversion. The Tunku, in particular, was known to feel that Communist insurgency fed on the frustrations that accompany low levels of economic performance. Both in his handling of

[10] Federation of Malaya, ASA, *Report of the First Meeting of Foreign Ministers* (Kuala Lumpur, 1961), p. 4. A Thai preliminary working paper circulated in 1959 also emphasized this point: "The cooperation will be *practical* in the sense that the South-East Asian meeting to be convened shall not deal with conflicts of ideologies and the so-called East-West issue, except as passing references. . . . Such meeting shall concentrate its attention and efforts mainly on matters which affect directly the region as a whole or some countries of the region, and on questions whose solutions will directly benefit the region or some of its members."

domestic development and in his strong advocacy of regionalism he has never denied the root political imperatives of developmental programs. Another quasi-ideological purpose lay behind the decision to build a regional organization: this was the belief that Southeast Asian states do constitute a geographical and cultural family distinct from others. Many leaders in Southeast Asia subscribe to the belief that centuries of Western involvement have distorted and destroyed historical ties among the peoples of the region. One recurring purpose of association—characteristic of ASA, MAPHILINDO, and most recently ASEAN—has been the concern to rediscover old linkages and promote on that basis a new sense of regional identity.

But the leaderships of the ASA nations, the Thai and Malaysians in particular, are eminently practical men, and it was the goal of cooperation for economic development that was stressed during the period of the Association's activity. After a brief examination of the group's history, we will give some attention to some of the projects that characterized ASA—especially those that probably will be considered by its successor, ASEAN.

1. ASA History, Purposes, and Structure

ASA had its origins in 1959 when the Prime Minister of Malaysia and President Garcia of the Philippines met in Manila. In their own capitals both leaders had already expressed interest in the idea of Asian regionalism, and soon after their meeting the Malaysian leader, Tunku Abdul Rahman, began to circulate a proposal for a Southeast Asian regional organization. For a long time little came of his efforts although every Southeast Asian government (with the exception only of North Vietnam) was invited to join. The idea did, however, catch the attention of the Thai government and its foreign minister, Thanat Khoman, in particular. As a result, he took the lead in preparing draft proposals for the outlines of the proposed new organization, and at the same time he attempted to attract the cooperation of several other Southeast Asian governments for the proposal. He was especially interested in Burma.

None of this was successful, however, and for a time it seemed that even Thailand might not join if the new group was to be restricted to too few governments. But by 1961 it was finally agreed that Malaysia, Thailand, and the Philippines would proceed anyway with its establishment, and ASA was created in a meeting held in Bangkok in July.

ASA's experiences for the next two years were uneven. At the beginning the organization set itself a series of wide-ranging and, in many cases, very idealistic goals. There was talk of a common market, a free trade area, and such appealing ventures as a cooperative three-nation airline and shipping line.[11] On a less grandiose level a number of meetings were held to plan for cooperative ventures in educational exchange, in the joint training of technicians in fields related to agricultural and industrial development, and in several other areas in which cooperation might be both feasible and useful in economic development. While there was also early interest in social and cultural cooperation, it was soon clear that aside from educational exchanges, most interest centered on projects in the economic field. This was consistent with the thoughts that President Garcia and the Tunku had in 1959: to build a regional organization for economic cooperation. As a result, the most interesting planning within ASA in 1962–63 and the subject matter that seemed to be of most interest to higher levels in each of the three nation's ministries fell into fields related to economic cooperation.

By early 1963 a sufficient number of ASA meetings had taken place so that its broad outlines were now discernible. Its structure, for example, developed on three separate levels. The first, the one that had given ASA its establishment initially, was an annual Foreign Ministers' meeting. The second level of ASA's organizational structure was comprised of a group known as the "Joint Working Party." This body represented some of the most senior officials in various ministries in each of the three Southeast Asian governments, and since the group reported directly to the ASA Foreign Ministers, its recommendations essentially structured the final agreements reached by the Association.

But it was not even in the "Joint Working Party" meetings, which lasted for only a week or so, that the detailed discussions and examinations of cooperative projects took place. Instead, this was the function of a series of "working-level" committees of the three governments, comprised of experts in functional fields. For example, some of the committees were concerned with shipping; trade liberalization; educational procedures; marketing; and with proposals for cooperation in such fields as agriculture and fisheries. Ordinarily these special committees, which represent the most pragmatic aspect of ASA planning, met in the autumn and winter months of each year. It was their

---

[11] See Bernard K. Gordon, *The Dimensions of Conflict in Southeast Asia* (Englewood Cliffs, N.J.: Prentice-Hall, Inc., 1966), Chapters V and VI.

purpose, following the ASA Foreign Ministers' meetings in July, to act upon the mandate they received from the ministerial level.

In mid-1963, when this structure was becoming apparent, ASA was forced to cease most of its operations. This cessation was caused by the Philippines' territorial claim to North Borneo, which served to aggravate and upset relationships between leaders in Manila and Kuala Lumpur. From the viewpoint of ASA development, this was an especially poor time for an interruption because the new organization had just completed its first year. During that year ASA had undergone a "shaking down" process, and some of the most senior civil servants in each of the three governments had begun to develop pragmatic ideas of what could and what could *not* be accomplished within the ASA format. Because ASA represented such an unprecedented experiment in Southeast Asian communications among governments and their senior officials, this was itself no mean accomplishment. Indeed, the Association was just beginning to outline some creative steps when the break came, and one of these steps was the "ASA Fund."

The fund was initially subscribed at a level of $3 million (a million dollars from each government), and it was expected that the money would be used to finance joint research projects. That, too, was an unprecedented development and suggested that the three governments were beginning to look upon the small subregional group with genuine, if limited expectations of accomplishment. Nevertheless, all this had to come to a temporary halt in the wake of disturbed Philippines-Malaysia relationships. In a sense ASA operations went into a deep freeze in mid-1963 but seemed to re-emerge relatively unscathed in 1966.

That recovery is in itself one of the most compelling signs that regional cooperation in Southeast Asia had a certain dynamism of its own and that ASA, in particular, represented a special strain in the breed of Asian regionalism. This became very clear in 1964–65 in the author's discussions with Foreign Ministers and senior civil servants in each of the ASA nations. That was, of course, a period in which ASA was not operating, for by 1964 the Philippines and Malaysia had severed diplomatic relations. Nevertheless, it was the most widely held view that ASA—in the words of one foreign minister—was merely in a period of "hiatus."

It was confidently expected in Kuala Lumpur, in Manila, and most certainly in Bangkok that ASA would be revived quite soon. Malaysian officials, in particular, were at pains to point out that they had not disbanded their ASA staffs. Instead they had continued to develop plans for cooperative ventures, essentially along the lines of the projects that had been agreed upon when ASA formally ceased operations the year before. A similar view was expressed by the Foreign Minister of Thailand. Although he complained that his prime minister had asked for the bookkeeping "return" of the $1 million allocated to the ASA Fund, Thanat Khoman stressed that his prime minister had assured him that, once ASA was re-established, the $1 million Thai contribution to the fund would be immediately restored. In sum, a temporary conflict in 1963–65 between two of the ASA governments was not regarded, even by leaders in those governments, as sufficiently important to destroy a subregional association to which they attached great value.

Their judgment was supported by developments after late 1965. One of these was the simple fact that the Philippines' claim to North Borneo (Sabah) had not been effective; indeed, among the many Filipinos who strenuously opposed it was the Senator—Ferdinand Marcos—who became President of the Republic in the November, 1965 elections. Although in 1968 President Marcos associated himself with a Philippines Congressional initiative on the claim (thereby leading to renewed irritations with Malaysia),[12] his succession to office and his first two years was a favorable development for regionalism. It allowed for resumption of ties with Malaysia, and helped lay the groundwork for rebuilding a degree of mutual trust. At about the same time there occurred the attempted coup in Indonesia, which led over the next few months to the gradual "toppling" from power of President Sukarno, and further important change in the Southeast Asian political climate.

As that event took place, it meant, too, the end of Indonesia's confrontation of Malaysia, a confrontation with which the Philippines had indirectly associated itself. Thus, while events in the Philippines were already moving in the direction of a Manila-Kuala Lumpur

---

[12] The Act, not Presidentially inspired, announces that North Borneo is regarded as part of the Philippines, and that its "claim" is still valid. Marcos expected a weaker bill, but—as a new election campaign began to take shape and at the risk of appearing to lack nationalist sentiment—he could not avoid signing the version presented to him. These nuances have not comforted Kuala Lumpur, although (unlike the 1963 instance) both governments have refrained from a diplomatic break. There are, moreover, in this second dispute greater external forces urging a peaceful resolution than in 1963. Indonesia in particular has added its voice to that of Thailand in steps designed to end the dispute, and in November, 1968, Foreign Minister Malik specifically offered Indonesia as a mediator (*Washington Post*, November 3, 1968). In December, 1968, Manila and Kuala Lumpur agreed to shelve the issue for at least one year.

rapprochement, that trend was facilitated by Indonesia's own cessation of its anti-Malaysia policy. Consequently it was not surprising that by mid-1966 Malaysia and the Philippines were once again speaking about reviving ASA.

Accordingly, in July, 1966 the third ASA Foreign Ministers' meeting was held, following meetings of the Joint Working Party. Then from October through December of 1966 a series of special committee meetings took place—designed to pick up regional planning where it had been left three years earlier. But now there was a new sense of urgency; among participants there was a clear conviction that ASA would need to make up for the time lost, and to prove that it was a viable institution. The Working Party, fearful that by grasping at every suggested cooperative venture ASA would spread itself too thinly, now gave priority status only to those proposals with a good chance of early accomplishment. Others, including some esoteric-sounding research projects (one concerned seasnake venom) were de-emphasized and eventually disappeared from the agenda of later meetings. An indication of the change in focus is reflected in the report handed to the Foreign Ministers in 1966: it contained only 34 recommendations in a brief document of 24 pages. The 1962 report was nearly three times that length, and included 171 recommendations.

2. ASA Projects and Future Implications

An examination of some of the specific projects recommended in 1966 will suggest the range of activities on which any Southeast Asian regional body is likely to concentrate. It will also suggest some of the most vexing problems that must confront any such effort. This is perhaps most clearly seen in the field of trade.

Trade among Southeast Asian nations is notoriously low and ASA attempted to improve the environment for trade expansion—through improved contacts among business leaders in the three nations as well as through a formal trade liberalization agreement. By mid-1967, when ASEAN was formed, the ASA countries were expecting to approve an essentially "most-favored-nation" agreement on tariffs, and initial attention was also being given to a potentially more far-reaching preferential agreement. An ASA committee that met in late 1966 considered a proposal for a free trade area, and early in 1967 the Subcommittee on Trade Liberalization announced agreement on the "general principles" that would underlie a Free Trade Agreement.

Such an agreement, even in a small number of commodities, would go considerably beyond the "most-favored-nation" treatment; it could mark a first step towards realization of ASA's "common market" dream. The amount of trade expansion in those commodities subject to free trade could become an important indicator of the utility of a wider Southeast Asian free trade area, or even a common market.

If such a goal is far from being achieved, there are lower-level benefits from trade talks among developing Asian countries. The ASA Conference on Commerce and Industry, for example, recommended that a Board of Commercial Arbitration be established—a proposal likely to be repeated in the ASEAN context as that body gets underway. An Arbitration Board would provide machinery for conciliation of differences among businessmen in the nations involved, and in the Southeast Asian context this seemingly minor arrangement could be of very considerable value. The reason, of course, is that there are almost no patterns of experience among traders and businessmen in these countries; they still know far more of procedures in Amsterdam, San Francisco, and London than they do of business conditions in Bangkok, Kuala Lumpur, and Manila.

The ASA group also sought ways by which cooperation could help in achieving a better return for their exports. At the time ASEAN was created, some ASA participants were again considering joint exhibits at trade fairs and exhibitions, joint trade missions abroad, and voting blocks in international economic organizations. Like exchanges of data on the production and utilization of their primary products, such joint ventures can promise economic benefits and require little or no national sacrifice. It is likely that they will be continued and enlarged in the new ASEAN format.

One of the most interesting aspects of the ASA experience, as we suggested just before, was the decision to create a joint fund of $3 million. This grew out of very early discussions on the prospects for "external financing" which could supplement locally raised funds devoted to joint projects, and it is very probable that the creation of the Asian Development Bank gave added impetus to the idea. Indeed after the ADB was established in 1966, ASA created an *ad hoc* committee and charged it with the task of identifying suitable projects for submission to the Asian Bank. The projects proposed included a feasibility survey of joint industries, a mineral survey, expansion and improvement of port facilities, a proposal for a "Marine Fisheries Training and Development Centre," a Public Health Institute, a "University of Southeast Asia," and a regional institute for the teaching of science and mathematics. There were others, and in large part these same projects will probably be given priority attention by ASEAN. The request by President Johnson (in September, 1967) for a $200 million *additional* U.S. contribution to the ADB increases the likelihood that genuinely joint development projects can be financed in Southeast Asia.[13]

Another project under consideration since the Association's formation is the concept of a joint shipping line. All Southeast Asian countries are very dependent upon foreign companies to ship both exports and imports. This has resulted in considerable hard-currency expenditure and irritation with schedules set in Europe. The Philippines are considerably more advanced than other Southeast Asian countries in the building of a merchant marine, partly because some private companies operate interisland services and also because its National Development Company began a ship-buying program in 1955. Yet even in the Philippines, domestic shipping accounts for less than ten per cent of total tonnage leaving and entering Philippine ports.

Table 2 TONNAGE OF MERCHANT MARINE*

Country	Tonnage	
	1961	*1964*
Philippines	255,955	393,000
Thailand	9,877	14,000
Malaysia	0	3,000

* Data for *Tables 2* and *3* are drawn from working papers presented at the Second Meeting of the Ad Hoc Committee on Shipping Line, Kuala Lumpur, 1966. For assistance in preparing these tables, and for other data in this section, I am indebted to Mr. Charles E. Morrison, my former graduate student at the Johns Hopkins University.

The ASA countries also objected to what they consider discriminatory and arbitrary "Conference" freight rates, which sometimes make charges to nearby Asian countries higher than those to European and North American ports. Some Asian leaders, moreover, have argued

[13] Although the U.S. Congress failed in 1968 to approve this request, the U.S., along with Japan, is already pledged to a $200 million contribution to the initial capitalization of the Asian Development Bank. The President's 1967 request for the additional $200 million stipulated that its use would be for special, including joint, projects primarily on a long-term, low-interest basis.

Table 3 TONNAGE MOVED BY DOMESTIC SHIPPING, 1964

Country	Exports			Imports	
	(1) Total Tonnage	(2) Moved by Domestic Shipping	Per cent Moved by Domestic Shipping	(4) Total Tonnage	(5) Moved by Domestic Shipping	Per cent Moved by Domestic Shipping
Philippines	10,008,038	648,909	6.48	7,453,619	739,295	9.92
Thailand	4,463,688	232,071	5.20	3,552,507	11,367	0.32
Malaysia	Data not available, but domestic shipping insignificant					

that the development of a merchant marine is essential to their national defense.[14] For all these reasons, ASA spokesmen gave priority to the idea of a joint shipping line, and to explore the idea, a special meeting was held in Kuala Lumpur in October, 1966.

The Philippines was particularly active in promoting the project and presented a draft agreement on the shipping line. In this plan, each of the ASA countries would initially contribute $5 million for a down payment on 12 merchant vessels, and to cover costs of operation.[15] Ships of identical type and specifications would be purchased in multiples of three, with one registered in each country's name.[16] The Philippines hoped that within five to ten years the ASA line would have a tonnage of about five million and be able to handle half the foreign trade of the ASA countries. Filipino delegates pointed out that Norway (with a population much smaller than that of any of the ASA countries) had over 13 million tons of merchant shipping.

With Indonesia's participation in ASEAN, and with that country's drastic shortage of shipping, much of the future direction of this proposal may depend on Indonesia's attitude. All Southeast Asian countries, it should be stressed, are critically dependent on the structure of their shipping arrangements, and in the case of Indonesia especially, the long-term developmental goals of the country relate very closely to shipping facilities. Indonesia's economy has suffered greatly since the ejection of Dutch firms and vessels, and Djakarta may want to participate in almost any shipping arrangements that can help in the movement and marketing of its commodities.

Additional ASA projects and proposals might be mentioned, but it has been our intention here only to suggest the types of cooperative ventures likely to be considered by a regional organization in the area. Clearly, developing nations have a number of goals that can be improved through joint ventures, and some of these suggest truly dramatic possibilities that would result in a Southeast Asian region far more cohesive than today. Already, for example, officials have turned their attention to the possibilities opened up by the advent of communications satellites, and even in the ASA framework progress

[14] The argument is that in case of a major war, other countries would commandeer their vessels for their own use and the ASA countries would be left with insufficient shipping to move their goods in a time of national emergency.
[15] The Filipino draft also outlined a management scheme (a multinational Board of Governors would be the ruling body) and the legal status, immunities, and privileges of the line.
[16] The ships would fly national flags, but be identified by the ASA emblem painted on their funnels and the name "ASA SHIPPING LINE" painted on their sides.

was made toward a direct microwave link between Bangkok and Kuala Lumpur. Even before ASEAN was established, Indonesia was participating in the international communications consortium sponsored by the COMSAT Corporation, and it is likely that satellite communications will become especially important to that 3000-mile long nation of islands. The creation of ASEAN raises the prospect of integrating that interest of Indonesia with the almost equally pressing communications requirements of the other four nations; it is in the nature of broadcast communications satellites that multination cooperation is essential if they are to be effectively utilized.[17] Like other projects that ASA considered, for example, in large-scale industrialization efforts and in certain fields related to agricultural research, significant progress is likely to be quite dependent on cooperation among a number of national economies.

3. Survival as Success

Although ASA achieved few tangible results, it can for at least three reasons be counted as a success. It represented an unprecedented and indigenous Asian effort, and second, it helped set the programs and procedures for likely future steps. But perhaps most important are the favorable circumstances under which ASA was superseded by ASEAN, for this underlines once again that the concept of regionalism has a remarkably strong appeal to the indigenous elites in Southeast Asia.

This appeal must be weighed against the political, cultural, and economic obstacles that impede cooperation. In ASA, the political problems were not insurmountable—the Philippines' claim to North Borneo was shelved, and the newest outbreak of this dispute, if a face-saving mediation procedure can be arranged, is also likely to be overcome. It is instead the set of divergencies in cultural and administrative patterns, and the presently low levels of economic interaction, which will slow cooperation in Southeast Asia. The small volume of intraregional trade militates against initially broad commercial contacts, but the similarity of economies increases the scope for exchanges of technical information and joint research related to economic development. It also enhances the opportunities for what

---

[17] Only in a genuinely enormous nation like India, and perhaps another like Brazil, is it likely to be feasible to consider the application of broadcast communications satellites as applicable to one nation alone—and even in the Indian case there will be "spill-over" effects in Ceylon, Pakistan, and Burma which may have to be taken into account.

some economists and senior ECAFE specialists call "harmonization of industrial development" among Southeast Asian nations.[18]

As long as ASA was restricted to only three nations, however, it was unlikely that significant progress could be achieved along such grandiose lines. The absence of Indonesia in particular made it difficult to accord ASA genuine potential. Indeed, it was partly in the hope of ultimately attracting the neutral Southeast Asian states, especially Indonesia, that the three ASA members regularly avoided mention of the fundamental political reasons that had led them to attempt regional cooperation. For it should be understood, before this discussion of ASA is completed, that its ostensibly nonpolitical label was never altogether accurate.

One overriding political goal—the restriction of communist appeals by improving Southeast Asian living standards—had been involved from the outset. This is apparent not only from the private memoranda circulated (in 1959) before ASA's birth, but also from a public statement made by Abdul Rahman at the April, 1963, Foreign Ministers' Meeting:

> We are determined to make a success of this organization because we believe sincerely that the best possible way of preventing the Communists from trying to destroy the lives and souls of our nations is by improving the lot of our peoples. Believing this thoroughly we must make ASA an inspiration and an example of sustained effort in growth and development. We must not allow anything to come in our way or to distract us from our common purposes.[19]

There are three implicit premises underlying this statement: (1) Containment of communism in Asia involves primarily combatting internal subversion (and in this it differs tactically from containment in Europe where strategic balance plays the principal role). (2) Internal subversion is facilitated by economic discontent and low standards of living. (3) Regional cooperation is one of the instruments that can be used to improve standards of living.

Communists in Asia have emphasized internal subversion as their primary vehicle for expanding influence, and the ASA countries—

[18] For a fascinating discussion of trade harmonization prospects, see Hikoji Katano, "Direction of Intra-Regional Trade Harmonization in the ECAFE Region," *Economic Bulletin for Asia and the Far East*, XVIII, No. 2 (September, 1967), 1–43. Based on intensive mathematical analysis, Katano concludes that "almost all the countries under review are in a position to gain more from trade by promoting intra-regional trade, as compared with trade with the rest of the world (p. 14)."

[19] Federation of Malaya, *ASA, Report of the Second Meeting of Foreign Ministers* (Kuala Lumpur, 1963), p. 30.

because they cannot by themselves hope to effect the overall strategic balance—probably judged correctly that their best contribution to security would lie in reducing the environment for subversive appeals. When they determined (with Indonesia and Singapore) to establish ASEAN in 1967, they continued to stress the connection between co-operation and improved developmental prospects—although it could not yet be said that ASA had brought them any tangible economic gains.

In political terms, however, it is reasonable to conclude that ASA brought some benefits. Among the most significant of these is the increased level of communications among its members. Without question, for example, the role that Thailand played in the Philippines-Malaysian dispute was enchanced by their common ASA membership. Both Filipino and Malaysian leaders frequently stressed their stake in the continuation of ASA, and developments in that difficult period do suggest that an informal peacekeeping role can be one of the most useful by-products of an ostensibly economic grouping. But ASA's most significant political contribution lies simply in its survival, for that reflects the remarkably strong appeal of the regional concept to indigenous Southeast Asian elites. Indonesia's participation in ASEAN is one of the best evidences of that appeal, and by virtue of Indonesia's membership it is now possible to say, for the first time, that the regional concept may acquire genuine political significance. For Indonesia's participation helps remove two of the major drawbacks of Asian regionalism (and of ASA) through 1967: too small a membership and a too clearly "Western-oriented" membership. Aside from adding the world's fifth largest state to the group, Indonesia's participation can help make it more feasible for neutral states like Burma and Cambodia ultimately to consider participation in the ASEAN format.

From Indonesia's standpoint, the goal of Southeast Asian regional cooperation has much to commend it. The concept provides a legitimate format within which to exercise what some Indonesians regard as a proper leadership role in the region, and participation in ASEAN has met with wide endorsement in both military and civilian circles. Foreign Minister Malik takes a strong personal interest in ASEAN,[20] and General Panggabean surprised many observers with a proposal

[20] Adam Malik, "Promise in Indonesia," *Foreign Affairs*, 46, No. 2 (January, 1968), 301–2. As we will show later, Dr. Malik devoted considerable portions of his own efforts to the creation of ASEAN, and in two conversations with this author he has left no doubt as to the depth of his feeling that regional cooperation is a major objective for him, and not a mere tactic for Indonesia, as was the case during the Sukarno period.

(expressed late in 1966) for Southeast Asian defense cooperation. Military endorsement for the goal of cooperation is especially important, for it must be assumed that the Army will remain the dominant political group in Indonesia, at least through the early 1970's.[21]

C. ASEAN: The Product of MAPHILINDO and ASA Combined

Indonesia's willingness to participate in new efforts in Southeast Asian regionalism, we have suggested already, represents a most important change in the Asian political environment. The Association of Southeast Asian Nations (ASEAN) is the reflection of this change, and it is not too much to say that the new group was created *for* Indonesia, since leaders in Djakarta have preferred to view ASA as a "Western-inspired" organization with which they could not associate. That was not true, but the Indonesian belief made it clear, nevertheless, that Indonesian participation in regional cooperation would depend on the creation of an entirely new organization. That new organization, moreover, would have to incorporate at least some of the appearances of the only other Southeast Asian regional group with which Indonesia was affiliated—the loose institution known as MAPHILINDO.

MAPHILINDO was created in 1963, and although it was only a loose consultative body of the three "Malay" nations (MAlaya, PHILippines, and INDOnesia),[22] it caught the attention of outsiders rather more than ASA ever did. The explanation lies in the two relatively useful

[21] General Suharto, who, since the fall of Sukarno, had been "acting President" of Indonesia, was given the formal title of President in March, 1968, as well as formal authority to lead the nation for a five-year term (*Washington Post,* March 28, 1968).

[22] The origins of MAPHILINDO cannot be discussed in detail here. I have, however, examined the subject in an earlier work (see *The Dimensions of Conflict in Southeast Asia*, pp. 22–23, 70–71, and 188–89).

It is sufficient here to point out that unlike ASA, MAPHILINDO was a dead letter almost from the beginning. It was primarily the result of Sukarno's desire to elicit the Philippines' cooperation in his anti-Malaysia campaign, and the parallel interest of Philippines President Macapagal in preventing the formation of Malaysia. Macapagal hoped to forestall the incorporation of North Borneo into Malaysia, and proposed the notion of a Philippines-Malayan "confederation." He asked that the University of the Philippines prepare a study detailing the concept, and parts of that study were later adopted by President Macapagal. Much of it now appears in such documents as the Manila Declaration and the other instruments that created MAPHILINDO.

by-products of MAPHILINDO. First, Indonesia's participation did represent a change in policy, for until 1963 its leaders had carefully avoided anything that smacked of regional cooperation in Southeast Asia. The utility of this by-product became apparent during 1966–67, the period when President Sukarno was being gradually toppled. During that uncertain time, it was possible for his successors to speak about *their* plans for regional cooperation without fear of breaking entirely new ground.

The second useful by-product of the MAPHILINDO experience—and this may help explain why MAPHILINDO gained more attention than ASA—lies simply in the fact of Indonesia's participation. The dramatic summit talks of June, 1963, which gave birth to MAPHILINDO, reminded observers once again of Djakarta's importance in the region. More specifically, MAPHILINDO helped bring home the point that without Indonesian participation, any effort at regional cooperation in Southeast Asia—such as ASA—would at best be a limited achievement.

That thought led me to argue in 1965 that because of Indonesia's potentially destabilizing role in the region, the approaches symbolized by both ASA and MAPHILINDO should be combined.[23] And in fact, ASEAN seems to represent a melding of ASA and MAPHILINDO. The text of the ASEAN Declaration[24] shows that it will have a structure much like that of ASA, whereas its purposes—even including its affirmation "that all foreign bases are temporary"—reflect the imprint that Sukarno and Subandrio gave to the Manila Declaration and MAPHILINDO four years earlier. Because this melding makes ASEAN the most promising Southeast Asian development in years, events that led directly to its creation should be explained.

The idea for a new Southeast Asian group can be traced primarily to the new Indonesian government—in particular to Foreign Minister Adam Malik. Malik was in the forefront of those who were urging

[23] In a concluding chapter called "Prospects for Stability in Southeast Asia," I wrote that "stability in the region probably would be enhanced if Indonesia became regularly associated with a continuing regional organization" (see *ibid.*, especially pp. 191–92). Such a melding, it seemed likely, might help "to internalize the role of Indonesia within the system of Southeast Asia's international politics." The ASA experience represented the pragmatism essential for successful cooperation, but MAPHILINDO also had advantages. The most important of these obviously was Indonesian participation itself. Consequently, I proposed the formation of a new Southeast Asian group, named so as to reflect both ASA's and Indonesia's imprint. The proposed new grouping was dubbed "ASANEFOS" to take into account Sukarno's acronym for his concept of the "New Emerging Forces" (NEFOS).

[24] The copy of the *Declaration* Text used here was provided by the U.S. Embassy, Bangkok.

President Sukarno's removal from power: he was anxious to bring a quick end to President Sukarno's "confrontation" with Malaysia, and as we suggested, he appears to have a strong personal interest in the concept of Asian regional cooperation.

The opportunity to express these sentiments arose late in 1965 and continued through the early months of 1966 as Indonesian officials, anxious to end *Konfrontasi,* inaugurated a series of informal "peace feelers" with the Malaysians.[25] "Regional cooperation" clearly was one of the agenda items when formal talks took place under Thanat Khoman's auspices,[26] for Malik announced in June, 1966, that he had proposed a new regional group and that the three ASA countries had already decided to join.[27] Although officials probably were considering a new "Southeast Asian Association for Regional Cooperation" (privately termed SEAARC), Malik's estimate was premature, for little more seems to have been achieved until the end of 1966.

The reasons for the delay centered on Indonesia and the question of precisely in what way Djakarta would associate itself with states which were already members of ASA.[28] Essentially the problem was whether Indonesian leaders, who tend to assume that their nation is the natural leader of the region, would be willing to "ask" for membership in a new regional group. Such a request might have the appearance of humbling Indonesia before Malaysians and Filipinos, and until Sukarno was removed it was especially important to avoid any charge that Indonesia was aligning itself with Western-associated nations.[29]

[25] Malik, it should be pointed out, is a relative of *the senior Malaysian official responsible for foreign affairs,* Tan Sri Ghazalie Bin Schafie. Ghazalie has described Malik to me as his "cousin," but I am not certain how close the family tie is. The two are, however, on a friendly basis; Ghazalie feels quite at home in Malik's house.

[26] For reports on these negotiations and discussions, see articles in the *Washington Post,* May 19, 1966, and May 31, 1966, as well as *The New York Times,* June 7, 1966.

[27] *The New York Times,* June 3, 1966.

[28] In an interview in October, Thanat Khoman suggested that although there were difficulties, he expected to find a format for Indonesian participation in a "new Asian group" (conversation with the author, New York, October, 1966).

[29] In March, 1966, while still in power, Sukarno attempted to persuade the Filipino government not to reestablish its diplomatic relations with Malaysia (*Washington Post,* March 8, 1966). By May, when his power was in rapid decline, Sukarno expressed his discontent with the talks then taking place with Malaysian leaders in Bangkok. It was apparently at this time that the Indonesian President was requested to make no more speeches on foreign policy subjects (*Washington Post,* May 31, 1966).

In addition, as late as August, 1966, other leading Indonesians complained about the ending of the confrontation, and they were not all closely aligned with

By late summer of 1966 a way was found out of this dilemma, perhaps as a result of talks between Malik and Thanat Khoman. When Thanat arrived in Djakarta late in August, he said that part of his visit was in connection with an Asian search for a Vietnam solution, but that regional cooperation, too, was very much on the agenda.[30] When he was asked whether that meant SEATO, he said emphatically, "I did not come here to discuss SEATO." Indeed, only several days before Thanat's visit, the Foreign Minister of the Philippines (Narciso Ramos) had also visited Foreign Minister Malik in Djakarta. Their joint statement reaffirmed "the importance and urgency of meaningful regional cooperation among the countries of Southeast Asia, especially in the economic, social, technical, and cultural field." [31] Given this background and Thanat's reputation for extraordinary negotiating ability, as well as his strong personal interest in Southeast Asian regionalism, it seems quite certain that much of his discussion with Adam Malik was oriented to regionalism. The question was, who would act, and when?

The approach that the two leaders apparently agreed upon called for Malik to make his views known to Thanat, who would then circulate a Thai invitation to the ASA members. This would spare Indonesia from having to "ask" for ASA membership. The invitation would probably benefit also from Thanat's prestige in both Malaysia and the Philippines.

1.   The SEAARC Proposal

In late 1966 (probably in December) a "Draft Joint Declaration" was sent from Bangkok to Manila, Djakarta, and Kuala Lumpur.[32] The gist of the document can be summed up by saying that it represented a careful and conscious melding of the purposes of ASA with much of the style and flavor of MAPHILINDO.[33] The preamble, in

President Sukarno. For example, Mohamed Dahlan, Chairman of the Central Committee of the Moslem Scholars (a party which claims about 8 million members), demanded a return to the agreement signed in Manila in 1963. This called for elections in Sabah and Sarawak, and it implied that Indonesia should not establish peaceful relations with Malaysia until Sukarno's demands of three years before were satisfied.

[30] *The New York Times,* August 30, 1966.

[31] *The New York Times,* August 24, 1966.

[32] At this stage Singapore, as a non-ASA member, was probably not contacted formally.

[33] The "Draft Declaration" was shown to the author by an official of one of the Foreign Ministries during a Southeast Asian visit in January, 1967.

particular, is distinctly reminiscent of the phrases incorporated more than three years earlier in the Manila Declaration, and those sentiments—in contrast to the organizational format of MAPHILINDO—owed much of their inspiration to former Indonesian Foreign Minister Subandrio. For example, when Subandrio met with the Malayan and Philippine Foreign Ministers in June, 1963, they issued a *Report*, which declared:

> The ministers were of one mind that the three countries share a primary responsibility for the maintenance of the stability and security of the area from subversion in any form or manifestation . . . .[34]

Only weeks later, Sukarno himself went to Manila, and because he wanted a specific reference to foreign bases, even stronger phrases were incorporated. Thus, to mollify Sukarno, Philippines and Malaysian leaders agreed in 1963 to words on foreign bases unlike anything their governments had ever said before.

It is very instructive to see today how those Indonesian-inspired sentiments have endured, for they are almost identical to the words Thanat Khoman of Thailand used in his 1966 and 1967 drafts, which led to ASEAN. The 1963 Declaration read in part:

> The three heads of government further agreed that foreign bases—temporary in nature—should not be allowed to be used directly or indirectly to subvert the national independence of any of the three countries. In accordance with the principle enunciated in the Bandung Declaration, the three countries will abstain from the use of arrangements of collective defense to serve the particular interests of any of the big powers.[35]

In comparison, Thanat Khoman began his new "Draft Declaration" with these words:

> The Ministers of Foreign Affairs in Indonesia . . . [and] Malaysia, the Secretary of Foreign Affairs of the Philippines . . . and the Minister of Foreign Affairs . . . [of] Thailand . . . .
>
> Believing that the countries of Southeast Asia share a primary responsibility for ensuring the stability and maintaining the security of the area . . .
>
> Being in agreement that foreign bases are temporary in nature

---

[34] This also appears as Paragraph 4 in the *Joint Communiqué* of the Foreign Ministers' Conference, Manila, June 7–11, 1963, and is published in *Malaya/Philippine Relations* (Kuala Lumpur, 1963), Appendix VII, p. 26. See also Gordon, *op. cit.*, p. 102.

[35] *Malaya/Philippine Relations*, Appendix VIII, in Gordon, *op. cit.*, pp. 100–104.

and should not be allowed to be used directly or indirectly to subvert
the national independence of Asian countries, and that arrangements
of collective defense should not be used to serve the particular interest
of any of the big powers . . . .[36]

If a side-by-side comparison is made of the texts of MAPHILINDO,
of SEAARC, and finally of ASEAN, part of the origins of the new group
becomes clear.[37]

Manila Accord July 31, 1963	SEAARC Draft December, 1966- January, 1967	ASEAN Declaration August 8, 1967
The Ministers were of one mind that the three countries share a primary responsibility for the maintenance of the stability and security of the area from subversion in any form or manifestation	Believing that the countries of Southeast Asia share a primary responsibility for ensuring the stability and maintaining the security of the area	Considering that the countries of Southeast Asia share a primary responsibility for strengthening the economic and social stability of the region and ensuring their peaceful and progressive national development, and that they are determined to ensure their stability and security from external interference in any form or manifestation in order to preserve their national identities . . .
Manila Declaration August 5, 1963	Being in agreement that foreign bases are temporary in nature and should not be used to serve the particular interest of any of the big powers	
The three heads of government further agreed that foreign bases— temporary in nature— should not be allowed to be used directly or indirectly to subvert the national independence of any of the three countries.		Affirming that all foreign bases are temporary and remain only with the expressed concurrence of the countries concerned and are not intended to be used directly or indirectly to subvert the national independence and freedom of states in the area . . . .

Indeed these evident similarities helped delay the establishment of
ASEAN until August, 1967, because neither the Philippines nor the
Malaysian government was initially enthusiastic over Thanat's effort
to mollify Indonesia again. The Philippines misgivings probably de-

[36] From the draft, "Joint Declaration, Southeast Asian Declaration for Regional
Cooperation," probably mid-December, 1966. It is also interesting to note that
Indonesia is listed first in the "Introduction" to the Draft Declaration.
[37] The texts are derived from previously-cited sources.

rived in part from President Marcos' tentative thought about proposing his own format for regional cooperation, and also from his uncertainty about the prospects for Sukarno's return to power in Indonesia.[38] Marcos' doubts about the new proposal cannot be readily explained otherwise, for it has to be said that the SEAARC proposal did not borrow much more than the preamble from MAPHILINDO. The rest of it, especially the structure and purposes of the proposed group, were clearly patterned after ASA.

Yet these same anxieties existed in Malaysia, reinforced by the Prime Minister's still-negative view of Indonesia, grown out of the confrontation. Thus when Thanat Khoman wrote to Tunku Abdul Rahman late in December, the Premier began his reply with the phrase, "I have certain grave misgivings . . . ." He went on to caution about the dangers of associating too closely with Indonesia: "As long as Sukarno is there . . . it would be dangerous for us to embark on such an enterprise." But his letter made it clear that more was involved in his negative response than merely doubt about Sukarno's role and his potential return to power (still an anxiety in early 1967). For the Tunku took pains to reaffirm in this letter his enthusiasm and interest in ASA; he wrote to Thanat, "I would not like to see us sacrifice ASA . . . to create a wider regional association, which I am convinced in the present circumstances has little chance of success." He added, finally, that although it was a noble goal to try somehow to help Indonesia (and the stability of the region, too) by incorporating Djakarta into a new regional group, this could be a mixed blessing. The Tunku apparently felt that Indonesia's own interests and behavior

---

[38] Early in 1966—shortly after President Marcos took office in Manila—he asked for and received from Foreign Secretary Ramos a memorandum outlining a Philippines posture toward regionalism. Ramos wrote that "if it is intended to divorce from the past and from existing rivalries in Southeast Asian power politics, there seems to be a need for a fresh approach to Asian problems under the new administration." After noting that Manila was well-suited to take a lead in new approaches, partly because the Asian Development Bank had just been established there, Ramos wrote that: "The fact remains, however, that with the prospective resumption of normal relations between the Philippines and Malaysia, the reactivation of the ASA will become a pressing issue. While the Philippines is committed to all that the ASA stands for, it would not be to its national interest to pronounce a sentence of doom for MAPHILINDO, which Indonesia might construe as a rebuff against her.

"Hence, it seems rather advisable if in favoring its reactivation, ASA *should be spelled out as a transitory arrangement, a stepping stone, toward the formation of the Organization of Asian states,* with a call for wider collective action to achieve Asian progress" ("Memorandum from Secretary of Foreign Affairs, Narciso Ramos, to President Ferdinand Marcos, January 6, 1966, Subject: Proposed Organization of Asian States" [typescript; emphasis added]).

patterns might so diverge from those of the three ASA nations that the risks involved in a new regional group might outweigh any potential benefits. Among other things, he reminded Thanat, "Indonesia's behavior has been to leave any organization when and as it suits her." [39]

Over the next six months these misgivings were softened, *largely because Thailand and Indonesia were willing to give a remarkable amount of time and energy to the task of creating a new multination association for regional cooperation.* Indonesian Foreign Minister Adam Malik and his senior deputy (Anwar Seni) made a series of trips throughout the region in April and May with two purposes in mind. The first was to inform the neutral states of Burma and Cambodia of Indonesia's plans for a new regional group. Djakarta hoped either to gain their support or at least persuade them not to publicly condemn the effort. The second purpose was to undertake with Thai, Malaysian, and Filipino leaders the specific negotiations necessary to launch the regional group.[40]

Thanat and Malik divided their responsibilities, and both tasks were reasonably well accomplished. Malik, although unable to gain Burman or Cambodian participation (unlikely anyway at that early stage), was pleased to have their assurances of friendly interest in the proposal.[41] And Thanat, almost up to the eve of ASEAN's creation in August, was required to bend all his efforts to persuade the Malaysian premier to accept Indonesia's new foreign policy course. Many others in the Malaysian government, however, were already prepared—even eager—to resume intimate ties with Indonesia: for there is apparent in the younger generation of Malaysia's elite and bureaucracy a strong identification with Indonesia. One of the most promising aspects of Southeast Asian cooperation in the future is precisely the strong likelihood that Indonesian-Malaysian relations will be quite close.[42]

[39] From draft letter of January 3, 1967 (typescript).
[40] Reports of Malik's travels appeared in *Antara* (Indonesia's press agency) dispatches of April 12, 16, and 21, 1967. In Bangkok, Malik announced that preparations for the new group "are almost complete," and added that it would cover technical, economic, and cultural fields and "be more perfect than MAPHILINDO."
[41] Accounts of Malik's talks in Rangoon and Phnom Penh, as well as letters between General Suharto and Prince Sihanouk, appear in *Antara* dispatches of May 16, 25, and 31, 1967. Prince Sihanouk, in a reference to the divisions resulting from the Vietnam war, said, "Cambodia will fully cooperate with Indonesia to promote the cooperation in question after all nations in Southeast Asia have again received their free and complete independence . . . ."
[42] Many Malaysians have family ties in Indonesia, and some of these ties are politically significant. The Permanent Secretary of the Malaysian Foreign Ministry

In 1967, however, the Tunku's understandable pride in having initiated the steps that led to ASA also led him to resist its inevitable disappearance once ASEAN was formed.

Thanat Khoman, on the other hand, although equally responsible for ASA's creation, understood, even in 1959, that ASA was not to be seen as an end in itself. To Thanat, regional cooperation is only an instrument for far more basic political purposes. Thus in 1967, and in contrast to the Tunku, Thanat was quite willing to bury ASA in favor of a wider grouping. He recognizes and stresses that tight bipolarity in Asia is not only dangerous, but especially uncomfortable to Thailand, and for that reason he hopes for a return to multipolarity as the structure of East Asian international affairs. Multipolarity in turn requires a more cohesive Southeast Asia, and it is with that goal also in mind that Thanat has so enthusiastically worked for regional cooperation.

2. ASEAN and the Concept of Subsystem in Southeast Asia: Implications for American Policy

The creation of ASEAN must be seen as something of a triumph for aspirations that the Thai Foreign Minister has entertained for several years. But it is potentially much more than that, for ASEAN is the first *general, indigenous,* and politically *neutral* effort in Southeast Asian regional cooperation.

Its characteristic as a potentially *general,* or multipurpose organization means that ASEAN must be distinguished from regional groups devoted to a specific functional purpose, such as the Mekong Development Committee and the Southeast Asian Ministerial Conferences on Education (SEAMES) and Transport. Such bodies have the support of the particular ministries involved, and can probably achieve certain specific cooperative tasks of importance—but there is little evidence that they attract wide and high-level participation and interest in each government. In essence, and in contrast to the sort of political support that led to ASA and ASEAN, such single-purpose ventures are narrowly based.

(as we noted earlier) is a cousin of Indonesian Foreign Minister Adam Malik and of other leading Indonesians. Tan Sri Ghazalie bin Schafie, although extremely critical of Indonesian policies under Sukarno, has been among the most active in pressing for a long-term stable relationship with Djakarta—sometimes pressing harder than the Tunku might have preferred. But aside from Ghazalie, it is clear that the dominant strain in Malaysian foreign policy thinking about the region, in both the bureaucracy and Malay political circles, strongly favors quite warm relations with Indonesia.

The *indigenous* nature of ASEAN must also be stressed, for this is the single most important characteristic missing from all other existing efforts at regional cooperation in Southeast Asia. Even the newly created Ministerial Conferences on Transport and Education just mentioned, to say nothing of the obvious cases of SEATO and the Colombo Plan, have been fundamentally based on the support, and frequently the initiative, of states outside Southeast Asia. The *ad hoc* groups created by these Ministerial Conferences commonly draw at least half their fiscal support from the U.S., and it is altogether un-likely that they could exist were it not for the constant encouragement of the U.S. This is not to condemn such efforts—but the judgment that ASA and ASEAN reflect high-priority local interests stems from the consideration that those two organizations, in contrast to all others, are entirely the work of the Southeast Asian governments themselves.

Finally, much of the potential significance of ASEAN derives from Indonesia's participation, which helps remove the "Western" stigma that afflicted ASA. ASEAN represents a large departure in the nature of Indonesia's foreign policy, and for the first time it is possible to expect that its considerable foreign policy energies can be channeled within the region. For its own benefit, moreover, participation in ASEAN opens the possibility for Indonesian collaboration with states that have had successful developmental experience. Thailand and Malaysia stand out in this regard, and the August, 1967 statement of ASEAN's "aims and purposes" suggests that—like ASA—the group will emphasize quite pragmatic goals. Of ASEAN's seven declared "pur-poses," most aim for cooperation in fields directly related to develop-mental needs, as this excerpt will show:

> To promote active collaboration and mutual assistance on matters of common interest in the economic, social, cultural, technical, scien-tific and administrative fields;
>
> To provide assistance to each other in the form of training and re-search facilities in the education, professional, technical and administra-tive spheres;
>
> To collaborate more effectively for the greater utilization of their agriculture and industries, the expansion of their trade, including the study of the problems of international commodity trade, the improve-ment of their transportation and communications facilities in the raising of the living standards of their people.[43]

Within a few months after that Declaration was announced, the

[43] This is from the text of the ASEAN Declaration, August 8, 1967.

five governments agreed to designate Indonesia as host of the "ASEAN Standing Committee" during its first year, and soon afterwards groups of experts began meetings in Djakarta. By February of 1968 this Committee had identified a series of projects on which initial work was to proceed, and the list clearly suggests the purposes which the five nations envisage for the new organization.[44]

First efforts, for example, will concentrate on food production and supply, in which ASEAN is expected to facilitate data exchanges and loans of specialists; trade expansion measures, in which it will be the function of ASEAN to organize combined ASEAN trade missions outside the region; meetings of business organizations in order to achieve trade liberalization measures; and a variety of other personnel and data exchanges in such fields as transport and telecommunications, publishing, and so on. Moreover, a number of steps were taken to exchange defense information, and early in 1968 several leaders offered suggestions for some form of defense and security cooperation.[45]

These steps represent a considerable change in the Asian political environment, and it is important to understand the political forces responsible for elevating the previously vague concept of "Asian regionalism" to its present level of interest. In many cases the explanation is the simple recognition that the paramount task for leaders in Southeast Asia—economic development—can probably be aided greatly by collaboration with neighbors. Another major task these leaders increasingly face, however, is the problem of providing for improved defense and security. For leaders coming to grips with this problem for the first time, cooperation with neighboring states seems almost as logical as economic cooperation. It is no accident, for example, that Indonesian and Malaysian leaders have begun to take the lead in speculating openly about "regional defense cooperation."

In both the Indonesian and Malaysian cases it appears that these new patterns of thinking have been kindled by an important catalyst:

[44] From *Antara,* reporting the February 23, 1968 meeting of the ASEAN Standing Committee.

[45] Prospects for defense cooperation will be separately discussed in the next chapter: it will be sufficient here to point out that proposals for security cooperation appear to have originated with a speech of Indonesian General Panggabean, Chief of the Army Staff (see *Djakarta Times,* February 28, 1967). In March, 1968, General Suharto, the new Indonesian President, publicly endorsed the concept, and added specifically that ASEAN could provide the "basis for defence understandings" (see *Antara,* March 7, 1968). The same reports carried the endorsement of Tun Abdul Razak, the Malaysian Deputy Prime Minister. President Marcos of the Philippines, while visiting Indonesia, similarly called for ASEAN members to "join in a defense arrangement . . . on a basis consistent with the principles and purposes of ASEAN" (*Washington Post,* January 14, 1968).

the disappearance of certain fictions that characterized the immediate postindependence and postwar era. In the Malaysian instance the fiction was that Britain, because it had so gradually phased out its colonial role, somehow would continue to look after the security of Malaya and Singapore. But leaders in Kuala Lumpur and Singapore must now face the fact that Britain simply does not have the will or capacity to play that role. In the case of Indonesia the fiction was the belief that a foreign policy consisted of repeated calls for "Afro-Asian solidarity" against the imperialist West. But the recognition has grown in Djakarta that the "West" is less a source of threat than a source of greatly needed assistance. To the extent that a threat exists, it is now more clearly perceived in Indonesia to emanate from Peking and its local supporters; the past exhortations for solidarity among the "new emerging forces" are no longer seen as responsible approaches to the problem.

Thus, for different reasons, both Indonesia and Malaysia are forced to the recognition that they must take steps to help ensure their security. Like Singapore and Thailand they are unwilling to rely permanently on the United States for security, and this has led all four to search for ways in which regional cooperation might contribute to defense needs. With somewhat less urgency, Philippines governments have also begun to seek closer ties in Southeast Asia. Presidents Garcia and Macapagal, in particular, helped alter Manila's traditional relationship with the United States and tried to establish a new Asian "identity." And early in 1968 President Marcos himself suggested while visiting Indonesia that "an interim security arrangement be made within the framework of ASEAN." [46]

These foreign policy trends will be singled out in the next few pages, because they point to new and *systematic patterns* of relationships among several Southeast Asian nations. The system created as a result may have very great significance for politics in the entire Asian region. This is the case despite the fact that some of the new relationships derived initially, not from a desire to cooperate, but from conflicts, or from what appear to have been "special circumstances." Manila's new emphasis on Southeast Asia, for example, can mistakenly be explained away as a "special case" with little meaning for the essential thrust of Philippines foreign policy. Policy under Macapagal (his desire to upset Malaysia's plan to incorporate North Borneo) did, of course, lead to the unprecedented and close relationship between the Philippines and Sukarno's Indonesia. But although

[46] *Antara,* January 13, 1968.

that specific objection is valid, it is essentially beside the point. For Manila's foreign policy—like that of all but one country in ASEAN—has been undergoing striking change in the mid-1960's, and the trends already visible show no sign of being reversed.

The exception to that statement is Thailand, for whom the emphasis on Southeast Asia represents not a striking change but a logical product of the main principle of Thai foreign policy: that Thailand should never become too dependent on *any* great power. Even in the period when Thailand forged its closest military relationships with the United States, its Foreign Ministry gave equal attention to the ultimate goal of forming some kind of Southeast Asian regional group. It has always been predictable that, when circumstances allowed, Bangkok would seek to reduce the sole dependence implied in the American relationship.

Foreign Minister Thanat symbolizes this double approach. Most hawkish of all men on the Vietnam war, he has nevertheless taken the lead in fostering the concept of regionalism ever since he was approached by President Garcia and the Tunku with the 1959 proposal that later became ASA. Thanat has always emphasized pragmatic achievements as the product of regionalism, and as ASA developed between 1961–64, the group showed the Thai imprint more than any other. The soundest planning for regional economic cooperation has come from Bangkok, as many other articulate Thais, reflecting Thanat's example, have also endorsed the concept. It was, moreover, to keep the idea alive that Thanat has so often undertaken the role of diplomatic broker in Southeast Asia, as a few illustrations will suggest.

Thailand's role in mediating *Konfrontasi* (Sukarno's "confrontation" against Malaysia) was critical to its resolution, and the early and most difficult Indonesian-Malaysian contacts took place under Thanat's good offices in Bangkok. Earlier, in the Sabah dispute between the Philippines and Malaysia, his function was similar: he served as a vital communications link. The former Vice-President of the Philippines referred to Thanat during that period as "our ASA Ambassador." [47] Similarly, as our discussion of SEAARC and ASEAN showed, Thanat played the vital role of "introducing" Indonesia into the new efforts aimed at creating a new group. For example, when the Tunku had doubts about Indonesia, more likely than not it was the Thai Minister

[47] Author's interview with then Vice-President Pelaez, Manila, July, 1963. Five years later, in December, 1968, Thanat performed a similar function. He arranged for meetings at his home in Bangkok between Malaysian and Filipino leaders.

who acted to allay those doubts. This was also the pattern when President Marcos appeared to have some second thoughts regarding proposed SEAARC terminology dealing with foreign bases. Here, Thanat was able to point to his own membership in SEATO and the military installations at Sattahip as evidence that ASEAN (or SEAARC) would not compromise the continuing Thai and Philippine security reliance on the United States.

These considerations are not mentioned simply to praise the Foreign Minister of Thailand, although his record as a diplomat is certainly striking.[48] My purpose has been instead to underline a point: that a deeply etched network of political contact and communications was established during the 1960's in Southeast Asia, and every indication suggests that the resulting pattern is becoming more and not less intense. Events set in motion in 1963–64 (when Indonesia embarked on her conflict with Malaysia) help explain this, for the *Konfrontasi* had an immense effect on each of the five nations now in ASEAN. It was in many respects a catalyst for the international politics of Southeast Asia, for it helped, as we noted earlier, to bring each of the states there into far more "tight" contact and communications than ever before. ASA had just begun to do that for three of them, but not necessarily on matters of high political sensitivity. *Konfrontasi*, on the other hand, forced each of the region's top leaders to reflect—much more than he had been required to do before—about his role in the region's affairs.[49]

The explanation for the catalytic importance of the confrontation, which can now be seen more clearly in retrospect, probably derives from the severe tensions that the conflict generated. In each of the three nations primarily concerned, many doubted the wisdom of steps their governments had taken, and this led to more careful internal scrutiny of national foreign policies and purposes than was ever required before. Leaders like Macapagal ultimately backed away from their first policy directions, and there is evidence that Sukarno and Subandrio, too, were searching for ways out of the conflict just a few months after it began. Throughout the entire affair, each of the

---

[48] The degree of professionalism in Thailand's Foreign Ministry is equalled nowhere else in Southeast Asia and is surpassed in Asia only by the *Gaimusho*, Japan's Foreign Ministry. Thai leaders, unique in their region, reflect a deep and self-conscious foreign policy tradition, and those responsible for foreign policy feel a deep sense of pride in the skills represented in the last century by King Chulalongkorn, Prince Damrong, and Prince Devawongse—pride in the fact that under those leaders Thailand preserved her independence.

[49] See Richard Butwell, *op. cit.*

states seemed to be looking for means, at a minimum, to restore peaceful relations, and if possible to forge some kind of regional cohesion after the dispute. In this respect *Konfrontasi* was a severe learning experience, and it is quite clear that ASEAN—probably the first genuinely important step in Asian regional *cooperation*—is a direct by-product of the contacts and communications created by the Indonesian-Malaysian *conflict*.

In Malaysia, for example, the confrontation experience reinforced the views of those who already suspected that Malaysian foreign policy under the Tunku had paid too little attention to Indonesian sensitivities in the past; it is very unlikely that this oversight will be repeated. In the Philippines also a number of lessons were learned. One was that Manila, if its leaders hope to establish their Asian "identity," must do much to overcome the view that they are mere puppets of the United States. Another lesson—and this was brought home to President Marcos in the months just before ASEAN was formed—was that any lack of enthusiasm his government then felt about Southeast Asian regionalism was not shared in Bangkok and Djakarta. The negotiations that led to ASEAN in the spring of 1967 showed that in the event of consensus on the part of Indonesia and Thailand, very little foreign policy latitude remains for Singapore and Malaysia. As a result, Philippines leaders, to the extent that they are convinced they cannot count forever on the protective umbrella provided by the United States (in trade and security matters, for example), have been forced to conclude that increasingly close cooperation with Southeast Asian neighbors is the only feasible foreign policy posture for their country. As the *Manila Times* warned just before ASEAN was formed:

> Western, particularly American, presence in Asia is not going to be a permanent thing, and farsighted Asian leaders are looking forward to the day when Western presence is removed, in which case the Asians themselves should be prepared to fill the "vacuum" left by the withdrawal.[50]

Aside from the fact that this is increasingly the view held by leaders in the five ASEAN nations, an equally important consideration is that this conviction has led to patterns of understanding and contact that would have been almost unthinkable in the 1950's. ASEAN reflects this, and it reflects, too, the existence of a developing *system* of nations in Southeast Asia. Indonesia, Thailand, Malaysia, the Philippines and Singapore comprise that incipient system, and even though their

[50] Editorial, *Manila Times,* July 15, 1967.

trade and economic profiles do not yet heavily reflect this sense of "region" or "system" (after several generations and even centuries of European-inspired commerce and production this is hardly surprising), their political and cultural outlooks are oriented more and more within the region. The change that has taken place was summed up well in President Johnson's remark that "the nations of Asia are casting off the spent slogans of earlier narrow nationalism . . . one after another, they are grasping the realities of an interdependent Asia." [51]

The President's word "interdependent" precisely fits attitudes among leaders and elites in the five ASEAN states—so much so that if a very large political change came to any of them, it would be reacted to far more intensely today than even five years ago. Putting this another way, it is reasonable to expect that a major political change, say in Burma or Cambodia, would be felt less intimately in the ASEAN capitals than would the same event if it came to one of the ASEAN states. Burma, Laos, and Cambodia, in other words, are less intimately a part of the Southeast Asian subsystem that has been developing in recent years. As ASEAN continues, and hence reinforces and regularizes the patterns that already have been created, this system effect of interdependence will be intensified. One outcome can already be anticipated and has major implications for American foreign policy in Southeast Asia: it relates intimately to the concept of *regional dominance* introduced earlier.

Consider as an illustration the possibility that Burma or Cambodia, through a change in government leadership, might so alter its political orientation that it could be concluded that effective influence over the nation's affairs resided with China. To the extent that Burma or Cambodia had not become a part of the increasingly tight system of relationships likely to result from ASEAN, such an outcome can be projected to have significantly less meaning for the ASEAN states than it would were Malaysia or Philippines the affected state. This is not to say that Thai leaders, for example, would not experience increased anxiety if Burma or Cambodia became incorporated within a Chinese sphere of influence. It is to say that the shock effects of the "loss" of Burma or Cambodia would be less intimately perceived in the ASEAN group, because the "lost" state was not a participant in the existing patterns of communications and political relationships. In effect the "loss" of Burma or Cambodia would be felt through an insulating layer—an insulation, however, which would *not* be present

[51] From the October, 1966, speech in Honolulu.

to dull the perceptions of ASEAN members in connection with a system-participant like Malaysia.

If such a system were to exist, with the attendant in-group perception consequences that I have suggested, one meaning for American foreign policy seems clear. It suggests that a Burma or Cambodia "lost" to China's influence would very likely have far fewer ramifications for the outcome of *Southeast Asia as a whole* than would be true were any of the ASEAN states "lost" or similarly threatened. The further and systematic development of ASEAN during the next decade suggests that the *effective region* of Southeast Asia will have a meaning equivalent to those states participating in a regular pattern of relationships. The present ASEAN group even now represents the overwhelming bulk of population, land mass, and resources that comprise the geographic Southeast Asia region. If the ASEAN group comes also to represent an interconnected and interdependent regional subsystem, such that Southeast Asian events outside it have few implications for the nature and shape of the subsystem as a whole, it will be appropriate for the United States to restrict its security concerns with "Southeast Asia" to the five nations and 200 million people in ASEAN. Put bluntly, if leaders in the five ASEAN states were themselves to conclude that the "loss" of Burma and/or Cambodia to Chinese influence did not portend a likely or necessary outcome for them, this would in effect suggest that the "loss" of Burma and/or Cambodia was essentially irrelevant to the structure of East Asian politics as a whole.

The implication for the United States, as we will suggest in a later chapter, is that on the basis of regional relationships the United States can begin to discriminate among the nations in Southeast Asia. For the concept of regional dominance with which the United States is concerned in East Asia does not require that Americans be concerned with outcomes in each and every one of the nations in that geographical region. It implies that the United States must be concerned with likely outcomes for the region as a whole, and if developing patterns of regional cohesion lead to a condition whereby some Southeast Asian states are essentially not a "part" of the region, the relevance of those states to the national security interests of the United States can accordingly be reduced very drastically.

3. *Likely Trends in ASEAN*

But even at the present time, when the existence of a Southeast Asian regional subsystem is just beginning to take shape, Southeast

Asian trends toward cooperation represent a positive development for
the United States. For Southeast Asia, where the interest in regional
cooperation is strongest, is the weakest of East Asia's parts, its nations
are the most tempting to subversive efforts supported by China, and
they are the most susceptible to a variety of security threats. In a word,
and in strong contrast to both India and Japan, the Southeast Asian
nations are precisely the states that can benefit most from cooperative
efforts with their neighbors.

The main uses of regional cooperation for these nations will probably
be found in two fields, both ultimately related to stability and security in East Asia. It is likely that the first uses of collaboration will relate to economic development, and it is important to stress again that
a large number of Asian and Western specialists strongly believe that
regional economic cooperation can bring marked advantages to the
development programs of relatively small states. States in Southeast
Asia, with strong outside support, are already operating on this assumption.[52]

Based on these trends toward economic cooperation related to development needs, it is prudent to expect that a somewhat more cohesive
Southeast Asia is a likely outcome before the 1980's. To deny this is to
deny the meaning of important steps taken since 1965, most notably
the establishment of the Asian Development Bank (with very strong
Japanese and American financial support); the creation of ASEAN; and
(despite some irritants, as in the Sabah claim), the marked reduction
in intraregional political tensions. These steps reflect and represent the
major political forces in Southeast Asian international affairs, and
there are few indications that these forces will decline significantly
during the next decade.

Consequently, although it is impossible to predict precisely the outlines of economic cooperation, it is reasonable to expect that by 1970–71
major planning steps will be well underway to coordinate specific de-

---

[52] A striking illustration came recently when the leadership of the Thai government visited the United States. Accompanying the Prime Minister was not only
Foreign Minister Thanat Khoman, but Pote Sarasin, now Minister of Development, and a potential premier in the future. In a speech to business executives,
in which foreign policy was *not* the topic of the day, Pote Sarasin concluded his
remarks with an emphatic endorsement of Thailand's emphasis on Southeast
Asian regionalism: "With regard to regional economic and political cooperation,
we are convinced that herein lies the future of Southeast Asia. Thailand has already taken the lead in promoting regional groupings such as ASEAN . . . we are
exploring the possibilities of a product by product approach to regional economic
cooperation" (*Press Release* No. 37, Permanent Mission of Thailand to the U.N.,
May 7, 1968; emphasis added).

velopmental efforts in Southeast Asia.[53] It is likely that concrete measures for "harmonization" of industrial efforts, especially in certain light-industrial fields, will be undertaken early. Similarly, early in the 1970's measures can be expected to establish joint research centers, especially in fields related to the agricultural and industrial productivity of the region. Only in the late 1970's is it likely that intraregional trade patterns will be perceptively affected by these and related steps. Nevertheless, it is possible to project that increased intraregional trade, especially in consumer goods and products of light and medium industry, will result from industrial programs even now underway, and industrial harmonization and improved transport will accelerate this tendency.

By the early and mid-1980's, therefore, it is probable that Southeast Asia will show considerably greater economic interaction than is presently the case. The necessary first steps, for example in outlining the preferred and feasible forms of economic cooperation, have been started in the 1960's. These have been the result of remarkable political support for the concept of cooperation, even in a period when there has been little or no real achievement to show. If achievements in economic cooperation are reflected in accelerated rates of economic growth—and these are its present justification—then it is reasonable to expect a continuation, and probably an enhancement, of political support for regionalism. Simultaneously, an improvement in economic conditions, although often a source of some dislocations and instabilities, should help reduce the appeals on which insurgents and subversives have relied since the 1950's. This was the basic assumption which led Tunku Abdul Rahman and President Garcia to propose ASA in 1959.

Yet even in the face of progress, it has to be assumed that Southeast Asia will remain a relatively fertile field for subversive efforts through the 1970's. Consequently, and although combating subversion is already a high-priority concern of several Southeast Asian nations, any visible benefits from patterns of economic interaction and political consultation may bring an important side-effect: intensified interest in regional defense measures. As I suggested earlier, interest in defense cooperation

[53] As an illustration, a number of transport and telecommunications projects were considered at the meetings of the Ministerial Conference on Transport in Kuala Lumpur in September, 1967, and the U.S. alone has offered up to $5 million for feasibility studies in 1968–69 having to do with roads, railways, harbors, and so on. Major additional funds will be sought from the Asian Development Bank, which has already made clear its strong support for projects in this sector.

is already apparent, although only at the earliest stages of discussion. Compared to cooperative measures in trade and development, which could take concrete shape in the mid-1970's (because they have already been talked about for a decade), regional defense measures ought not be expected in the same time frame. Nevertheless, the lines along which Southeast Asian defense collaboration could proceed are discernible even now; they derive from the forces—discussed up to now in this book—that give political reality to the concept of regionalism in East Asia. Against that background, and having already suggested the relevance of Asian regionalism to the U.S. interest in a multipolar Asia, we can now deal more specifically with the relationship between security and regional collaboration. For genuine multipolarity in East Asia can be achieved only in an Asian political structure in which the United States is not the only source of resistance to China's capacity for direct and indirect influence.

Eight

REGIONAL SECURITY PROSPECTS
FOR THE 1970's

As recently as 1964–65, when Southeast Asian leaders discussed regional cooperation, most denied that it was useful even to speculate about the relationship between regionalism and security. Instead they always stressed the purely "economic and cultural" aspects of the subject.

By early 1967, however, leaders in Indonesia, Thailand, the Philippines, Malaysia and Singapore, while continuing to stress the major economic purposes of regional cooperation, no longer regarded defense and security functions as necessarily inconsistent with other aspects of the concept. Foreign Minister Malik is only one of several leaders who projected (even before ASEAN was formed) that if a new body were established along the lines suggested by SEAARC, "cooperation for defense would be an inevitable later step." [1]

This does not mean that leaders in the region expect any immediate shift toward locally sponsored and significant joint defense operations. It does, however, mean that Southeast Asian leaders themselves will be considering what aspects of their overall security problem might be susceptible to joint efforts, and ASEAN—though it was formed only in mid-1967—is already the subject of much speculation in this regard. General Suharto, now the President of Indonesia, is one of many who began suggesting in early 1968 that ASEAN may be the catalyst for joint defense efforts. Speaking to a Japanese correspondent, he is reported specifically to have said that "ASEAN could be made more effective by developing it into a body of military cooperation." [2]

Philippine President Marcos, as we noted earlier, has spoken in a similar vein; and when Thailand's very powerful Deputy Premier

[1] Interview with the author, Djakarta, January, 1967.
[2] Suharto's interview with *Mainichi Shimbun* was reported by *Antara,* March 6, 1968.

(General Praphas) visited Manila early in 1968, he, too, endorsed the suggestion that defense cooperation had soon to be considered by the Southeast Asian nations who had formed ASEAN.[3] Malaysian leaders, perhaps most immediately affected by Britain's imminent withdrawal from Singapore, have echoed these same thoughts. Tun Razak—the Deputy Prime Minister—has specifically mentioned ASEAN in this connection, and although Malaysia will also be interested to see what prospects may lie in defense cooperation with Pacific Commonwealth members (Australia and New Zealand), Tun Razak's thinking appears to closely parallel that of General Suharto.

The views of other prominent Southeast Asian leaders, endorsing the same general notion, could be presented here at length, and it is likely that leaders will continue to speculate on the possibilities for developing some form of defense cooperation. Yet it will not be easy to score concrete achievements, especially in the early future, for the very idea of defense cooperation labors under much ambivalence in Southeast Asia. The term "military pact," for example, is widely opposed, and even leaders who generally endorse the concept of defense cooperation find it necessary to stress their opposition to "pacts." Thus when General Suharto said that ASEAN could be developed into a format for military cooperation,[4] he said almost in the same breath that Indonesia is "not moving towards any military pact." [5]

Much of the explanation for this ambivalence lies in the deeply negative image of SEATO, and this attitude will exercise a dampening influence on any new consideration of the prospects for defense cooperation in Southeast Asia. To many, if not most observers, SEATO seems at best an ineffective vestige of an earlier era, and for some it has a far worse image. Even among U.S. officials SEATO is generally regarded as moribund, and the net effect of this widespread view is to complicate any fresh assessment of the future utility of the concept of Asian defense cooperation. Yet it will represent an unfortunate irony if Americans— precisely when Asians themselves are beginning to give new thought to the concept of defense cooperation—discount its prospects too heavily. To avoid that, and to ensure that the prospects for Asian defense cooperation are realistically evaluated, it is essential to identify several factors likely to influence both Asian and Western thinking on the subject.

[3] *Antara,* March 11, 1968, citing Manila press reports.
[4] Indonesian Radio Broadcast, March 2, 1968, reporting General Suharto's interview with the Japanese newspaper *Mainichi Shimbun* of February 28. See also *Antara, ibid.*
[5] Quoted in the *Far Eastern Economic Review,* April 25, 1968, p. 207.

The SEATO image, for example, has to be considered, because it does continue to color any consideration of defense cooperation. It will be necessary for both Americans and Asians to identify just what that organization was intended to be and, perhaps even more important, what it was *not* intended to be. Secondly, it will be essential to determine just where in the overall framework of Asian stability and security the concept of defense collaboration fits. Does it relate meaningfully to the problem of general nuclear deterrence and strategic deployment, or merely to the most local kinds of peacekeeping? Does Asian defense cooperation perhaps fit somewhere in between? That question needs to be answered before we can say whether Asian defense cooperation is feasible. And third, if elements of utility to the interests of the United States do seem to derive from possible Asian defense groupings, what steps can Americans contemplate to enhance the creation and effectiveness of such collaboration? We will try to examine each of these considerations here, beginning with the one effort at defense cooperation in Southeast Asia that is most familiar—SEATO.

A. SEATO: DULLES' EFFORT TO BUY TIME

There is a widespread conviction that the Southeast Asia Treaty Organization demonstrates how difficult it is, if it is possible at all, to apply the concept of defense cooperation in Southeast Asia. To those observers who already doubt that there are any genuine prospects for security collaboration among Asian nations, the SEATO experience is regularly cited as a ready-made "proof" of their case. For SEATO, as its critics always note, has had only partial Asian membership. It has never developed a defense potential analogous to NATO, and its two Southeast Asian members, Thailand and the Philippines, appear to rely far more heavily on their bilateral ties with the United States than on any SEATO guarantees.

Yet much of the criticism of SEATO, which after all at least sounds like NATO, rests on the assumption that it was genuinely expected to apply familiar principles of collective security to Southeast Asia. It was not, and to assume that SEATO can be compared usefully to NATO seems to misjudge not only the initial purposes of the Manila Pact, but also the underlying purposes of U.S. security policy in East Asia, of which SEATO was just one reflection in 1954.

It has to be recalled that SEATO was created immediately in the

wake of the Geneva settlements, which Secretary of State Dulles regarded as the dismal reflection of a very distressing Asian environment, and with which he refused formally to associate the United
States. It was in that context that he hastened to Manila, not to create
an Asian equivalent of NATO, but to underscore a point. The point was
simply that the United States, despite the French defeat and withdrawal, intended to play a continuing and potentially larger role in the
defense and security of Southeast Asia.

The method Dulles chose to make this point was the creation of the
Southeast Asia Collective Defense Treaty, but he was never under any
illusion that Asian conditions allowed for collective security and defense burden-sharing arrangements along the lines set out in Europe.
Indeed, both he and his predecessors had resisted the earlier urging
of some Asian and Pacific nations for just such a multilateral security
pact. Australia had wanted one, as had the Philippines, as early as 1949.
But American policy had been instead to undertake bilateral guarantees on a quite selective basis—satisfying Australia and New Zealand
with the ANZUS Pact, and others (like the Philippines) with bilateral
commitments.[6]

At Geneva, however, Dulles stated that if the armistice arrangements
reached by the French were unsatisfactory, if they "provide a road to
a Communist takeover and further aggression . . . then the need will
be even more urgent to create the conditions for united action . . . ." [7]
Dulles clearly regarded the Geneva arrangements as less than satis-
factory, and consequently he sought at Manila to restore some of the
confidence which he felt had been destroyed in Geneva. At Manila,
however, he resisted efforts to establish a NATO-like structure:

> At the Manila Conference in 1954 the United States was not in favor
> of the establishment of a unified military command and a standing
> force; it did not want an Asian NATO with joint headquarters, joint
> military forces, and a common strategy . . . . Washington was op-
> posed to earmarking American forces under the proposed Manila Pact
> for specific areas in the Far East; such a step was considered neither
> necessary, practical, nor desirable.[8]

The reason that Dulles adopted this posture, so different from the

[6] These treaties took effect on August 30 (with the Philippines), and on September 1 (with Australia and New Zealand), 1951.
[7] Speech of May 7, 1954, in *Department of State Bulletin*, May 17, 1954,
pp. 739–44.
[8] Russell Fifield, *Southeast Asia in United States Policy* (New York: Frederick
A. Praeger, Inc., 1963), p. 131.

one in Europe, was precisely his recognition of the difference in circumstances between the two regions. American *interests* in Europe and East Asia, as we have stressed repeatedly here, have not been fundamentally different—in both regions the United States has sought to prevent any one-nation dominance—but as Dulles said about Southeast Asia (which could never be said about Europe): "We have a material and industrial strength which they lack and which is an essential ingredient of security." [9]

These sentiments should make clear the U.S. purpose in creating SEATO: to stake a claim, as it were, to the defense and security of the region, and to put others on notice that the U.S. would not shrink from providing the major military force necessary to prevent dominance in Southeast Asia. It was decidedly not Dulles' purpose to bind Southeast Asian nations into an orthodox collective security arrangement to which they could not usefully contribute. It was for this reason, for example, that he even resisted calling the Manila Pact by the name that has since been given to it. "He made an effort to have it nicknamed MANPAC, for Manila Pact, by way of emphasizing that it differed from NATO, but SEATO stuck." [10]

Despite the SEATO label, however, the differences between it and NATO need to be remembered. In Europe, at the time NATO was formed, the Red Army and Soviet policies represented a more massive and more immediate level of potential threat to the security of the Western European states than was the threat in Southeast Asia when SEATO was formed. These circumstances of the European environment and the purposes envisaged for NATO both called for and allowed for the permanent stationing of sizeable American *and* allied military forces. That was an appropriate response in that environment because for some years a conventional Soviet military move was seen as one of the more likely threats to European security. In East Asia, on the other hand, a similar conventional military threat was not among the likely threats at the time SEATO was formed, nor was a permanent and collective military deployment an appropriate response. The most that

[9] From Geneva Speech of May 7, 1954, in *Department of State Bulletin,* May 17, 1954.

[10] John R. Beal, *John Foster Dulles* (New York: Harper & Row, Publishers, Inc., 1957); see also Fifield's comment that "Dulles, in fact, tried to avoid in the early stages of the pact using the word 'SEATO' lest an organization like NATO be implied" (Fifield, *op. cit.,* p. 126). I have since confirmed this interpretation of Dulles' SEATO views with the State Department officials responsible for compiling the Dulles papers, and with Professor Fifield in a conversation of October 6, 1967.

seemed feasible and necessary was almost precisely what Dulles set out to do: to convey the message that the U.S. remained committed to the security of the region, and to do this in a way that would bolster the confidence of small Asian nations.

Compared to NATO, these were quite limited purposes, and because of these limited goals the United States never tried to bolster SEATO with the sort of infrastructure and joint military forces that characterized its European alliance—and Washington's posture toward that alliance. It seems clear from that evidence (or rather the lack of any evidence suggesting that the United States pressed for significantly intensified efforts in SEATO), that the Manila Pact was not expected nor intended to become a conventional alliance system. The United States expected instead that should a high-level threat develop (from China, no doubt), the major defense and deterrent role in Asia and the Pacific would continue to be a function of American air and naval forces.

At the low end of the threat spectrum, that is, in terms of subversion and insurgency, the U.S. hoped that its essentially bilateral military assistance programs would enable each potentially threatened state to manage on its own resources. Certainly few, if any, efforts were made to develop joint programs for collective defense on the ground, and in the few cases where outside troop assistance was implemented—as in Thailand, Laos, and Vietnam—the U.S. deployed American ground units on the basis of bilateral agreements.[11] The SEATO framework was almost incidental to those decisions, although within the American domestic context it may have been useful to point to the treaty as an added justification for these actions.

---

[11] It is worth noting, too, that even in the heyday of Secretary Dulles' alleged propensity for collecting allies and building "pacts" (some have referred to this as his "pactomania"), the United States did not seek to enlarge the formal membership of SEATO. Cambodia, for example, is reported in the immediate and depressing aftermath of the 1954 Geneva Settlements to have sought more specific defense guarantees from the United States. Prince (then King) Sihanouk, according to some sources, even expressed his willingness to join a "Western security system for Southeast Asia" if an American guarantee went with it (Virginia Thompson and Richard Adloff, *Minority Problems in Southeast Asia* [Stanford, Calif.: Stanford University Press, 1955], p. 189). Michael Leifer, a very close student of Cambodian affairs, similarly reports that "Cambodia was the most anxious of the Indo-chinese states to be militarily associated with the United States" (Michael Leifer, *Cambodia and Neutrality* [Canberra: Australian National University, 1962], p. 23). Much the same point is made in Roger M. Smith, *Cambodia's Foreign Policy* (Ithaca, N.Y.: Cornell University Press, 1965). See the section "Cambodia Seeks an American Commitment," pp. 68–72.

Despite Cambodia's interest at that time, the United States was singularly unreceptive to efforts to extend its guarantees on the mainland beyond Thailand, and certainly was not seeking to enlarge the formal coverage of SEATO.

B. The Nonapplicability of SEATO
in the Future

In sum, SEATO did not represent an American aim to duplicate patterns that had been applied to Europe, and in all important respects it has simply not been comparable to NATO.[12] SEATO is better understood as an effort in image-building, and, at most, as an annex to and a restatement of the many bilateral arrangements that the U.S. has concluded in East Asia. In that context SEATO may have played an important and general deterrent role since 1954—not because it was a formidable collective defense agreement, but because it symbolized a high-level American military commitment in Southeast Asia. Any deterrent effect during the years of SEATO's existence must be traced to a Chinese (and perhaps Soviet) perception of American will, in which SEATO *per se* can have had only marginal meaning.

That condition—that deterrence against major conventional and certainly nuclear aggression in Asia will continue to be largely an American function—is likely to remain essentially unchanged for the foreseeable future. That reality is increasingly understood in East Asia, and this implicit American defense umbrella—instead of detracting from indigenous interest in regional cooperation—appears to enhance those trends toward defense cooperation to which we pointed in the previous chapter. This should be a welcome development for American foreign policy, especially in light of the U.S. objective of encouraging multipolarity in East Asia.

It needs to be stressed, however, that the type and style of any emergent patterns of Asian security cooperation are likely to be fairly unique, or at least quite different from collective defense efforts that have been tried elsewhere. This reflects the widespread negativism throughout Asia toward the concept of defense "pacts," and also reflects certain security conditions specific to Southeast Asia—the Asian subregion where interest in defense cooperation is strongest. Both factors suggest the lines along which military cooperation is most likely to develop, for at least the following three boundaries, or parameters of discussion, can even now be identified.

---

[12] In terms of its geographic scope alone SEATO cannot usefully be compared with NATO—for an Asian security framework that does not include Japan, Taiwan, and Korea hardly expresses the full range of U.S. defense interests and guarantees in East Asia.

First, it is clear that SEATO will provide no model for foreseeable Asian defense efforts, because SEATO was essentially a unilateral American guarantee with merely the color of multilateralism. Leaders in contemporary Southeast Asia reject that model; they seek instead to disassociate themselves as much as possible from too heavy dependence on the United States or any other great power.

Second, it can be safely presumed that future defense arrangements will in all likelihood grow out of presently discernible patterns of Southeast Asian regionalism. Asian leaders are extremely unlikely to embark on an *ad hoc* collective defense arrangement, or create a new organization specifically for defense purposes. Instead, there is increasing evidence that today's leaders realize that defense cooperation is the most difficult form of international collaboration, and they recognize as a result that much common experience and trust is required before this more difficult form of cooperation can be attempted.

This is, of course, precisely the opposite of the process that developed in SEATO, CENTO, or NATO. Each of those bodies, and SEATO in particular, has striven to find new "nonmilitary" tasks and functions to perform, as if by so doing it could polish a tarnished image. But that is a difficult (if not impossible) transformation to achieve, and leaders in Southeast Asia today appear to recognize that defense cooperation will be more soundly based if it grows from other forms of collaborative experiences. Foreign Minister Thanat Khoman has said as much in his recent calls for devoting much more intensive efforts to ASEAN. Mutual interests developed through "economic cooperation and . . . joint projects," he has begun to emphasize, will provide the ASEAN nations "with something they want to join together to defend." [13]

Finally, it is reasonable to predict that regional security arrangements, because they will center on Southeast Asia, will be *primarily concerned with defense against low-level or insurgent threats*. No responsible leader in Southeast Asia deceives himself into believing that the full range of defense functions can be met by the Southeast Asian nations themselves. Most of them recognize (reluctantly perhaps, but at the same time realistically) that the ultimate element of security against, for example, "nuclear blackmail" or large-scale aggression, can be provided only by the United States, and this is the *sine qua non* for their own efforts. Indeed, if they are to become increasingly willing to shoul-

[13] *Bangkok Post*, March 8, 1968. It was for this reason that the Thai Foreign Minister (whose devotion to regional cooperation cannot be questioned) called for "more planning, more work and more sacrifices" to make ASEAN a "going concern" if it is indeed to lead to a regional defense arrangement.

der a greater share of local defense burdens, these leaders must at the same time be assured that the overall strategic umbrella provided by the United States will not be withdrawn.

These characteristics suggest an ambivalance about the U.S. security role in Asia that must be regarded as one of the region's most important political features. There *is* a strong desire to loosen dependence on the United States, but this is tempered by the belief of many that Washington should continue to play some sort of protective role. In Southeast Asia especially, much of the contemporary interest in regionalism grows directly from the first part of this attitude: from an intense concern to reduce dependence on the West, particularly on the United States. This conviction is no doubt most strong in Thailand, and only slightly less so in Indonesia, where the interest in regionalism also derives from Djakarta's concern to play a role of some leadership. And even among those nations which do not yet give priority to regionalism (like Burma and Cambodia), there is, nonetheless, agreement on the need to reduce dependence on the West. All, that is, would subscribe to the three-fold thesis in the 1967 ASEAN Declaration that:

(1) The countries of Southeast Asia share a primary responsibility for strengthening the . . . stability of the region
(2) . . . that they are determined to ensure their stability and security from external interference . . . [and]
(3) that all foreign bases are temporary . . .

C. Factors Influencing Future Defense Cooperation

These sentiments make it clear that in any future defense arrangement, no outside great power, and perhaps not even a middle-range power like Australia, is likely to be acceptable as a formal participant. The reason, of course, is the widespread conviction that great-power participation is too reminiscent of the SEATO model. Many Asian leaders feel, as we have mentioned already, that the SEATO model was inappropriate even in 1954; today it certainly is regarded as not in keeping with attitudes that stress the "primary responsibility" of the Asian states themselves for the security of the region. Americans who are concerned with developing improved arrangements for Asian security will need to appreciate the force of this conviction; it means, for example, that recent Congressional proposals for a "little NATO" in

Southeast Asia are not likely to be welcomed by most Southeast Asian leaders.

Such a proposal has been suggested by Congressman Zablocki, a senior member of the House Committee on Foreign Affairs and Chairman of its Subcommittee on the Far East. Representative Zablocki, who is well aware of the need for revised security arrangements in East Asia, has pointed out that the Singapore government, deeply affected by Britian's impending withdrawal from East Asian defense responsibilities, has already suggested the creation of a new collective defense arrangement for Southeast Asia.[14] In this plan the members would be exclusively those in the British Commonwealth: Singapore, Malaysia, Australia, and New Zealand. Representative Zablocki has "urged serious consideration of the idea,"[15] and he has in turn proposed that the plan could be broadened to include Thailand, the Philippines, "and perhaps Indonesia."

The potential difficulty in this plan lies in the Southeast Asian view that Australia and New Zealand are insufficiently "Asian" to be acceptable to the non-Commonwealth Southeast Asian states. Indonesian Foreign Minister Malik, for example, has on several occasions stated that the United States clearly could not be regarded as a potential member of ASEAN, and when questioned about Australia, he has answered emphatically that "ASEAN remains the Association of Southeast *Asian* Nations."[16] Australian leaders are well aware of this Indonesian view, and although they will endeavor to be responsive to Malaysia-Singapore defense anxieties flowing from the British withdrawal, they are most unlikely to take steps which might alienate them from Indonesia. The new Australian Prime Minister (John Gorton) is reported, for example, to have told a departing Indonesian Ambassador that "any defense and security agreement would be useless without Indonesia entering it."[17]

[14] See, for example, a discussion on Premier Lee's proposal by James Reston, *The New York Times,* January 16, 1968.

[15] *Press Release* from the office of Hon. Clement J. Zablocki, January 24, 1968. Soon afterwards the Congressman sponsored a series of Congressional Hearings on this and related subjects, with a view to developing legislation in support of Asian initiatives that look toward greater Asian responsibility for the defense and security of the region. Among many others, this author testified.

[16] From Malik's statement to the press, November 23, 1967, reported by *Antara,* November 24, 1967. On this occasion, as on many others since, Dr. Malik carefully pointed out, however, that in his view ASEAN would welcome assistance from both the United States and Australia.

[17] *Antara* despatch from Canberra, April 6, 1968, reporting on talks between Prime Minister Gorton and former Indonesian Ambassador Major General R. A. Rosasih.

As a result, Australia is likely to reinforce its bilateral agreements with its Commonwealth partners in Asia (if they seem to insist on that), but will probably resist joining with them in a new and formal collective defense arrangement—partly for fear that such a step would detract from ASEAN. Indeed, the most feasible approach for Australian participation in Asian security arrangements will probably lie in an indirect relationship with a genuine Asian group—along the lines, for example, that Representative Zablocki has suggested for the United States. The United States, he has said, "could play a vital role in back-stopping such an organization . . . our military aid to participating nations could be channeled through the organization." [18]

An indirect role of that sort, unlike formal participation by white nations like Australia and the United States, is likely to be welcomed by Southeast Asian leaders. Although they believe their states should have "primary responsibility" for the defense of the region, those leaders have not deluded themselves regarding their present and potential military capacity. Indeed, while they may disagree on many other subjects, Southeast Asian leaders tend to agree wholeheartedly on this proposition: for *ultimate* security there is no substitute for the United States and the air-nuclear power symbolized and deployed by its Pacific Fleet. This has been one of the strongest impressions the author has gained from a number of discussions during the last several years with most Southeast Asian Foreign Ministers and other ranking officials.[19]

In the Philippines, of course, it was no surprise that senior officials have stressed the need for continued dependence upon the U.S. Rhetoric aside, the Philippines will be the most reluctant of all Southeast Asian states to cut "prematurely" its defense ties with the U.S.[20] But even in Indonesia, among officials who have often expressed deep misgivings about American actions in Asia, it was nevertheless stated that "general security" and "overall defense against China" must continue to be the function of the United States.[21] Else-

---

[18] From *Press Release*, January 24, 1968.

[19] Conversations held in Manila, Djakarta, Singapore, and Bangkok early in 1967 revealed that officials with different views on global politics consistently stressed precisely that point.

[20] Leaders interviewed on this subject in Manila in January, 1967 included Under-Secretary Seyquio in the Defense Ministry; the Foreign Secretary (Narciso Ramos); the Chairman of the House of Representatives Committee on Armed Services; and the Executive Secretary of the President's Office, Mr. Rafael Salas.

[21] A perfect illustration is Mr. Anwar Seni, Director-General for Political Affairs in the Indonesian Foreign Ministry, who was interviewed in Djakarta in February, 1967. His immediate superior, Foreign Minister Malik, has expressed

where in Southeast Asia today, it is most commonly heard that although Asian states may possibly be able to assume greater defense responsibilities against subversion—either separately or in combination—for other purposes the continued military "presence" of the U.S. will be required for years to come.

These views reflect the growing consensus among elites in Asia (especially in Southeast Asia where internal stability problems are so acute) that the overall security equation is best understood at two distinct levels. The first level relates to the general strategic balance. At this level it is frankly hoped that the United States will continue to effectively limit Chinese ambitions and efforts toward direct aggression and aggrandizement. Admittedly, Asian thinking on this point is vague and often contradictory; those who accept the need for an American military "presence" often have given little thought to the operational requirements of such "presence." Many tend to believe, for example, that while American air and naval installations are not desirable on their own national territories, somehow other Asian states will find these installations less objectionable.[22] Of course, Asian trends generally are not favorable for the continued presence of clearly "foreign" bases in the region, and it would be prudent for Americans to assume that in ten years (and certainly by the mid-1980's) even the Philippines is likely to ask that direct U.S. control of bases there be relinquished. In Thailand, the giant American-built complex at Sattahip (U-Tapao) is subject to even more doubts, for all bases in Thailand are *Thai* bases, always subject to effective insistence on American reductions and withdrawals.[23]

These considerations, although they may pose difficulties for the U.S., are not necessarily inconsistent with long-term American strategic requirements and objectives. Even now, American policy-makers are acutely aware of the problems that come from the continuing use

---

similar views about the long-term and broad security role in Asia of the United States.

[22] Prince Sihanouk illustrates this point perfectly. When it appeared that hostilities might be reduced in Vietnam, he announced his hope that the U.S. would continue to "occupy" Thailand, the Philippines, and "other countries in the area." After speaking with the Prince, Stanley Karnow wrote that Sihanouk had said "he would welcome a continued American presence in Southeast Asia . . . provided the United States did not occupy his country" (*Washington Post*, November 4, 1968).

[23] For a discussion of the extent and scope of U.S.-built bases in Thailand, see my article, "Thailand: Its Three-Fold Meaning to the United States," *Current History*, January, 1967.

of bases on territories where there are concentrations of population, and where the presence of American military equipment and men causes domestic difficulties for a host government. Reportedly, consideration is already underway for the development of a military site in the Indian Ocean, for the support of strategic air, missile, and naval forces,[24] and some have suggested a site on Australian territory. One very well-informed writer has specifically proposed that a "suitable small base . . . could be developed . . . around Diego Garcia," an island 1100 miles South of India,[25] and Australian papers have reported that the United States had "partially surveyed" that island "recently." [26] Insofar as *strategic strike forces are concerned*, therefore, it is reasonable to assume that in the 1980's the U.S. will not require full-time control over bases within Southeast Asia. Instead, as the Vietnam war illustrates so well, the major value of installations in the Philippines, in Thailand (and even on Okinawa) is in their relationship to air and logistic support for conventional and subconventional war. American military needs and foreign policy objectives will be enhanced in the 1970's and 1980's by the continued existence, maintenance, and upkeep of modern military installations in Southeast Asia, but these objectives do not require *de jure* or even *de facto* U.S. control.

That judgment is based on the assumption that the likeliest forms of military involvements in East and Southeast Asia will continue to be actions designed to defeat insurgent forces. In the event of general war, on the other hand, the major reliance of the United States for SAC airfields and missile launching sites certainly will not be on installations within Southeast Asia. Dependence for those purposes will instead be on installations on Guam, in Hawaii, Australia, the con-

---

[24] See "Australia Takes a New Look—And Turns Towards U.S.," *U.S. News and World Report*, April 18, 1966, for a discussion of negotiations on sites and bases. During the same period Australian newspapers referred to an "unpublicized 50-year agreement" between Britain and the U.S. for joint use of certain Indian Ocean territories.

[25] Hanson Baldwin, "After Vietnam—What Military Strategy in the Far East?" *The New York Times Magazine*, June 9, 1968.

[26] *Canberra Times*, August 14, 1968. This report notes that in 1966 Britain announced that islands within the British Indian Ocean Territory "would be available for construction of defense facilities by the British and U.S. governments," and that some initial attention was given to the island of Aldabra, north of Madagascar. Writing from Washington, the Australian correspondent noted that "The U.S. is quietly surveying the possibility of establishing some military presence in the vast area of the Indian Ocean, once dominated by the Royal Navy."

tinental U.S. itself, perhaps the Indian Ocean at such potential island
sites as Diego Garcia, Aldabra, or Cocos,[27] and possibly, but not necessarily, on Okinawa.

Installations within Southeast Asia will, on the other hand, continue
to be useful in connection with support for less-than-general war
efforts. The U.S. Army's Ninth Logistical Command at Khorat is a
good illustration of what will continue to be needed in Southeast Asia
during the next twenty years. There, in central Thailand, matériel for
a force close to divisional size has been prepositioned. But such pre-
positioning, and the ability to operate militarily within Thailand and
Laos, depends upon a road and supply infrastructure far larger than
Thailand has had until now. These are provided by the complex of
new docking facilities at Sattahip, the oil pipelines and roads from
that port through the center of the country, and the relatively small
airstrips fed by those recently built facilities. The naval base at Singapore, with its related airfields, repair shops, barracks, and warehouses,
also represents the kind of facility which—*if maintained*—could allow
the quick deployment and supply of forces designed to defeat insurgencies in Southeast Asia.

But bases and installations exist only to support men and their
weapons, and if it is posited that future security requirements in
Southeast Asia will require the capacity to defeat insurgencies, the
question must immediately arise, from what quarter will counterinsurgent forces come? Certainly it is not likely that they will be available from the United States; one of the surest consequences of the
Vietnam war will be a powerful American disinclination to once again
engage large U.S. combat forces in that region for counterinsurgency
purposes. It is equally clear that forces will not be available again
from Britain, as they were in the Malayan "Emergency" from 1948–56
and in the Indonesian *Konfrontasi* with Malaysia from 1963–65. Britain
no longer possesses the capacity to intervene on behalf of its former
colonies and the United States has no desire to be engaged again with
its own forces in that region.

It is at this point that the concept of Southeast Asian defense cooperation, tailored primarily to meet insurgent threats, becomes most
attractive—from the viewpoint of both the regional nations and the
U.S. Although the concept of defense cooperation has long been the
subject of interesting speculation (and even taking into account the

[27] A brief discussion of the Indian Ocean installations and other "East of
Suez" considerations is found in Dick Wilson, "The Indian Ocean Frontier,"
Far Eastern Economic Review, September 14, 1967, pp. 517–23.

extremely active pattern of non-defense cooperation to which we have
pointed), there is today a new and powerful convergence of political
trends apparent in Southeast Asia. This "convergence" of trends could
be catalytic for the development of genuine and practical regional
security cooperation, and this will become more clear if we recapitulate
four major elements that we have already identified in the East Asian
security and political environment.

First, the major security requirement in the region during the next
decade and more will be for counterinsurgent forces, and the likeliest
areas to be threatened by insurgency are in Southeast Asia. *Second,*
in the aftermath of Vietnam, the United States will seek to reduce
the need for commitment of its own combat forces for counterinsurgency actions in that region. *Third,* Southeast Asian perceptions
of the need to meet insurgent threats have been heightened recently
—partly by the increasing estrangement of China from even those
nations formally friendly to Peking, and also by Britain's withdrawal
from Singapore (and East Asian defense responsibilities generally)
after 1971–72. *Fourth,* the formation of ASEAN in 1967 brought together most, and probably the most important, nations of Southeast
Asia in a group dedicated to regional cooperation. The fact that five
nations formed this group reflects not only a widespread anxiety over
China's aims, but a strong indigenous conviction that the developmental goals of Southeast Asian states make it necessary for them
to pool their resources—if their ultimate security is to be preserved.

This conviction, it should be clear, provides a favorable political
base from which to develop a locally sponsored Southeast Asian regional defense capacity, and it is in this sense that an impressive convergence of trends seems to exist. The convergence strongly suggests
that if goals are not set too high, and if outside powers (such as the
United States, Japan, and Australia) provide relevant assistance, the
1970's could witness the development of meaningful defense cooperation in Southeast Asia.

D. BRITAIN'S WITHDRAWAL AND SINGAPORE: NEW LEASE AS AN ASEAN BASE?

In mid-1967, when Great Britain announced plans to vacate its base
at Singapore, and ultimately to withdraw from most defense responsibilities "East of Suez" by the mid-1970's, Asian leaders and American

policymakers were forced to re-examine many of their most basic assumptions. Within six months Prime Minister Harold Wilson further announced that the mid-1970's was not soon enough. When he revealed that except for a token garrison in Hong Kong, Britain would complete its withdrawal from all Asian posts by the *end of 1971*, the "totality of Britain's military pullout . . . stunned some and vastly disappointed others." [28] In the wake of the earlier announcement, the reaction was even sharper: critics in London argued that it was hardly necessary to make the announcement in so public and formal a manner (it came in a Defence *White Paper*). This method, critics suggested, would serve only to convey to insurgent leaders in Southeast Asia that somehow a clear path had been opened for their ambitions.

But even if that were not the case, it could not be denied that Southeast Asian fears and anxieties had been heightened by the announcement—and this was especially clear in Malaysia and Singapore. Malaysian leaders immediately announced that Britain's decision would cause them to rethink much of their defense orientation, and within days they contacted Australia and suggested joint meetings to discuss a new "Commonwealth Defense Arrangement." [29] In Washington the decision was seen as the final installment on an American policy that had failed—failed, that is, to persuade the British that Malaysian and Singapore defense should continue to be *their* responsibility and should not be shunted off to the already burdened shoulders of the United States.[30]

In Singapore itself the decision—although no major surprise—was nevertheless the source of much distress, and at this writing the dust has not yet settled on some of the irritants that it caused. Most immediately upsetting to the government of Lee Kuan Yew was the likeli-

[28] *Washington Post*, January 17, 1968, in a dispatch from London on January 16, the day of the British statement.

[29] A senior Australian official remarked to the author that Kuala Lumpur had been "rattled" by Britain's announcement, and soon afterward informal meetings were held in Australia. In June, 1968, formal talks took place in Malaysia, and new Australian assurances were extended to Singapore and Malaysia. Canberra insists, however, that Singapore and Malaysia must coordinate their own defense thinking, will make no commitments beyond 1971, and is anxious to avoid any steps that will irritate Djakarta (see *Far Eastern Economic Review*, June 20, 1968).

[30] Author's conversation with the Officer for Malaysia-Singapore Affairs, Department of State, Bureau of East Asian and Pacific Affairs, August, 1967. As *The New York Times* also reported, "In the months preceding the Labor Government's decision . . . the Johnson Administration has been urging the British to remain as a force for stability in these regions at least until the Vietnam war is concluded . . . ." (*The New York Times*, January 20, 1968).

hood of severe economic dislocations as a result of the impending base closure. The economy of the island-state is dependent on expenditures related to the base for perhaps as much as 25 per cent of its income, and the British announcement came when Singapore had not nearly recovered from the economic impact of the 1963–66 *Konfrontasi* with Indonesia. Partly as a result of that policy, in which Indonesia had aimed to end its dependence on Singapore's commercial facilities, there were some 80,000 unemployed there. Thus, in the first reaction to the British decision, Singapore authorities were very concerned to find some sort of substitute for the income that has come from the base, and they have sought to gain direct British aid for the island's economy.[31]

In addition, Premier Lee Kuan Yew, who only months before had been very critical of the United States, now made his first visit to Washington since Singapore's independence. His comments, both private and public, made it clear that although he did not seek a direct American military role in Singapore, he "was known to have asserted in private that some 'outside underpinning' was needed to provide security."[32] The Premier said openly that Singapore was ready to help build an Asian regional "framework for common prosperity and mutual security." Later, when Britain stepped up its withdrawal timetable, the Singapore Prime Minister literally rushed to London, hoping to persuade the British to delay their 1971 deadline. On this occasion he made it clear that, serious as were his economic worries deriving from the first announcement in the *White Paper,* economic aid was no longer his first priority. "My main worry is continuing security and defense . . . . All I am asking for is a few more years of British defense."[33]

Britain, of course, has refused to reverse its decision on withdrawal "East of Suez." When Premier Lee arrived in London, officials there emphasized "that the government's decision to quit the Far East . . . has been taken and will be changed by Lee's pleas only in minor detail."[34] That proved to be the case, and as a result the early months

[31] Reports appearing in the *Straits Times* during October, 1967, however, suggest that there will be major difficulties. British authorities have begun to stress that *private investment* in Singapore will be encouraged and facilitated; Singapore authorities, on the other hand, insist adamantly that London assured them of *aid,* and they have announced that they will not regard private investment as a substitute.

[32] *The New York Times,* October 19, 1967. For other reports and comments on Lee's visit, see Chalmers Roberts in the *Washington Post,* October 24, 1967.

[33] *The Washington Sunday Star,* January 14, 1968.

[34] Associated Press report in *The Washington Sunday Star,* January 14, 1968.

of 1968 found the Singapore government in the forefront of those in Asia who were concerned with developing new patterns of security arrangements. The economic impact alone should not be minimized— for the unemployment rate in Singapore even before Britain's announcement was 12 per cent,[35] and as we noted earlier, at least one-fifth of Singapore's earnings have been traced to British expenditures in connection with the base there.

These considerations are mentioned here for two reasons: first, to demonstrate that the intended closing of the British base has already helped bring forth a good deal of defense rethinking, and second, to suggest that this major and quite modern defense installation should not be allowed simply to go out of existence as scheduled. For the Singapore base, especially in connection with the prospects for regional security cooperation in Southeast Asia, could help fill an important need in overall East Asian defense planning. It might even, for example, be reconstituted as an "ASEAN Defense Headquarters," with remarkable facilities for training, billetting, communications, and the stationing of equipment relevant to counterinsurgency operations.

Given the fact that Malaysian and Singapore leaders have already called for new defense arrangements, as well as the important consideration that Indonesian military leaders have informally proposed the creation of a regional security arrangement in Southeast Asia, it seems difficult to ignore the ideal role which the base at Singapore could play in these developing trends. In that perspective, and despite the criticism that has been leveled at the British withdrawal announcement, it might be more appropriate to regard the British decision as a highly useful development. For Britain's withdrawal, like heightened perceptions of China's great-power ambitions, has helped to catalyze the Asian environment for collective defense. Today, as never before, new patterns of security are being sought, and the historic withdrawal of Great Britain from the region is one more ingredient forcing Asian leaders to consider the extent to which they must become more self-reliant for the defense and security.

In this context, the particular relevance (and attractiveness) of Singapore becomes most apparent if the base there is seen as the hub of a joint ASEAN force. Singapore's location is nearly ideal in both strategic and political terms, and, of course, it already contains most, if not all the facilities that a joint regional security arrangement in

---

[35] See *Washington Post*, January 17, 1968.

Southeast Asia would otherwise be called upon to create.[36] Consider, for example, the site-location problems that might arise if the present ASEAN nations (the Philippines, Indonesia, Malaysia, Singapore, and Thailand) decided to extend their cooperative activities to defense and security functions. Given the presence of large American installations in both Thailand and the Philippines (and their SEATO membership), it is unlikely that a location in either of those places would be acceptable to Indonesia. An Indonesian location, on the other hand, would pose enormous supply and maintenance problems in the light of Indonesia's reputation for handling military equipment—even if Malaysian, Filipino, and Thai apprehensions about Indonesian "dominance" did not forbid locating a joint base in Indonesia.

Singapore, in contrast, is no threat to anyone, and it is not tied to the United States in any way. The island-nation, with its amazingly skilled urban population, already possesses the facilities that might have to be built elsewhere, and its leaders—as we have seen—are already worrying about the economic impact of closing the base. They have begun to cast about for ways to make alternative and profitable use of the drydock and other installations that will be vacated.[37] And,

---

[36] For some interesting descriptive information of the vast facilities which Britain built at Singapore, and for an impressive photograph of its naval base facilities, see the fascinating article by Terrence Smith, in *The New York Times,* October 24, 1968. It is clear that the installation can handle upwards of 35,000 troops at any one time. Among its most important facilities are those for repair and maintenance—they are the equivalent of "back to the factory" for even the heaviest of British military and naval ordnance. In addition, the naval, air, and communications facilities available at the base are striking. The airfields are capable of handling all contemporary British aircraft, and there are important jungle warfare training facilities. In most respects, the base would be ideal as a training center for a large counterinsurgency force, although full field exercises have been held upcountry in Malaya. The reason for this is that Britain always conceived of the Singapore installation as an integral part of its Malayan responsibilities—thus naval and air exercises have used both Singapore (Tengah airfield) and Butterworth in Malaya, which is capable of handling even the newest F-111's. This data comes from British embassy sources and from the *Defense Agreement* of October, 1957, between Malaya and the United Kingdom (Annex F).

[37] Late in 1968 the Singapore government contracted with the British ship-repair company, Swan Hunter, Ltd., for conversion of many of the base facilities into commercial ship-building and drydock functions. The firm hopes to retain between 3000 and 4000 skilled personnel already there and build a dock capable of repairing almost any ship afloat. The Singapore government, moreover, intends to build ships in the 15,000-ton class in numbers, with the potential to build vessels of up to 80,000 tons (*The New York Times,* October 24, 1968, and *Far Eastern Economic Review,* October 17, 1968, for report of joint Japanese-Singapore ship-building plans).

more than any other state in Southeast Asia, they critically depend upon close and friendly relations with their neighbors.

It seems not at all unreasonable, therefore, that the Government of Singapore could welcome an arrangement by which the base continued to be used, and in which some thousands of troops added to the economic life of this commercial city. Certainly the present leadership has made very clear its belief that regional cooperation is the best hope not only for Singapore but also for Southeast Asia. As Lee Kuan Yew has said on several occasions, the major value of U.S. involvement in Vietnam is that it can provide time for Southeast Asian states to develop and to build a format for Asian regionalism: "If you get that kind of [cooperative] situation emerging and we all gear in with each other, we may get something akin to what has happened in Western Europe . . . ." [38]

Finally, of course, Singapore is located nearly at the center of Southeast Asia; troops and forces stationed there would have more ready and quick access to likely trouble spots in the region than from any other single location. In a city as developed as Singapore, long accustomed to housing British, Gurkha, Malaysian, Australian, and New Zealand forces, it is likely that the impact of a joint force would be lower than anywhere else in the region. In sum, Singapore represents a ready-made military base capable of handling the full range of weapons and equipment likely to be used by Southeast Asian forces. The base is in many respects "up-for-grabs"; the possibilities for dovetailing its availability with the strong indigenous interest in adding defense functions to the ASEAN agreement are simply too impressive to ignore.

E. A JOINT ASEAN FORCE

But if Singapore represents a useful catalyst for achieving defense cooperation in Southeast Asia—and a unique practical asset as well—what kind of defense arrangements might be brought into being? What, in essence, is the likely nature and purpose of security cooperation in the region? The answer to that question is suggested by the nature of both national and international politics in Southeast Asia:

[38] Denis Warner, "Lee Kuan Yew's Fight for Survival," *The Reporter*, November 2, 1967, pp. 36–38. Mr. Lee made similar statements to an American audience when he spoke on a network interview program in October, 1967.

the likeliest form of defense cooperation is a *joint force to combat insurgency.* Regional security cooperation in Southeast Asia is unlikely, as we have stressed, to be closely patterned after collective security arrangements in other areas. If security cooperation in Asia is to be relevant to the defense needs of the region, it will instead have to represent a form of defense cooperation both lesser and greater than that reflected in the OAS, in SEATO, and in NATO.

One of the major purposes of the OAS, for example, is its consultative function—it is designed to mediate conflicts among Western Hemisphere nations. But the OAS has never played a significant role against external aggression, and partly for that reason it has not been necessary to create joint combat forces. Instead, and in a region where there are numerous opportunities for border and similar disputes, the OAS has, to a fairly high degree, developed procedures for intraregional "peacekeeping." [39] In Southeast Asia, and in the ASEAN context, informal peacekeeping arrangements are likely to be a by-product anyway, and if formal arrangements were made for the creation of a joint combat force, it is probable that a formal consultative machinery for intraregional mediation would also be included. But that is about as far as the OAS model is likely to apply in Southeast Asia; for unlike the Latin American nations, the Southeast Asian states need to be concerned not only with a major external military threat, but also with a China that is willing as well to assist indigenous insurgents. This is the problem, after all, in Burma (and possibly Cambodia) today, in Malaya earlier, and in Indonesia—as we saw earlier—when China apparently helped ship in arms under cover of "building materials."

In the Americas, on the other hand, the more immediate meaning of threat has been perceived to emanate from nearby states of relatively similar power status. In that environment it has been both unnecessary and unlikely to expect defense collaboration among these states—unlikely because their defense forces and elites are often distrustful of one another, and unnecessary because of the overwhelming protective interest of the U.S.

This is quite different from the environment in Southeast Asia. There, defense collaboration would have to include at least some of the attributes of a familiar defensive alliance, but there is only limited

---

[39] Detailed discussions, including treatment of the OAS role in the Honduras-Nicaragua conflict of 1957, is found in Jerome Slater, *A Reevaluation of Collective Security, the OAS in Action* (Ohio State University, Mershon National Security Program, 1965); Gordon Connell-Smith, *The Inter-American System* (London, 1966); and Pan American Union, *Inter-American Treaty of Reciprocal Assistance: Applications* (Washington, D.C., 1964).

utility in analogies to NATO or SEATO. SEATO, as we have seen, was never intended to be a defensive alliance with joint forces, but has instead been a convenient umbrella for underlining the security commitment of the United States. NATO, because it is the most highly developed of alliances, would appear at once to be the model furthest removed from anything that might be conceived in the Southeast Asian environment. For example, the threat which NATO was designed to deter and combat—a large-scale conventional aggression—is almost irrelevant to conditions in Southeast Asia; even were it to develop, the Southeast Asian states will never have within their resources the capacity to meet that unlikely event.

There is, nevertheless, an important similarity between NATO and a joint counterinsurgency combat force that might grow out of ASEAN. It is a similarity that is too easily overlooked because of the enormous differences in scale between the European and Southeast Asian security environments. Perhaps most obvious is the extent to which the cooperating states in ASEAN and the states that formed NATO have shared a common perception of the security threat in their respective regions. Common perception of the Red Army threat was probably the critical element in the West European environment in the 1950's; it helped make possible the creation of a NATO infrastructure and the earmarking of combat forces for NATO purposes. Today a roughly similar perception exists in Southeast Asia; there is little doubt that Southeast Asian leaders believe that China, and China's support for internal dissident groups, represents the main threat to their nation's security.[40] But another similarity is just as important. This is the extent to which a joint counterinsurgency force would be most *appropriate* to Southeast Asian threat conditions, for insurgency is likely to remain the critical problem there. In Western Europe, by the same token, a target of many NATO divisions was most appropriate to European threat conditions and the existence of the Red Army.

Similarly, the point to stress in Asia is that defense forces, and defense cooperation, must be relevant and appropriate to the scale of likely Asian security threats. Of course it is possible to dismiss the concept of Southeast Asian defense cooperation by comparing indigenous forces there to the massive armed strength available to China—

---

[40] This is not to deny that Prince Sihanouk still identifies Thai, and especially Vietnamese, ambitions as a potential threat to Cambodia, nor is it to deny that Malaysians are sometimes apprehensive about Filipinos and Indonesians. All these considerations, however, become of much less significance when weighed against the potential problem represented by China—as even Prince Sihanouk has often pointed out.

but that is a rather pointless comparison. It would be equivalent to weighing Soviet air and nuclear strength, in the environment of the 1950's, against the conventional combat forces available to the Western European states. Such a comparison, for military planning purposes, would not have been relevant; instead, it was always recognized that in the unlikely event of general war in Europe, the ultimate security of Western Europe depended—not on indigenous conventional forces —but on the air and nuclear strength of the United States. NATO ground forces, on the other hand, *were* meaningfully relevant to the more likely threat during the early years of NATO: for it was feared then that war in Europe would mean large-scale, but essentially conventional, land combat.

If roughly the same logic is applied to Southeast Asia during the 1970's, it will be apparent that since the most likely range of armed threat is of a subconventional nature, the ASEAN states possess the capacity to develop joint combat forces *relevant to the threat environment in their region.* This judgment is not invalidated by arguing that the Southeast Asian states do not and will not possess during the next decade the material resources to equip and train a joint counter-insurgency force. For the judgment is based on the expectation that the United States and Australia, and hopefully Japan, could find it squarely within their national interests to provide the bulk of logistic support and training for a joint ASEAN force.

Ideally such assistance would be in the form of sophisticated (and expensive) communications, air and naval equipment, as well as the training required for its effective use. Such a role, it should be pointed out, would not be significantly different in kind from vital functions performed by the United States in connection with NATO. U.S.-designed and supplied equipment has often been central to NATO resources, and for many years American military assistance enabled NATO members to equip and train their armed forces. There seems no major reason why, in Southeast Asia, the United States, Australia, and Japan could not similarly function as "off shore" suppliers to an ASEAN defense group.

The problem instead is to determine whether the forces presently and potentially available to a joint ASEAN force are appropriate to the magnitude of likely insurgent threats in Southeast Asia. Some guidelines for answering that question can be inferred from examining estimates of insurgent movements in the region today and then identifying the troop and equipment requirements for a force designed to meet that level of threat. For illustrative purposes, such an examination is presented in *Table 4* and although estimates of insurgent strength in Southeast Asia are subject to much questioning, figures re-

Table 4 ESTIMATED STRENGTH OF INSURGENCY GROUPS IN SEVERAL SOUTHEAST ASIAN NATIONS

Philippines:	Huk Movement*	
	Regulars	156
	Part-time guerrillas	136
	Communist party sympathizers	1000
	Sympathizers	26,000
Thailand:**	Northeast	
	Armed guerrillas	1000–1700
	Active supporters	2500
	Sympathizers	15,000–25,000
	Malayan Communist Party remnants in the Thai South	600
Malaysia:	Communists	
	Hard core	500–1500†
	Reserves	1000
	Sympathizers	20,000
Indonesia:‡	Sarawak-Kalimantan PBRS (Sarawak People's Guerrilla Troops)	400–500
Burma:§	White Flags (pro-Peking communists)	3000
	Red Flag (Trotskyist communists)	1000
	Karen National Defense Organization	5200

* *The New York Times,* April 16, 1967.

** *The New York Times,* August 18, 1966, November 27, 1966, October 8, 1967, and December 2, 1967, in which it was reported that terrorists numbered 2000.

† *London Times,* October 26, 1966, and Malaysian Embassy, Washington, D.C., November, 1967. This includes insurgents both in mainland Malaya and Sarawak, and if perhaps a high estimate, it was repeated in a Malaysian White Paper in late 1968. This charged Peking support for 500 terrorists in Thai border areas (see *Washington Post,* November 10, 1968).

‡ Djakarta radio, September 23, 1967. No doubt there are others elsewhere in Indonesia; the figure presented here represents an estimate of *armed* insurgents.

§ *The New York Times,* May 6, 1967.

leased by army and police units in several nations provide at least rough guidelines.

As the table suggests, insurgent groups are small in number; in no one of the five ASEAN states do the armed terrorists yet number more than 2000. More commonly they are counted in the hundreds. Yet in rural Southeast Asia, where the infrastructure of government is very, very undeveloped and where peasant discontent is quite common, these small numbers[41] of insurgents are readily able to obstruct the normal conduct of life and government. For example, in the North-eastern provinces of Thailand, especially since 1965, several clusters of armed terrorists have required increasing levels of attention on the part of the Bangkok government. Thai experience in attempting to cope with this problem points to some tentative characteristics of insurgency, among them what might be called the notion of a "crit-ical mass." By that I mean that insurgents, when they consist largely of roving armed bands of quite small numbers, are not likely to pose insuperable problems for most governments in Southeast Asia. When, however, the number of insurgents exceeds several hundred and begins, as in the Thai case, to approximate one to two thousand, the scale of the problem has apparently begun to strain not only local police capabilities but Army resources as well.

It is at that point that outside assistance is most likely to be called for—as, in the Thai case, it has been sought from the United States. In part the explanation lies in the need of government forces for modern communications and transportation equipment, but numbers alone may be an even more important explanation. It is instructive, after all, to recall that the proportion of government troops required to combat terrorists effectively, or merely to prevent an increase in their numbers, is quite high. A ratio frequently mentioned is 15:1. With the exception of Indonesia (where the Army numbers more than 325,000), a 15:1 ratio helps explain why Southeast Asian countries are likely to find that even "small-scale" insurgency will seriously tax any one of their separate national military establishments.

If, for example, an insurgent movement were made up of 2000 armed men, a government force of roughly 30,000 would be indicated to meet it—and armies in Southeast Asia generally number less than 50,000. In some nations they are much smaller. Cambodia, for example, was reported in 1967 to have an Army of less than 35,000; Malaysia,

---

[41] In testimony before a Congressional subcommittee in 1968, former American Ambassador to Thailand, Kenneth T. Young, Jr., prudently suggested that all press estimates of guerrilla strength be doubled. In the past, he pointed out, officials have invariably learned that their guesses of insurgent strength proved to be far too low. Let it be said again that the figures and estimates provided in the accompanying table are designed to be illustrative rather than definitive. Estimates constantly change, and vary with the source providing the figures.

27,600; and the Philippines Army reportedly has only 17,000. In Malaysia there are reserves of perhaps 20,000, and in the Philippines the Constabulary of approximately 17,000 adds to the total strength. Even Thailand, which reports total armed forces strength of 125,000, has not much more than 80,000 in the Army. It is only in Burma and Indonesia that genuinely large-size armies are found, and considering that both nations are military-dominated governments, the size of their armies can in part be explained by the many civic functions performed by army personnel.[42]

If, on the basis of these figures, we project an insurgency of even 2000 terrorists, it is not difficult to understand why outside assistance is likely to be sought. It is also not difficult to see how valuable might be a combined, or joint "ASEAN Force," specially trained and equipped for counter-insurgency operations and numbering perhaps 30,000–35,000 men. Even partial deployment of such an ASEAN force, in increments of perhaps 10,000, could be exceptionally valuable to any one of the states now in ASEAN. For a quickly available and self-contained force of 10,000 men would represent just the sort of added stiffening that would enable an ASEAN member-state to respond quickly and effectively to an armed insurgent problem in its early stages. It would mean, for example, that one of the threatened states, able on its own to field as many as 20,000, would have available (with the ASEAN joint-force contribution) a total of 30,000—and that, as we suggested earlier, is likely to be the number required to cope with an insurgent group that numbered only 2000 guerrillas.

If, moreover, we conclude that Ambassador Young is correct in warning that estimates of insurgent forces are regularly low, and that terrorists might number as many as 3000, our rule-of-thumb ratio suggests the need for as many as 45,000 government troops. That is so clearly beyond the capacity of most Southeast Asian nations that the potential value of a joint ASEAN force, with a pool of 35,000 or even 50,000 men becomes strikingly apparent.

[42] The Burmese Army reportedly consists of 100,000, and as indicated already, the Indonesian Army includes (with reserves) as many as 325,000. Yet considering Indonesia's population of more than 105 million, this should not necessarily be regarded as excessive. Japan, for example, has a somewhat smaller population, a near-total American defense umbrella, and a "no-war" constitution which provides only for "Self-Defense Forces." Yet Japan has an "army" whose regular forces of more than 180,000 are not much smaller than Indonesia's regular army of about 200,000. Most of the data in the paragraph and this footnote are based upon *Appendix I* in D. E. Kennedy, *The Security of Southern Asia* (New York: Frederick A. Praeger, Inc., 1965) and "The Military Balance, 1967–1968," *The Institute for Strategic Studies* (London, 1967).

A force of this size is not beyond the combined resources of the five ASEAN nations, though, of course, tiny Singapore would not be expected to make nearly the contribution that might come from Indonesia.[43] Consider, however, that in 1968 Thailand felt able to increase the size of its combat contribution in Vietnam to at least 12,000,[44] and that the Philippines has had a force of 2500 there for more than two years. Consider, too, that around Djakarta alone the Indonesian army maintains elite battalion forces numbering approximately 30,000 men, and that the Indonesian government under President Sukarno was willing to dispatch highly regarded forces to the Congo in support of a U.N. peacekeeping operation. Moreover, in response to this author's question early in 1967, the Indonesian Foreign Minister replied that his government might be prepared to consider sending quite a large contingent to Vietnam as part of a similar post-hostilities peacekeeping force. Since the size of the Indonesian Army is approximately 300,000 men, Mr. Malik suggested that the number which might be "spared" for such an operation was 50,000.[45]

These considerations suggest that there *is* a potential capacity within the ASEAN nations to develop an elite combined force of 50,000 or more men. That such a step is not a remote possibility is suggested by the political trends and indigenous interest in regionalism discussed in the preceding chapter. Because the pace of these trends has been so rapid, it is no longer accurate (as it was even in 1964–65) to say that although "developments in Asia since 1954 have increased the concern of individual countries for their own security . . . it is less certain that any sense of common responsibility has been evolving." [46] Instead, Southeast Asian leaders increasingly speak of their own nation's destiny as integral with that of the region as a whole, and also

[43] Present planning in Singapore calls for the creation of a six-battalion force, and Israeli instructors are already there to assist (*Far Eastern Economic Review,* August 12, 1967).

[44] Press reports have varied on the size of the additional Thai contribution in Vietnam, which by late 1967 was approximately 2500. One account suggested that an additional 18,000 would be sent (*Washington Post,* October 20, 1967), but this was followed by an announcement that the level of U.S. assistance required for such a contribution would only allow for an additional 12,000 (*Washington Post,* October 30, 1967). Seemingly final reports (in news agency dispatches from Bangkok on November 11, 1967) suggest that the total *additional* force will be 10,000. Since the total size of the Thai army is 84,000, a force of 12,000 in Vietnam will represent a very sizeable contribution.

[45] Interview in Djakarta, February, 1967. This conversation focussed only on a possible peacekeeping force, but it must also be said that many civilian leaders in Indonesia would not object to an arrangement which saw parts of the Army sent abroad and paid for by somebody else!

[46] Kennedy, *op. cit.,* p. 238.

speculate openly about cooperation for the defense and security of
the region. Part of the reason, of course, is that China is now widely
understood to be the relevant security concern, and even when leaders
shy away from specific proposals related to defense cooperation (because of the association with cold-war "pacts"), they acknowledge the
need for some form of collective response for security. This was precisely the sentiment recently expressed by a member of Indonesia's
parliament. In his view, it is still "premature" to add military functions to ASEAN, although "he was fully aware . . . that the People's
Republic of China constituted a menace to ASEAN member states." [47]
The extent to which this perception of China, and security threats
related to China, is common and widespread in Southeast Asia cannot
be stressed too much. This, probably more than any other reason,
helps to explain why Asian interest in regional cooperation has accelerated so much since 1965. As a very cautious American newspaper
remarked recently—in an article titled "Non-Red Asian Nations Shape
New Unity Effort"—"the pace has quickened over the past three
years." [48]

As a main result of this change, the concept of defense cooperation
—possibly including even the sort of joint ASEAN force proposed in
this chapter—is no longer an alien and unacceptable topic for the
region's leaders. Even now Malaysia has formal and informal arrangements with Indonesian army units for cooperative and joint actions
around Sarawak,[49] and with Thai armed forces and police units in
the Thai-Malay border provinces. Similarly, Philippines naval units
are cooperating with both Indonesian and Malaysian patrols in an
effort to supress piracy and smuggling.[50]

[47] The speaker was Chalik Ali, a member of the NU (Moslem Scholars Party),
reported in *Antara*, January 21, 1968. He was speaking in his capacity as a
member of the Committee on Defense, Security, and Foreign Affairs.
[48] *Christian Science Monitor*, February 27, 1968.
[49] Djakarta recently announced that the operation of its 12th Tandjungpura
Regional Military Command had forced Sarawak guerrillas into Malaysian territory, where they then came under the pursuit of the Malaysian Third Infantry
Brigade. The commander of that Brigade then announced that "the Malaysian
armed forces have agreed to give logistic support to Indonesian forces carrying
out operations against communists in the Malaysian-Indonesian border region.
The troops will be assisted through the Indonesian liaison team in Kuching
[Malaysia]." The Djarkarta report concluded that the *Malaysian* officer had
"made these statements . . . following a *regular meeting* with . . . General
Witono [commander of the Indonesian forces]" (Djakarta Radio, September 23,
1967; emphasis added).
[50] For example, on April 19, 1968, the Philippines and Indonesia "agreed in
principle to implement fully their revised agreement on direct liaison and
coordinated naval patrol operations in areas lying between their countries." Indo-

The Indonesian arrangement with Malaysian forces is especially interesting, for it has long seemed that Indonesia would pose the most serious obstacles to pragmatic cooperation. Under the arrangements apparently arrived at on North Borneo, however, Malaysian forces (in order to help combat "communist" insurgents near Malaysian Sarawak) provide logistic support to a battalion of Indonesia's well-known Siliwangi division.[51] In addition, and unrelated to any need for joint patrolling operations, the Indonesian government began early in 1968 to invite numbers of Thai officers and military students for extended visits to Indonesian military training installations. Visits back and forth have become quite common,[52] and as an Indonesian source reported, "proposals were made recently that Southeast Asian countries encourage combined military training, including exchanges of students and technical know-how on regional strategy." [53] The Indonesian Military Attache in Bangkok said, for example, that although a "pact" should be avoided, "existing military cooperation should be promoted further." [54]

Aside from the technical cross-fertilization among military elites effected by these exchanges, the willingness to undertake these efforts —especially the joint patrolling activities—has to be regarded as encouraging. It suggests that the region's military leaders probably would not oppose a proposal, if initiated by their political authorities, to broaden cooperation by creating a joint counterinsurgency force. Indeed, it is likely that leaders like Indonesian Army Chief Panggabean would enthusiastically support the idea.

It seems clear, too, that such a force could be of remarkable utility, considering the many places in Southeast Asia where insurgency must be anticipated during the foreseeable future. Security prospects would certainly be greatly enhanced were there regularly available, as a supplement to national forces, an airmobile unit, for example, that could on very short notice be deployed to Sarawak, to Central Luzon, or to Northern/Northeast Thailand. As we have seen, the base at

---

nesian and Philippines ships, according to the Commander-in-Chief of the Indonesian Navy (Admiral Muljadi), will participate in joint patrols. As part of this agreement, a radio network will be created linking several points between the two countries (Radio Malaysia, April 4, 1968, reported in BBC *Summary of World Broadcasts*, April 23, 1968).

[51] *Antara* dispatch from Pontianak, West Kalimantan, September 26, 1967.

[52] *Antara* reported on March 1, 1968 that 55 Thai Air Force cadets and officers were visiting Indonesian installations, and that in February "a 67-member study group of the Indonesian Naval Defence College visited Thailand."

[53] *Antara* dispatch from Bangkok, March 1, 1968.

[54] *Antara* dispatch, quoting Col. Sugeng Djarot, March 7, 1968 (from Bangkok).

Singapore can without difficulty house and maintain the equipment for a force of up to 35,000 men; no stretch of the imagination is required to envisage a ready force of, say, 10,000, deployable from Singapore to anyplace in Southeast Asia within 48 hours.

1. An ASEAN Force in Operation: A Scenario

For purposes of illustration, let us assume that such a force were created by the end of the 1970's, that members' troop contributions had been decided upon, and that joint training exercises had been held in and around the Singapore facilities and related installations nearby in Malaysia (for example, at the jungle-warfare school near Malacca). Assume further that at any one time approximately 10,000 ASEAN troops are stationed in and are undergoing advanced training exercises near Singapore. Such a force, let us also assume, has been equipped primarily through military assistance loans and grants made by the United States, Australia, and Japan. Conceivably, this burden could be allocated as follows: United States—45 per cent; Japan—25 per cent; Australia (as administrator of a British Commonwealth contribution)—30 per cent. In practice Britain would bear a 10 per cent burden and New Zealand a 5 per cent burden, so that Australia's own share would represent the remaining 15 per cent. These proportions are shown in the accompanying diagram. Instructors, let us assume, have been provided by each of these nations.

PROPOSED EXTERNAL FINANCING AND ASSISTANCE FOR THE ASEAN FORCE

Major aspects of this assistance, in addition to a variety of vehicles and communications equipment, have come in the form of sufficient helicopters and ground attack aircraft to compensate for the probably thin combat deployment of the ASEAN force and for the lightness in artillery support typical of Southeast Asian forces (as compared, for example, with European armies). Ideally, that is, the 10,000 men on ready-alert in Singapore would comprise an ASEAN airmobile unit, and the major categories and quantities of equipment suitable for such a force can be estimated. If it approached divisional size, for example, an ASEAN ready-force would require approximately 1500 trucks, 400 helicopters, more than 500 machine guns, and almost 2500 radio and communications units. These are not precise figures, but they indicate the scale of military assistance which would be required from non-ASEAN states in order to bring such a force into being. These matériel requirements, moreover, relate primarily to the ready-force; that force would comprise less than one-third of the total 35,000–50,000-man force proposed here. Considerable additional matériel requirements would obviously be generated to meet the larger goal and to provide a capacity for meeting more than one contingency simultaneously.

Assuming the existence of this force and the presence in Singapore of the 10,000-man airmobile unit, let us, finally, posit a scenario in Thailand. We may assume that in view of increased sightings of large helicopters making secret landings in the Northeast with reinforcements and supplies for the guerrillas, the Thai Government has decided that the threat to national security warrants an all-out effort to crush the insurgents and pacify the entire region.

Were such an event to take place today, it is quite clear that the Thai government would seek to invoke its American guarantees. We must assume, however, that Thailand will continue to seek to *reduce* its dependence upon the United States. That trend reflects a constant and central foreign policy objective in Bangkok[55]—one that has led to Thailand's remarkably active role in promoting regionalism during the 1960's. It can, therefore, be posited that Thailand will give strong support to a program to create an effective ASEAN counterinsurgency force. Let us suppose, therefore, that the steps to create this force are taken by 1973–75; by 1977–80 it should have achieved combat-readiness.

At that point in time the Thai government, if pressed along the lines described in the scenario, could be much less inclined than now to seek direct military help from the United States. We can assume instead that if an ASEAN force existed in the middle or late 1970's, the Thai government would request *its* help. In the Thai case this is an especially plausible assumption: Bangkok is the strongest advocate of regionalism in the area, and much of its enthusiasm grows directly

[55] For elaboration on this basic point, see Kenneth T. Young, "The Foreign Policies of Thailand," 1965 (mimeo.).

from reluctance to continue for too long Thailand's dependence on a great power like the United States. Let us then assume that the ASEAN standing committee concurs with the Thai request and agrees to dispatch an initial 10,000-man force from Singapore to assist in the counter-insurgency effort in the Northeast. The essential factor leading to this decision is the conviction that the threat in Thailand constitutes a regional threat, as well as one to the security and independence of Thailand.

The guerrilla stronghold can be presumed in this case to lie in the area between the Laotian border and the Phu-Pan highlands. This is an area of traditional alienation from the central government in Bangkok and one that by the mid-1970's will still be far less prosperous than other regions in Thailand. It is relatively thinly populated, but its terrain—with numerous forests and caves—is well suited for tactics dependent upon ambush and hiding places. We can assume, for this illustration, that guerrilla raids have undermined the confidence of the rural population in the government's ability to provide security, and it is estimated that roughly 15,000 people can be identified as sympathizers of the insurgency. Indeed, the Thai government fears the 2000 insurgents less for their immediate military threat than for their long-term destabilizing effect on the Northeast. It is the desire to drastically reduce the insurgency, and especially to prevent recruitment of additional cadres, that has led the Bangkok government to decide on greatly increased measures on this occasion.

A force of even 10,000 men from ASEAN would represent a very significant contribution to this effort. It would have the equipment, training, and doctrine necessary for quick action; presumably its hallmark would be very high mobility. The major manpower load would continue to be that of the Thai army itself, and in all likelihood foreign troops would not be expected to participate in a pacification program.[56] Among the major advantages of an ASEAN force, however, would be its potentials for almost immediate deployment and quick reinforcement. For, under the proposal of an initial total ASEAN force of between 35,000–50,000, we assume as well that the 10,000-man

[56] The Thai government has recently created a "Communist Suppression Operations Command," which in 1967 included civilian administrators, police officials, and, of course, Thai Army and Air Force personnel. This command is also able to call upon border and provincial police and a Village Defense Corps of 25,000. (For this and certain other data mentioned in the scenario, I am indebted for research assistance to Kenneth Myers, doctoral candidate at Johns Hopkins University.)

unit that had departed for Thailand would be almost immediately replaced and billeted in Singapore.

To depart for a moment from the scenario, it should be pointed out that Thailand will soon possess the facilities to receive such a force. In part this results from the large American-financed military construction program there during the past several years—symbolized, for example, by the base complex to be completed at Sattahip (on the Gulf of Siam) by 1970. U-Tapao airfield there, which includes 11,500-foot runways, can already accommodate the largest troop-transport aircraft, and from U-Tapao the ASEAN force could be readily ferried to Khorat. This could be accomplished by helicopter or by road, for Khorat is linked to Bangkok and the South by an excellent road and supply pipe line. From Khorat an additional highway stretches to Udon Thani near the Laotian border, and even today a number of important airfields are in the Northeast. The Thai Air Force already maintains an operations center at Sakol Nakhon; this center, as well as a Thai Air Force Base at Nakhon Phanom on the Mekong, has been used even in the 1960's for major antiguerrilla and air-support operations.

To return to the scenario, an ASEAN force would have the general task of assisting regular Thai forces in patrolling the Thai-Lao border against infiltration.[57] Because of the nature of its training and equipment, it would also, no doubt, participate significantly in "search and destroy" missions, with the purpose of ensuring government control of given areas. After achieving that task, it is probably reasonable to assume that Thai-ASEAN forces would be replaced by strictly Thai teams. The primary mission of an ASEAN force, that is, would not be posthostilities policing, although it could be available for that purpose. Instead it would gain most of its value from its capacity, as a combat element with very great firepower and mobility, to be *added* to the forces that any ASEAN government would normally maintain. Over the next fifteen years it is not at all difficult to envisage situations of insurgency in Malaysia, the Phillippines, Thailand, and Indonesia, where such a combined force could be critically important.

Yet this book is not the place to speculate in further detail on how such a force might operate in every conceivable instance. It is only necessary to restate that since 1948 Southeast Asia has been marked

[57] Interestingly, in mid-1968 (after the above passage was written), the Thai government announced its intention to "close" the border with Laos. It is impossible to say yet how effective this effort will be.

by insurgencies and that nothing readily foreseeable during the next decade and beyond suggests a disappearance of this phenomenon. It is instead far more likely that there will remain a critical requirement for effective counterinsurgency forces in this region, and so long as it is a major American interest to prevent the general toppling of certain governments in Southeast Asia, it will also be of considerable interest to the United States that insurgencies not succeed. The more operative question will, therefore, be how and with what military forces insurgencies can best be frustrated, and it is in that context that an ASEAN force has attractions.[58]

At the minimum, the security environment in Southeast Asia would be enhanced by the constant availability of at least 50,000 highly equipped and specially trained counterinsurgency forces. Moreover, each of the ASEAN governments has already had considerable national experience with counterinsurgency operations, and on that basis there are probably important lessons which Filipinos, Malaysians, Thais, and Indonesians can impart to each other. The United States Government recognizes this, for it has given some attention already to the potential for a special Counterinsurgency Center in the Philippines.[59] Indeed, Filipino leaders welcome this possibility precisely because it is recognized that *joint* training in counterinsurgency, drawing on existing Southeast Asian experience, is likely to be very valuable.

But such a Philippines-American initiative, however valuable, would probably represent considerably less than could be achieved and much less than needs to be accomplished. For the collaborative environment in Southeast Asia now encourages security cooperation on a basis wider than that represented by the traditional pattern of bilateral American assistance. Indeed, bilateral relationships are increasingly inhibited by the domestic environment in the United States, as well as by attitudes in Southeast Asia. Thus, even if the United States sought to extend the scope of its commitments (and that is hardly likely), Southeast Asian nations not already tied militarily

[58] Nothing in this discussion should imply that major armed response by government is proposed as the only or "best" way to deal with insurgency. Instead, if the appeals of revolutionaries are to be blunted, main reliance should still be on effective local administration; an in-touch rural police force with excellent intelligence; and of course firm evidence that government is achieving locally-identified popular needs. But even the best efforts will not always succeed, and overwhelming and effective armed force *can* contribute to the defeat of an insurgency where other, and preferred, methods have not been sufficient. It is in the recognition that such situations are likely to arise during the 1970's in Southeast Asia that an ASEAN force is recommended.

[59] President Johnson appeared, in his statements to President Marcos in Washington late in 1966, to give support to this proposal.

to the United States would not be receptive to the offer. Singapore, Malaysia, and Indonesia, to say nothing of Burma and Cambodia, well illustrate this point; even in the wake of Britain's military withdrawal, leaders in Kuala Lumpur and Singapore stressed that although they hoped to design some alternative to the resulting "vacuum," they certainly did not intend to ask for direct American military guarantees.[60]

Similarly, it should be clear by now that the negative view held of SEATO makes that format, or anything too much like it, unsuitable as the framework for defense collaboration of the sort proposed here. SEATO officials, of course, are quite conscious of the declining prestige and role of the organization, and it may be expected that some of them will insist that any new proposal for defense cooperation in the region be undertaken within their framework. But the SEATO label, it is even more certain, would prevent the participation of Indonesia, Singapore, and Malaysia in the sort of joint force proposed here. These and other considerations suggest that the most appropriate format for security cooperation in Southeast Asia must have the political endorsement of the region's major states, and the ASEAN framework fits that requirement particularly well.[61] Because of its strongly indigenous nature, moreover, ASEAN seems especially consistent with an important objective of the United States: to encourage multipolarity in Asia. In our concluding chapter, therefore, we should examine the interrelationships between American objectives and those political trends in Asia that have been discussed up to now.

[60] As Lee Kuan Yew put it, "The surest way to get insurgency is to have an American garrison" (*Washington Post*, January 14, 1968, reporting on Lee's visit to London).

[61] Although he has not spelled out specific applications, Donald Nuechterlein has also given consideration to the potential role of ASEAN in helping to meet Southeast Asian counterinsurgency problems. See his "Prospects for Regional Security in Southeast Asia," *Asian Survey, VIII* (September, 1968), 806–16.

Nine

TOWARD DISENGAGEMENT
Asian Defense Cooperation
& United States Policy

In the preceding two chapters I have aimed to develop two main points: first, that an ASEAN counterinsurgency force would represent an appropriate response to the likely ranges of threat in Southeast Asia, and second, that defense collaboration will be a feasible step for ASEAN soon after the new organization establishes itself. By that I mean that ASEAN will have to demonstrate a capacity for tangible achievements, and considering the pressures in that direction from Thailand and Malaysia, it is reasonable to expect such achievements—primarily in certain sectors of economic cooperation—by the early 1970's. It is now appropriate, therefore, to consider how the proposal for an ASEAN counterinsurgency force relates to the system of international politics in East Asia and to the national interests, objectives, and policies of the nations that comprise that international system.

To begin with, it should be stressed that an ASEAN counterinsurgency force was not proposed here as a way to "contain" China. No forces available to the Southeast Asian nations, we have said, will be able to "contain" China if China determines to embark upon a massive military aggression aimed at the conquest of Southeast Asia. In the exceedingly unlikely event that Chinese leaders might contemplate such a step, only the air and nuclear forces of the United States, and perhaps fear of strategic reprisal from the Soviet Union, too, could act as effective deterrents.[1] Regional cooperation, however, and regional security cooperation, in particular, can contribute toward the *counterbalancing* of China. It can do this by improving the security of the still weak states on China's rim. Most specifically it can help ensure

---

[1] For elaboration on this point and on the "three levels" of potential conflict situations in Asia, see the final two chapters in Kennedy, *op. cit.*

the defeat of the subconventional military measures likely to be the major manifestation of China's aims in those nations.

This limited task of helping to shore up relatively small and weak states which could otherwise come under China's predominant influence should be seen as part of a process of creating counterweight in Asia. For it is counterweight or counterbalancing, rather than "containment," which is in any event most deeply in keeping with American national interests in East Asia—and it is also counterweight in that sense that is likely to be achievable. It should be stressed, after all, that the United States does *not* require that China be permanently confined and restricted from significant participation in East Asian affairs, even if that were possible. Indeed, even if possible, such a goal would require long-term and direct American opposition to most Chinese roles in Asia, and would also imply a continuation of the already dangerous condition of bipolarity in East Asia. As China becomes more powerful militarily and develops a limited but real capacity to endanger directly American territory, such tight bipolarity would represent even greater dangers than today. It is likely for that reason that the United States will seek to reduce the likelihood of confrontations with China, as well as the conditions which lead to confrontations. *But it will also be essential for the United States to ensure that China is neither encouraged nor allowed to bring into her orbit the bulk of Southeast Asian states.*

This implies that American goals in East Asia are essentially negative and preventive; it implies, too, that the United States can accept an East Asia in which both China and America "live and let live." [2] The task, of course, is to achieve conditions in which Chinese leaders will conclude that they, too, can be satisfied with "live and let live." Chinese leaders are not likely to reach that conclusion if the Southeast Asian states near and adjacent to their borders are not only intimately

---

[2] Nicholas Katzenbach, then Under Secretary of State, reaffirmed this essential consideration of American policy in 1968. Taking into account that Chinese leaders are probably apprehensive about an American security threat, Katzenbach sought to reassure leaders in Peking, as well as those in the United States who feel that the American posture in East Asia has sometimes been too provocative: "I cannot stress too strongly . . . that no basis for such a fear exists.

"If we actually wanted to threaten Communist China, would not repeated opportunities have presented themselves? Could we not have attacked it on the many occasions when the mainland was weak or wracked by internal problems? . . . given normal and sensible restraint on both sides, there is absolutely no reason why the United States and Communist China should come into conflict" (From a speech to the National Press Club, March 21, 1968, reported in the *Washington Evening Star,* May 22, 1968. Also see *The New York Times,* May 22, 1968).

tied to American military postures, but also contain on their territories American bases with strategic capabilities. On the other hand, if Southeast Asian states, through cooperation, reduce their susceptibility to subversion and improve their internal security, that situation— although not pleasing to China—would be extremely difficult to construe as provocative.

A. REGIONAL DOMINANCE AS AN OPERATIONAL CONCEPT

The dilemma, of course, will lie in reconciling the deep desire to avoid a conflict with China with the equally deep-seated requirement to prevent a condition of dominance from arising in East Asia. A resolution of that apparent dilemma may, however, be found in the concept of "regional dominance," to which this book alluded in its first pages, where it was also suggested that the concept could be understood in East Asia in terms of the region's three parts: China, Southeast Asia, and Japan (with Korea).

Because today it is Southeast Asia and not Japan that is directly threatened, the instrumental key to the resolution of the dilemma lies primarily in Southeast Asia. The term "instrumental" applies to Southeast Asia because of Japan's much greater objective weight in international politics. Japan's economic might and its military potential far outweigh anything that can be envisaged for Southeast Asia during this century; but at the same time it has to be recognized that Japan's international posture is not independent of events elsewhere in East Asia. Instead, Japan is likely to be deeply affected by the outcome of events in Southeast Asia. Were Southeast Asia unprotected by the United States or were American guarantees in Southeast Asia clearly to fail, it can reasonably be expected that Japan would face its own agonizing foreign policy reappraisal. In part this would arise from Japan's concern that an American failure in Southeast Asia (perhaps in the wake of a Vietnam defeat) would signal a general withdrawal from East Asia and an inability to make good on its commitments to Japan as well.[3] Japan's concern would be sensitized specifically by an

---

[3] As a knowledgeable correspondent has remarked, there is "a concern shared by many Japanese that the United States may at some point pull out of Asia, leaving Japan to fend for itself. If the Vietnam war leads to a resurgence of

American withdrawal from Southeast Asia, for that would remove an effective obstacle to China's achievement of dominant influence in that region—or what Mozingo terms "a belt of weak, friendly, and pliant states."

1. Japan as Key State

In the face of that possibility, Japan would have one of two main choices, both of them distasteful from the perspective of the United States. One approach would be for Japan, recognizing the inability of the United States to support its commitments in such Southeast Asian states as Thailand and the Philippines, to "make its peace" with China. If that effort succeeded, and if as a result the enormous industrial, scientific-technological, and potential military might of Japan were allied with the hostility toward the United States which China represents, Americans would indeed be faced with the need to prepare for general war. For, as we have stressed from the outset, the *Level One* interest of the United States in East Asia is to prevent the dominance in that region of one power or group of closely aligned powers. Were the United States not prepared to risk war against a China-Japan combination, the era of the United States with a major role in the Pacific regions of the globe would certainly have come to an end.

Admittedly a Japan-China combination is not a likely development in East Asian politics. It is more likely that were Japan forced to reconsider its posture in the face of a Southeast Asia threatened by Chinese dominance, Tokyo would decide to rearm and attempt to frustrate China's ambitions.[4] But that, too, is an unsettling environment

American isolationism, this reasoning goes, Japan must be prepared to step into the breach and defend itself.

"Thus, *what Japan will choose in the next decade is seen to hinge largely on American Far East policy*" (*Christian Science Monitor*, April 27–29, 1968; emphasis added).

[4] It is possible to envisage a third choice for Japan: namely an attempt to align itself with the Soviet Union. The Soviets, for their part, might welcome an opportunity to work more closely with Japan in connection, of course, with Soviet apprehensions regarding China's intentions in North Asia. At the same time, many factors militate against a Japanese willingness to associate closely with the Soviet Union, not least of which are a number of outstanding territorial disputes in what Japanese term the "northern territories." Moreover, Japanese leaders retain a deep resentment against Moscow for what Tokyo sees as the Soviet Union's traitorous decision to enter the war against Japan in 1945—despite a nonaggression pact that had not expired and that required the U.S.S.R. to observe strict neutrality.

On balance, Japanese leaders probably would believe that their ability to

for the United States to envisage, not least because of the deep commitments which the United States government has repeatedly expressed to the security and integrity of Japan. A Japan rearmed, hostile to and suspicious of China, would be a source of danger for the United States. Decisions in Japan could lead to war, and because of the extensive Japan-U.S. security relationship and the obvious importance of Japan in the global context, the United States would find itself constantly in danger of being "pulled in."

It should, therefore, be the objective and purpose of American policy to avoid conditions which might require Japanese leaders to contemplate any one of the alternative postures just outlined. In that sense Southeast Asia is "instrumentally" a key to the question of East Asian dominance, and it is largely for that reason that the security of Southeast Asia—particularly those parts of it which appear to be indicators of the outcome for the region as a whole—is so important for the United States today. But, once again, the dilemma for the United States is how to provide for Southeast Asian security without, at the same time, provoking China, or reinforcing her belief that the United States has hostile intentions toward her. Statements of reassurance to China by American officials can do no harm, and in that respect the recent conciliatory remarks of such spokesmen as Messrs. Bundy, Eugene Rostow, and Katzenbach are to be welcomed. In more operational terms, however, a resolution of the difficulty can be found in two considerations: conceptually, in the notion of regional dominance (applied now to the Southeast Asia *subregion*), and pragmatically, in the concept and application of indigenous Southeast Asian defense cooperation.

2. System and System Determinants
in Southeast Asia

To make that more clear, let it be noted again that the concept of a regional international system implies that some components, or actors within that system, have "system-determining" characteristics. Some nations, in other words, either by virtue of their objective resources (population, size, industry, wealth, and war-making potential, for

influence China would be greater than their leverage on the Soviet Union, in the event that Japan ever were led to consider an alignment with either. Whatever the case, it is clear that from the perspective of the United States, a Japanese decision to consider a close relationship *with either China or the Soviet Union* would represent a disaster for American interests.

example), or by virtue of their relationship with other nations, can be considered as bellwethers for the regional system of which they are a part. Germany, for example, is such a state in Europe today; by virtue of its objective resources alone, were West Germany to become closely allied with the Soviet Union it would not be unreasonable for other Europeans to conclude that the Soviet Union had made a giant stride toward European hegemony. If, moreover, the circumstance that had led to Soviet dominance in Germany were a forfeiture by the United States on its guarantees to West German security, then other states in Europe would have little choice but to conclude that no American guarantee was worthwhile.

In East Asia there are similar bellwether states—of which the most prominent examples are Japan, Thailand, the Philippines, and for different reasons, South Vietnam and probably South Korea. Japan is an indicator of the trends in East Asia in its own right, that is, as a result of its possession of very major objective resources of wealth, population, and power potential. In addition, the economies of most Southeast Asian states are tightly linked, as noted earlier, with the trade and investment patterns of Japan. Within Southeast Asia, in contrast, the nations which can be characterized as "indicators" of trends are more difficult to identify, but some gross differences are apparent nevertheless. For example, there is a major difference, apparent to every observer, between the roles in Southeast Asia of Burma and Cambodia on the one hand, and Thailand, Malaysia, and the Philippines on the other.

As I suggested in an earlier chapter, few leaders in Southeast Asia would judge that China was the "wave of the future" because Burma had somehow been incorporated within the Chinese sphere of influence. But a very different estimate would be made if the same outcome applied, for example, to Thailand. This would be the case especially if a government like that presently in Thailand were overthrown and a pro-Chinese regime installed in its place—and all of this in part the result of a failure by the United States to honor the commitments it made to Thailand in 1954 and 1962.[5] But even in

---

[5] In 1962 Secretary of State Rusk agreed to a memorandum, known as the Rusk-Thanat agreement, which commits the United States to the security of Thailand as part of a bilateral agreement, regardless of any decisions in the SEATO format. The joint statement includes this sentence: "The Secretary of State reaffirmed that the United States regards the preservation of the independence and integrity of Thailand as *vital to the national interest* of the United States . . ." (Department of State Bulletin, March 26, 1962, pp. 498–99; emphasis added).

its own terms, and aside from specific American guarantees, Thailand has become a leading actor in a developing pattern of intraregional politics within the Southeast Asian subsystem. There is much interchange among the elites of Bangkok, Manila, Djakarta, and Kuala Lumpur, and leaders in the other capitals observe developments in Bangkok quite closely.

The same can be said increasingly about Malaysia, Indonesia, and the Philippines—for a pattern of political and economic communication has begun to take shape in parts of Southeast Asia. The result is that although there are a number of nations geographically "in" Southeast Asia, some are more a part of the region than others. Burma, Cambodia, Laos, and both Vietnams, although geographically within the region, are, as national actors, much less intimately involved with the region's affairs than any one of the nations that now comprise ASEAN. Indeed the ASEAN nations, as earlier chapters have stressed, have begun to form a sense of regional community *within* Southeast Asia. One result is that were any of the ASEAN states to come under the effective and exclusive influence of China (or to become "pliant" states as China expects as a minimum condition), the effects of that Chinese achievement would be sharply felt in each of the other ASEAN states. It can also be expected that were the same result to take place in Burma or in Cambodia, the reaction—although the event would be depressing and worrisome, especially to an adjacent state like Thailand —would be far less severe elsewhere in the region.

3. *The United States and ASEAN*

These considerations have important implications for Americans. For the United States, to the extent it has an interest in the security of the Southeast Asia region (in part because of the way in which Southeast Asia relates to Japanese perceptions of China's relative power), can begin on this basis to *discriminate* in its perception of what is important in Southeast Asia. If, for example, Southeast Asians themselves would not regard Burma or Cambodia in a "pliant" relationship to China as a development with adverse "system effects," then there would be no security-related reason for the United States to reach that conclusion. In contrast, the relationship of the ASEAN nations to the interests of the United States appears to be more direct; any one of those nations seems to include characteristics such that their submission to Chinese dominance would very likely have shattering effects for the ASEAN group as a whole.

For one thing, the ASEAN member-nations include the two Southeast Asian states to which the United States has made clear and firm commitments (Thailand and the Philippines). And further, the ASEAN group also includes those nations which can reasonably be regarded as having some of the characteristics of bellwether nations insofar as the region as a whole is concerned. For both reasons, the United States would appear to have a clear national interest in seeing to it that the security of the five ASEAN states is preserved. Beyond that, however, the implication of this analysis suggests that the United States has little or no reason to extend or imply commitments to any *other* nation in Southeast Asia.[6] On the assumption that the United States will not leave South Vietnam under circumstances which have the earmarks of a defeat, the more pressing question seems not whether the United States should consider *new* commitments, but, rather, what posture should this nation adopt toward Southeast Asia after the end of the conflict in Vietnam?

Formal commitments to nations other than Thailand and the Philippines must probably be ruled out—for certainly there is a strongly felt belief within the United States today that commitments in Southeast Asia—and other global areas—should not be enlarged. But, as we have seen so far, few, if any, nations in Southeast Asia are likely to desire formal security ties with the United States anyway. The increasing Southeast Asian interest in regional cooperation, including defense cooperation, reflects that attitude very clearly. It is an attitude which looks toward increasing self-reliance, and it would appear that the United States can hardly fail to benefit by encouraging that view. In practice this will mean that the posture of the United States toward Southeast Asia should increasingly aim at disengagement. Such a posture is likely to gain support from Americans who believe that their nation is already overextended. Just as important, however, is this consideration: a posture of American disengagement can help

---

[6] South Vietnam, of course, as we pointed out in an earlier chapter, exists for the United States at *Level One* of its national-interest scale, but that is in large part a result of the escalation of commitments on the part of the United States itself: from *Level Two* to *Level One*. Despite that, it remains essential—if the commitments of the United States are to have validity in East Asia or elsewhere—that South Vietnam not be incorporated within a North Vietnamese regime under circumstances that could reasonably be traced to a failure of will or capacity by the United States.

to galvanize Asians into accelerating their plans for self-reliance—
much as Britain's withdrawal from Asia led Malaysia and Singapore
to think seriously for the first time of indigenous collective defense
measures.

As applied by the United States, a posture of disengagement regarding the Philippines, for example, would help to remove the defense "crutch" on which Filipinos have up to now relied. It is no
accident that the Philippines (with traditionally the tightest American guarantee) has in recent years been more reluctant and hesitant
with regard to regional cooperation than its Southeast Asian neighbors.
This Philippines reluctance is probably proportionate to the extent to
which leaders in Manila feel no pressure—because of their American
guarantee—to move with more energy toward self-reliance. It would
be reasonable to predict that as Philippines leaders become less sure
of the present pattern of American guarantees, defense support, and
special economic assistance, to the same extent are their perspectives
on regional cooperation likely to resemble the more "Asian" attitudes
now found in Djakarta and Bangkok.

This is not to suggest, of course, that an American posture of disengagement can be applied without restraint, for precipitate withdrawals could lead to greater weakness and instability in Southeast
Asia than exists today. At the same time, a posture of disengagement—
if resolutely applied—could help to convince China that the United
States is not bent upon the most obnoxious forms of direct, American-
dominated "containment." To the extent that such an American posture
came finally to be believed in Peking, it could help in turn to reduce
China's incentives for supporting indigenous subversive movements
and forces in Southeast Asia.

To take an example, both Thailand and the United States will
benefit to the extent that China finds less reason to believe that the
Bangkok government is merely an American puppet. Yet only some
genuine reduction in Thailand's heavy military dependence on the
United States is likely to help produce such a change in thinking
among the Chinese leadership. An ASEAN force of the sort proposed
earlier would be one major step toward convincing the Thai military
leadership that it was feasible to reduce that present dependence on
the United States. If this decision helped in turn to persuade China
that Thailand was less provocative a neighbor than before, the effect
would be to reduce the level of relative threat. In that event a joint
ASEAN force of the size proposed could, with less uncertainty, be regarded as reasonably adequate for the levels of threat that must still
be anticipated in the future.

B. Conclusions: Three Implications
for American Policy

Three main policy implications for the United States stem from these considerations. The *first* is that *"groupings" of Asian states represent a development generally favorable to American interests* and probably should be encouraged. The assets to the United States fall into two broad categories. The first is that regional cooperation (especially in Southeast Asia) can improve the security of likely "target" areas—indirectly, through improved economic development, and directly, by raising the level of local counterinsurgency capabilities. The other favorable element is that regional defense cooperation, by increasingly substituting Asian forces where our units now stand, can help reduce the need for a direct American military presence. For China regards the armed presence of the United States, as presently deployed in certain parts of Southeast Asia, as among the most serious provocations to her security and prestige.

This is another way of saying that if it is successful, regional defense collaboration can play a role in restoring multipolarity in East Asia. The purpose of regionalism, it should be remembered, is to achieve a more cohesive Southeast Asia—one less balkanized and more capable of pooling at least *some* resources for the sake of more rapid development throughout the region. Such a Southeast Asia would be much better able than now to participate in a multipolar East Asian system, and such a system is not only acceptable to but is *identical* with American interests. For, as this book has said at several points, the United States requires no dominance of its own in East Asia; it requires only that *no* state or group of like-minded states achieve hegemony. Regionalism in Southeast Asia can contribute greatly to that goal by making more difficult the piecemeal absorption of the several individual states there, and also by facilitating the end of the region's near-total dependence on one great power. If that can be achieved, a major step will have been taken toward multipolarity, which in turn will represent the achievement of the most basic U.S. interests in East Asia.

The *second* major policy implication is that *regional security cooperation should not be seized upon as a justification for premature American disengagement*—for example, from the Philippines or Thailand. Because there are likely to be strong American pressures for withdrawal from Southeast Asia, especially in the wake of the Vietnam war, the existence of an ASEAN force could lead the United States to overestimate indigenous defense capabilities. Withdrawal from forward deployments in Southeast Asia, and the need to shift part of the defense burden to local powers, *does* provide the ultimate rationale for American support for regional defense cooperation. Nevertheless, if there were weakness where there appeared to be strength in ASEAN, and were this weakness "tested" by insurgents, the United States could be placed in a dangerous dilemma. America might again be faced with the choice of either foregoing the security of a critical area, say Thailand, or of involving its own armed forces to protect it.

The first would be dangerous because it could presage Chinese control of mainland Southeast Asia. The second would pose the danger of directly confronting a China more powerful militarily than she is today. Consequently, American foreign policy must understand that the concept of achieving regional security cooperation in East Asia may have inherent in it a gap of considerable danger. A point in time is likely to come when indigenous defense capacities may be just large enough to lend a sense of security (and hence lead to Southeast Asian and American pressures for base withdrawals), but not yet so large as to effectively deter China-supported insurgents. That point in time will be most critical and could require special but temporary defense guarantees.

Because there are these dangers, and problems of application, inherent in the concept of defense cooperation, we should not leap to the conclusion that the concept is inconsistent with American objectives in Southeast Asia. Rather, it can be said that the proposal for an ASEAN force is highly consistent with both American *interests* and *objectives* as they were defined early in this book. United States *interests* will be served to the extent that regionalism, by promoting a more cohesive Southeast Asia, also promotes East Asian multipolarity. American *objectives* will be served to the extent that regional defense cooperation, by shoring up the security posture of the area, prevents its incorporation into a Chinese sphere. The remaining question relates to steps the United States might take to help create an ASEAN force: What *policies* (to use the distinction supplied in Chapter II) will enhance the achievement of the American interests and objectives just identified?

The policies most appropriate seem self-evident. If the United

States is concerned to foster multipolarity in Asia (both as a long-range interest and as a mid-range security objective), and also to avoid needless confrontations with China, then it must look to states which have both the interest and the capacity to act in ways consistent with American goals. This means, in the first instance, that the ASEAN states themselves, some of whose leaders already are inclined toward defense collaboration, need to be strongly encouraged to move in that direction. But the ASEAN states cannot achieve that goal with their own resources, and for reasons already outlined it will not be most prudent for the United States itself to act as the major "outside" supporter of an ASEAN force. Thus the *third* main policy implication points to *increasing American reliance on proxies for the achievement of its Asian objectives.* The two nations in the Asia-Pacific region that have the capacity for this role, and sufficient interest in the creation of a secure Southeast Asia, are Australia and Japan.

1. The Special Roles of Australia and Japan

With the assistance of Australia and Japan, an ASEAN force of the type proposed here could be created. Australia alone probably does not have the material capacity for such a role, and just as important, an ASEAN force with only Australian-American sponsorship might appear too clearly to be only a variant of SEATO. Japanese sponsorship alone, from the viewpoint of several Southeast Asian states, might pose fears of Japanese dominance. Taken together, however, Japanese-Australian resources of both material capability and political acceptability could be combined in a most effective manner. Certainly leaders in both nations, as well as in the five states combined in ASEAN, share Washington's conviction that no single state should dominate the Asia-Pacific region. The national interests of those nations can, in that important sense, be said to be parallel with those of the United States. Indeed, in the Australian case it is fair to say that since January of 1942, all Australian leaders have recognized that the ultimate security of their nation depends intimately upon American actions.[7] It is for that reason that Australian governments, in the

---

[7] A journalist accurately summed up the position when he wrote recently that "Australia appears to have no alternative but to accelerate its trend towards closer alliance with the United States now that Britain has decided to withdraw from the Far East" (See *Washington Post*, January 17, 1968).

Korean War and in the Vietnam war, have responded quickly to American desires for military contributions.[8]

Furthermore, it is also clear that the Australian government is keenly aware that a conflict-torn and unstable Southeast Asia is inimical to its immediate interests. Australian troops were instrumental both in suppressing the Malayan Emergency and in defending Malaysia against Sukarno's "confrontation" policy. Australian officials have indicated, in the wake of confrontation's end and the British decision to vacate Singapore, their intention to continue to cooperate on defense matters with both Malaysia and Singapore in the future. As noted earlier, the speed with which Britain is leaving Singapore and Malaysia makes it likely that Australia will be pressed by those two nations to extend some special defense guarantee. It will be exceptionally difficult for Australia to resist such a request from her Commonwealth partners, and some special—even if temporary— arrangements must be expected after 1968.

At the same time, many Australians will argue against their nation making a commitment just to Malaysia and Singapore, and they will in particular be likely to argue that Australia does not have the resources, acting alone, to shore up Southeast Asian security. The new Prime Minister, John Gorton, has said publicly that "Australia and New Zealand [do] not have the capacity to take over the role that British forces had been playing in the area."[9] In a vein not very different, the leader of the opposition in the Australian Parliament has argued that Australia's unilateral commitment to Malaysia and Singapore should include no more than the granting of "sophisticated military aid rather than keep ground forces in the area."[10] It is highly desirable, he added, that "regional arrangements" should now be intensified. In the light of these considerations it is very likely that Canberra, which actively supports the concept of Southeast Asian regionalism, would find an ASEAN force—which she could help by providing military assistance—a most welcome contribution to East

[8] To this writer Australian relations with the U.S. have often resembled the behavior of an individual who keeps his insurance policy up-to-date and fully paid. Coral Bell, for example, similarly suggested recently that "Such measures of Australian policy as the troops in Vietnam . . . and the American communication base for Polaris . . . can be read in part as premiums paid for the security-insurance of the American alliance" (Coral Bell, "Southeast Asia Minus Britain," *Survival* [March, 1968], p. 75).

[9] *The New York Times*, January 13, 1968.

[10] From remarks of Mr. Whitlam, reported by Radio Australia (Melbourne), January 30, 1968.

Asian security and to continued good relations with such Australian neighbors as Indonesia.

Just as important, Australia possesses resources which can help bring that force about. Not only would Canberra be in a position to provide funds on probably greater levels than its present assistance to Southeast Asian states, but she clearly has the capacity to manufacture much of the matériel that such a force requires. In sum, it can be said that Australia is ideally suited to act with and for the United States in helping to bring about the creation of a joint ASEAN force. Politically, Australia's endeavors are somewhat more acceptable to some ASEAN members (Indonesia, Malaysia, and Singapore) than those of the United States and she poses no threat of great-power dominance to any of them. Moreover, Chinese fears of "U.S. encirclement" may to some extent be ameliorated if Australian training instructors, rather than Americans, play the largest "white" role in creating an ASEAN force.

But it is probably Japan which remains the largest unknown in the development of *any* form of Southeast Asian regional cooperation. Opinions of scholars and others vary considerably on the extent to which Japan is likely during the next decade to contribute just to the economic progress of the region. Beyond that, informed observers are in even less agreement as to the possible *security* roles that might be undertaken by the Japanese. Of the possible roles that can be envisaged, however, only the extremes seem very unlikely. It is unlikely, for example, that Japan will desire or be able to "opt out" altogether from playing *any* role in East Asian security matters. Similarly, it is unlikely that Japan will rise up completely from her low posture and undertake a full-scale program of rearmament, complete with nuclear weapons and air-missile capabilities.[11]

[11] It must be said, however, that the extent of Japan's "nuclear allergy" has seemed to decline somewhat in recent years, and the tone of Japanese debate, as reflected for example in the daily press, makes it clear that defense and security considerations are now at least widely discusssed, with much attention to potential Japanese roles. Even that was rare before the mid-1960's, and it is no longer uncommon for Japanese leaders to say privately that should an Asian nation like India decide to undertake a nuclear armament program, then "Japan would have to reconsider its own position." On this subject, and although considerable attention has been paid by the author to Japanese press and other written sources (in translation), I am greatly indebted to many conversations with Professor Donald Hellmann of the University of Washington, Dr. Young C. Kim of the Research Analysis Corporation, and Dr. George Packard, III, of Johns Hopkins University and the *Philadelphia Evening Bulletin*. Each is a Japanese language scholar, and all have recently been engaged in studies of the defense and foreign policy process in Japan.

Yet the sheer increase in Japanese economic might and its increasing involvement in the economies of Southeast Asian states would seem to indicate a growing concern for the stability and security of that region. So far, Japanese leaders have hoped to contribute to the economic progress and stability of Southeast Asia through commercial policies and moderate economic assistance.[12] Japan, that is, remains somewhat ambivalent toward Southeast Asia—sharing with the United States an interest in seeing the region remain outside China's orbit, and at the same time, not being willing to play an activist role in support of that interest. It is precisely because of this ambivalence that the concept of an ASEAN force, aided by Japan, could be extremely attractive to Japanese leaders.

Part of the reason for this attraction lies in the fact that Japan could make an important contribution to the security of Asia and the counterbalancing of China without becoming *directly* and unilaterally involved. There are important inhibitions within Japan against such direct involvement, and, of course, there are major inhibitions against major Japanese rearmament. At the same time, there are both conservative *and* leftist forces which, under different circumstances, could accept and even press for a greater security role for Japan, acting perhaps with others in Asia. Conservatives, already anxious to develop some greater security posture as a hedge against Chinese power, are even now beginning to rethink Japan's low posture.[13]

Support for an ASEAN force, in which such very friendly states as Thailand and Indonesia were major participants, could represent a highly acceptable mid-range step for Japan. Japanese technical assistance, training, and weapons supply to ASEAN could appear far less provocative to China (and to domestic doubters) than a Japanese de-

---

[12] An indication of Japan's interest is reflected in the estimate of the Director of Japan's Economic Cooperation Bureau who predicted recently that by 1971 Japan's aid to Southeast Asia alone would reach $1.4 billion annually (from Tokyo press reports of December 18, 1967, on a meeting of the Budget Committee in the Japanese House of Councilors).

[13] Within days of Richard Nixon's election in 1968, Selig Harrison reported from Tokyo that the President-elect's views have "made him a controversial figure here . . . *warmly admired by powerful factions within the ruling Liberal Democratic Party. . . .*" The views they admire stem from Mr. Nixon's long-standing conviction that Japan should be encouraged to revise its "no-war" Constitution. Harrison noted, first, that "Nixon first advocated revision of the . . . clause 15 years ago . . . and has consistently held to his conviction," and second, that in October, 1967, writing in *Foreign Affairs*, Mr. Nixon again suggested Constitutional "modification," because Japan—in Mr. Nixon's words—"will surely want to play a greater role both diplomatically and militarily in maintaining the balance in Asia." See *Washington Post,* November 9, 1968.

cision in favor of unilateral Japanese rearmament. Military support for ASEAN would have the further asset of providing a convenient rationale for maintaining Japan's arms industry at a useful and up-to-date level. Finally, a willingness to join with Australia and the United States would be consistent with Japan's strong disinclination to take unilateral initiatives in Southeast Asia. In terms of both Japanese support for the Asian Development Bank and contributions to the U.N. Mekong River Project, Tokyo's leaders have shown a marked distrust for Southeast Asian projects where they alone might be left "holding the bag." In security matters this tendency would in all likelihood be greater.

The preceding considerations suggest that Japanese support for an ASEAN force would not be forthcoming immediately, although the stated aims of Japanese leaders suggest that the purposes of such a force would be highly consistent with Japan's own objectives. Nevertheless, Japan's *will* to take such a step cannot be taken for granted. What can be taken almost for granted, however, is Japan's physical capacity to play the role envisaged here. There is little doubt, for example, that Japan could act as a major supplier for defense collaboration in Asia, and even now it may possess the capacity to equip an ASEAN force of the size proposed in the previous chapter. Recent reports indicate that during 1968–69 alone, as defense contracting resumes, Japanese firms will produce 60 fighter aircraft, 45 reconnaissance aircraft, 45 large helicopters, and 55 smaller helicopters. Thousands of trucks and small arms will be manufactured for the defense forces, and a naval building program, with several destroyers planned, is also underway. In its initial stages it "will make Japan the third most powerful naval power in Asia." [14]

In the light of these facts it can at least be said that Japan has the capacity to play a leading role in restructuring the patterns of security in Asia. She could easily fill the role of arms-supplier that I have outlined in connection with an ASEAN force; that the willingness to fill that role could be brought forth is strongly suggested by the

[14] "Japan: The New Arsenal," *The Economist* (October 28, 1967), pp. 434–36. By 1971, moreover, Japan will possess hundreds of Nike Hercules and Hawk missiles (three battalions each), and plans are being made now for production of the U.S.-designed F-4 Phantom fighter-bomber. A recent report concluded that "While defense production is geared to the domestic market, some arms manufacturers reportedly are watching growing export opportunities. *With the impending military withdrawal of Britain from Asia,* it is thought that the Southeast Asian countries in particular will look to Japan for help in building up their own defenses" (Charlotte Saikowski in the *Christian Science Monitor,* March 25, 1968).

widening debate on Asian defense and security that now characterizes Japanese politics.[15]

C. The Need and the Opportunity to Lessen America's Involvement

There is today in East Asia a convergence of factors highly favorable to both the immediate objectives and long-term interests of the United States. Precisely at a time when Americans are most anxious to reduce their unilateral role in East Asian affairs, nations like Japan and Australia have begun to achieve the economic output, and nations like Indonesia, Thailand, and the Philippines have begun to adopt the political outlook, that for the first time makes the concept of burden-sharing applicable in Asia. We have seen, for example, that there is an increasingly suitable political environment for regional cooperation in Asia, especially in Southeast Asia where the need is greatest. We have also shown that cooperation for defense and security is now a practicable goal, especially among the five nations in ASEAN. For all of these reasons this book has proposed the creation of an "ASEAN Counterinsurgency Force," and has suggested that the interests of the American people would be well served by United States encouragement and assistance for Southeast Asian cooperation as reflected in ASEAN.

What is proposed, therefore, is not a policy of American withdrawal from Southeast Asia, but a posture of declining direct American involvement in the defense and security of the region. This posture requires that something else fill in where up to now there has been a direct and quite clear American "presence," and that gap points to the role that can increasingly be played by indigenous Southeast Asian defense cooperation. For if Southeast Asians themselves can be encouraged and helped to assume more of the burdens in their own defense, it is not unlikely that a partial buffer will have been created between American and Chinese forces. This must, of course, be a secure buffer, and it will be important for this reason to ensure that an ASEAN force is not a paper tiger. Yet circumstances are now appropriate for Southeast Asian peoples to be encouraged to rely less

[15] For an excellent discussion of the defense debate in Japan, with reference to the possibility of nuclear armament as well as a conventional military role, see Charlotte Saikowski in the *Christian Science Monitor,* Weekend Issue, April 27-29, 1968.

upon American guarantees and more upon their own resources. American assistance will still, of course, be required—probably in very large quantities and at great cost. But the United States has long since shown, in Korea and in Vietnam, that it will sacrifice much American blood for the security of Asian peoples and states. Americans need no longer be apologetic in suggesting that Asian effort and Asian manpower become the primary means of providing for Asian security.

INDEX

ANZUS, 22, 23, 134
ASA, 74, 97–104, 108–19, 120, 122–23, 127–29
ASEAN, 73, 74, 91, 97–99, 103–4, 108, 110–12, 115–16, 118–21, 123–27, 131, 138–40, 145, 148, 151–53, 156–63, 165–66, 172–77, 179–83; and defense, 131, 138–40, 148, 151–53, 156–63, 165–66, 174–77, 180–81; environment for, 97–99, 110–12, 115, 118–19, 123, 125–26, 172, 179, 182
Asian Development Bank, 61, 65, 68, 73, 74, 87, 104–5, 117, 128–29, 181
Asian Relations Conference, 98
ASPAC, 68, 74
Australia, 60, 92, 132, 134, 139–41, 143, 145–46, 182; military aid, 145, 153, 156, 160, 178; security and U.S., 14, 22, 23, 28, 134, 139–41, 143, 145–46, 153, 156, 160, 177–79; see also Gorton

Balance of power, 12, 29, 31, 33–35, 37, 41, 44, 47, 49–52, 54, 57, 58, 63, 97, 166–67, 180; and national interest, 29–31, 34, 35, 37, 47–49, 51, 54, 57
Bandung Conference, 68, 82, 98
Bases, see Military
Bell, Coral, 23, 79, 178
Bipolarity, 6, 7; see Japan and U.S., China and U.S.
Britain, 12, 14, 20–22, 33, 34, 48–50, 56–60, 76, 122, 140, 143–48, 160, 165, 173, 177–78, 181; Asian withdrawal, 49, 122, 140, 144–48, 165, 173, 177–78, 181
Bundy, William, 69, 170
Burma, 78, 81, 82, 94, 126–27, 151, 154, 156, 171–72; and Chinese, 78, 81, 82, 126–27, 171; and regionalism, 74, 93, 96, 99, 110, 118, 126, 139, 172

Cambodia, 76–81, 94, 126–27, 136, 142, 151–52, 155; regionalism, 110, 118, 126, 139, 172; see Sihanouk
CENTO, 138
China, 6, 16, 18, 26, 39, 42, 60, 72, 78, 82, 94, 136, 145, 153, 158, 160–69, 182; in Asian view, 13, 14, 42, 71, 74, 78–84, 87, 90, 91, 97, 148, 152, 172; divided, 13, 19, 48–49, and dominance, 53–55, 70, 75, 80, 168–69,

172; influence, 126–27, 130, 171–72, 175–76, 180; and insurgency, 77, 128, 151–52, 154, 174, 176; and U.S., 1, 5, 6, 13, 14, 19, 31–35, 37–39, 41–45, 47, 51, 53, 55, 63, 70–71, 80, 137, 141–42, 166–68, 170, 174–77, 179–80, 182; see Open Door
Chinese, overseas, 11, 16, 17, 77, 81, 82
Commitments, 17–27, 54, 55, 173
Commonwealth Defense Arrangement, 146
Communications, technical, 20, 21, 107–8, 121, 153, 160
Communism, 14, 42, 77–80, 89–90, 109–10

Defense, 21, 61, 84, 90, 107, 110, 121–22, 129–38, 148–53, 155–65, 170, 172–80, 182; leaders on, 138, 141–43, 145–46, 158; and U.S., 131–38, 141–46, 151–52, 164, 174–75; see Regional Cooperation
Defense White Paper, 146–47
Disengagement, 6, 7, 173–76
Dominance, 10, 12–16, 17–20, 22, 51–56, 66–68, 168–70; and U.S., 10–16, 19, 20, 22, 24, 26–29, 31, 37, 41, 42, 44, 45, 51–54, 56, 58, 62, 63, 72, 126, 135, 168–70, 175
Dulles, John F., 73, 134–36

ECAFE, 74, 83, 85, 86, 92, 98, 109
Economic development, 65, 66, 94, 95; see Regional Cooperation
Europe, 34, 35, 37, 49, 51, 56, 94, 95, 105, 125; and U.S., 10, 12–15, 17–19, 26, 27, 29, 39, 48, 135

Fairbank, John K., 32–34, 42
Foreign policy, U.S., 2, 4, 5–10, 12, 14, 16, 19, 25–27, 29, 31–42, 44–54, 57, 58, 67, 71, 72, 86–90, 133–34, 136–37, 142–44, 146, 161, 171, 175–77; and balance of power, 31, 33–37, 41, 57, 63; and dominance, 31, 37, 41, 42, 45, 51–54, 126; and regionalism, 60–62, 86–90, 125, 146, 175
Fulbright, J. W., 1, 3, 4, 25

Garcia, Carlos, 99, 100, 122–23, 129
Germany, 12, 16, 47, 49, 57, 171

184